pages 11-43

STARTING POINTS

STARTING POINTS

A guide to basic writing skills

second edition

RICHARD SWARTZ

PRENTICE-HALL, INC.. ENGLEWOOD CLIFFS, NEW JERSEY 07632

Library of Congress Cataloging-in-Publication Data

Swartz, Richard.
Starting points.

Includes index.
1. English language—Rhetoric. 2. English language—Grammar—1950– I. Title.
PE1408.S786 1987 808'.042 86–9410
ISBN 0-13-843046-2 (pbk.)

Editorial/production supervision and
interior design: Marina Harrison
Cover design: Wanda Lubelska
Manufacturing buyer: Raymond Keating

Printed in the United States of America

10 9 8 7 6 5 4 3 2

ISBN 0-13-843046-2 01

Prentice-Hall International (UK) Limited, London
Prentice-Hall of Australia Pty. Limited, Sydney
Prentice-Hall Canada Inc., Toronto
Prentice-Hall Hispanoamericana, S.A., Mexico
Prentice-Hall of India Private Limited, New Delhi
Prentice-Hall of Japan, Inc., Tokyo
Prentice-Hall of Southeast Asia Pte. Ltd., Singapore
Editora Prentice-Hall do Brasil, Ltda., Rio de Janeiro
Whitehall Books Limited, Wellington, New Zealand

Contents

Part IV Mechanics

Preface

This second edition of *Starting Points* has undergone several major revisions, chief among them being the organization of the text. Out of a belief that students can profit from understanding that writing is a detailed and arduous process, I have reorganized *Starting Points* to emphasize the subordinate role grammar plays to writing.

In this edition, students explore the writing process in the very first chapter, without worrying about grammar and sentence structure; thus they see that it is their ideas, and how effectively they can express them, that are of primary importance. The grammar and sentence structure elements come into play, then, as tools that enable writers to express themselves more clearly and powerfully. The first chapter leads students through the steps of one process they may use in writing, while emphasizing that the process any writer uses must be tailored to that person's particular needs. The chapter ends with a reminder that the process does not end with the flow of ideas onto paper; rather, that is a beginning, while a finished product is a blend of content and correctness of expression.

Other major changes in this edition include new chapters on pronoun use (Chapter 9) and on essay writing (Chapter 11). In addition, Chapter 4—"Combine Sentences"—has undergone extensive revision, as has the entire section of the text dealing with verbs and verb tense (Chapters 6, 7 and 8). Chapter 10—"Learn Paragraph Organization"—has been expanded, with new sections on limiting topics, expanding support, using the definition pattern, and combining methods of development.

Students and teachers will find useful two new features in the second edition. First, selected practice exercises are noted with an asterisk, indicating that an answer key to the exercise is included in the back of the text. Also, in keeping with the book's emphasis on actual writing, many more practice exercises now require students to produce original phrases or sentences; thus, they will be analyzing their own writing. All of these exercises are marked by a bold **Write!** so that instructors who wish to use them exclusively can locate them easily.

It must be emphasized that no single book can make a competent writer out of a basic writing student. Rather, textbook, classes, personal conferences, and writing laboratories, in concert, provide the key to preparing the student to write effective sentences. With this thought in mind, more exercises have been included in the text than could reasonably be reviewed in class during a one-semester course. The exercises that are not covered in the classroom sessions can serve the needs of individual students who may require additional practice in a writing laboratory or conference setting.

Even as I have tried to emphasize the role of the full writing process throughout the text, I have been reminded of its importance in preparing this second edition. In professional writing, the process involves not only many steps but also many people. My thanks to Phil Miller, English Editor at Prentice-Hall, for guiding the process at each step along the way. Many of the significant improvements to the text were suggested by a team of very able reviewers, Therese Brychta, Sally Geil, and Judy Longo. Finally, to Marina Harrison and Bob Mony, the production staff whose specialty is the finishing touch in the long process, my gratitude and my admiration.

1 / Begin by writing

STARTING POINTS

What happens when you are asked to write something? Do you break into a cold sweat, plunge ahead, and begin writing your final draft? Or do you stare at the page waiting for an idea to pop into your head? These are common reactions people have to writing. In this section, we will explore a few methods of getting started on a writing assignment. These methods are offered as suggestions—as "starting points." They do not cover all of the possible methods of getting started because there are as many different writing processes as there are different writers. But these suggestions may give you a few ideas about how to get started with your writing.

UNDERSTANDING THE TOPIC

Perhaps the most important task in responding to an assigned topic is to understand what you are being asked to do. While this sounds like an obvious instruction, it is one that students overlook quite often. In most cases, your instructor will assign a specific topic. Let's look at a typical writing assignment to determine just what you as a writer are being asked to do.

PRACTICE EXERCISE

EXERCISE 1
TOPIC 1

Answer the questions about the following topic:
Do you like or dislike the community, neighborhood, or area you are living in now? Write a paragraph answering this question. Support your statement by providing reasons, details, or examples that explain your position.

1. What *subject* or *topic* does the assignment ask you to write about? ____

   ____

2. What are you being asked to say *about* the subject or topic?

   ____

   ____

This brief exercise shows one way to make sure you understand the writing assignment you are given. First, you must determine what **subject** or **topic** you're being asked to write about. In this case, the topic is "the community, neighborhood, or area you are living in now," so this is what you would write about. Check your answer to the first question in Exercise 1. Pay attention to special aspects of the topic that will limit the way you respond. Would an essay about the area you lived in ten years ago be an acceptable response to this question? Why not?

Next, you need to determine what statement, position, or point you are being asked to make about the topic. This will be your **main idea**. In this case, the instruction is clear: "State whether you like or dislike. . . . " That direction defines the question you must deal with: "Do I like or dislike my neighborhood?" Check your answer to the second question in Exercise 1. Your answer should express clearly whether you like or dislike your neighborhood.

The final instruction given in Topic 1 is to provide support for your position. That is, after you decide how you will answer the question "Do I like or dislike my neighborhood?", you must provide some reasons or examples that show why you feel the way you do. This is called **support**.

We will deal with the idea of topic, main idea, and support in greater detail shortly, but for now just remember that these are the three key elements to search for when you are given a writing assignment. (1) What *subject* are you being asked to write about? (In this case, your community or neighborhood.) (2) What statement are you being asked to make *about* the subject? (In this case, that you like or dislike your community or neighborhood.) (3) How will you support your statement about the topic?

PRACTICE EXERCISE

EXERCISE 2 *In the space below, indicate exactly what you are being asked to do in responding to Topic 2. You are not actually required to write on this topic; your task right now is just to decide what the topic asks you to do.*

TOPIC 2 *Describe someone you know who you believe is either a good friend or a bad friend. Explain why you view this person as a good friend, a bad friend, or a bit of both. Support your ideas with specific examples.*

LISTING

Now you know how to determine what a particular topic requires, but how do you get started with the writing? And how do you decide just what main point you want to make? One approach is to begin **listing** all of the ideas you have regarding the topic. Writing, of course, requires thought, and one way to get started on a piece of writing is to list all of the thoughts that come to mind about the topic.

Let's take a look at some possible lists in response to Topic 1. The following example shows one student's list:

Gwen's List

good schools
tree-lined streets
friendly neighbors
beautiful front porch
police and fire protection
There's a nice, old-fashioned movie theater just two blocks away from my house.
close to shopping centers
nice parks
comfortable climate

Notice that this list does not look like a finished paragraph on the topic. In fact, there is only one sentence in the list. The purpose of listing is not actually to write the paragraph or essay, or even to write the sentences that you will use. Instead, writing a list is a way to get your thoughts down on paper. Your list may be longer than this example. The longer your list is, the better it is likely to be, because the more items you have in a list, the more you have to choose from when writing your paragraph.

PRACTICE EXERCISE

EXERCISE 3 *Get started on Topic 2 (see Exercise 2) by listing all of the ideas you have about a friend of yours. Try to think of all of the things that make this person a good friend or a bad friend.*

THE MAIN IDEA

After listing all of the thoughts that come to mind about a topic, the next task is to try to organize the items in the list so that they help you to accomplish your purpose. For Topic 1, you will remember, the *purpose* is to state whether you like or dislike your community or neighborhood, and to support that statement.

As you can see, no single statement in Gwen's list answers the question asked in the topic or states what could be the **main idea** of the paragraph. Yet, a main idea underlies all of the items in the list. Take a moment now to write a sentence that states a main idea suggested by the *majority of the items* in Gwen's list. This statement will be the main idea for the paragraph.

Main Idea:

____

____

____

Because all of the items in Gwen's list appear to be positive, a general statement broad enough to cover the main idea of this list would give a positive answer to the question. For example, one statement of the main idea might be: "I like the neighborhood I'm living in now for a number of different reasons."

PRACTICE EXERCISE

EXERCISE 4 *Using the list you wrote for Topic 2 in Exercise 3, write a sentence that states a main idea suggested by the majority of the items in your list.*

SUPPORT: CONVINCING THE READER

After you have written a statement of your main idea, you must decide how you will support it. As we've seen above, Gwen's list provides just the kind of support that is needed, but how do you decide which items to use and how do you arrange them?

In most types of writing, support is the way a writer accomplishes his or her purpose. The purpose of most types of writing is to **convince** the reader of something. For example, in Topic 1 the purpose is to state whether you like or dislike your neighborhood or community and to support that statement. Your task as a writer is to convince your reader that you like or dislike your neighborhood or community.

Most writing, then, is an attempt to convince. When you write to persuade, for example, you are trying to convince your reader of the truth or appeal of your opinion. When you write to describe, you are trying to show the object or experience so convincingly that your reader will be able to see or feel what you saw or felt. Even when you write to explain something, you are trying to convince your reader of the accuracy of your information, the ease of your method, or the interest of your topic. Think of your writing, therefore, as an act of convincing.

Organizing: Sorting the List

If convincing is the purpose of writing, it becomes easier to decide which items in a list are more valuable than others. Your standard for choosing must be "Which is the most convincing?" In the case of Topic 1, we can state this question more precisely: "Which items are most likely to convince the reader that I like the neighborhood where I am now living?" Now go back to Gwen's list and rank the different items in terms of their power to convince. Put a "1" beside the most convincing item, a "2" beside the next most convincing, and so on. Also, identify any entries that would *not* help you write a paragraph on the assigned topic. Be prepared to explain why each item would or would not be useful.

You probably identified "beautiful front porch" as an entry that does not relate to the topic. There was nothing wrong with listing this idea, but it does not belong in a paragraph about community or neighborhood. Why? It is certainly a positive statement, so that's not the problem. The problem is that a beautiful front porch is not a reason for liking or disliking a neighborhood or community. It is a reason for liking a *house*, a particular place within a neighborhood, but not the neighborhood itself. This item should be scratched from the list as *too narrow*. Next look at "comfortable climate." What's wrong with this item? Do we normally speak of a community or a neighborhood as having a certain climate? Usually not. A term like "climate" refers to an area larger than a neighborhood, like a region. This item should be removed from the list because it is *too broad*. Take one more look at the items in Gwen's list to be sure that they all refer directly to the neighborhood or community.

Because we have taken care to understand the assignment, and because the assignment calls for only a paragraph, we can see that even the revised list contains too many items to use in a single paragraph. The next step, then, is to decide which of the other items can be scratched out. While this appears to be a problem, and sometimes makes for difficult choices, removing extra items from a list that is too long is always easier than adding items to a list that is too short to write a full paragraph. Examine the remaining items in the list and select the three that are most convincing.

Now let's take a look at another student's list on the same topic.

Harry's List

noisy neighbors
good schools
too much traffic
good police protection
low property taxes
little kids everywhere
houses are well maintained
old junker car in neighbor's driveway

What is the difference between Gwen's list and Harry's list? While all the items in Gwen's list state positive characteristics of her neighborhood or community, those in Harry's list have a mixed quality. Some items are clearly positive features, while others are negative. Harry, then, is faced with a task that was relatively simple for Gwen. That is, both students produced a list in response to the topic. But while Gwen's list clearly suggested a main idea, Harry's does not. So what will be Harry's main idea? This will depend on what conclusion he decides the various items in the list "add up" to. Take a moment to review Harry's list now. Place a "+" next to positive features and a "−" next to negative features.

You probably found that Harry has a mixed opinion of his neighborhood. He likes the schools, the police protection, the tax rate, and the condition of the houses around him. But he dislikes the noise level, the traffic, and the junker car in his neighbor's driveway. What about the little kids? Are they a positive or a negative characteristic? That, of course, depends upon Harry's opinion of children. Some people would view the presence of lots of children in the neighborhood as a definite plus, while others may view it as a negative feature.

Thus, in contrast to Gwen, Harry's list does not immediately suggest a clear main idea for a paragraph. But that doesn't mean that he has nothing to write about. Again, a list is a source of ideas about a topic, and a writer should depend on it to get started. In Harry's case he has two choices. He can decide which position he's going to take and use only those items that support his position. Or, he can decide that he has a mixed opinion of his neighborhood and make *that* his controlling idea. In that case, he could use most of the items in his list to convince the reader that his neighborhood has its good aspects as well as its bad ones.

PRACTICE EXERCISE

EXERCISE 5 *Return again to the list you prepared for Topic 2 in Exercise 3. Sort through the items in your list, eliminating those that are too narrow, too broad, or that do not support your main idea. Next, rank the remaining ideas in terms of their power to convince a reader of your main idea.*

Expanding the Support

Now that you have listed your ideas, sorted the items in the list, and decided upon a main idea, you can begin to expand the support. To see how this works, let's go back to Gwen's list and assume that you picked "good schools," "friendly neighbors," and "nice parks" as the three most convincing items in the list. This is a good start for organizing a paragraph. But just how convincing is the phrase "good schools" likely to be in a paragraph?

By itself, none of these items is likely to be very convincing to a reader, but, if expanded, each one has the potential to be quite convincing. And the way to expand supporting elements is to make them more specific, to **show** the reader what you mean. For example, to show what you mean by "good schools," you might mention the interest and participation of parents in school activities, the higher-than-average test scores earned by students, and the large number of books and computers in the school libraries. These **specific details** are an effective method of showing the reader that the schools in the neighborhood really are good. When it comes to writing, showing is just as important a word as convincing.

PRACTICE EXERCISE

EXERCISE 6 *Using the example discussed above, expand the support of the following two items from Gwen's list. Remember, the best way to expand the support is to show what you mean by giving specific details and examples.*

A.

Supporting item	*Specific details*
1. friendly neighbors:	______________________
	______________________
	______________________
	______________________
2. nice parks:	______________________
	______________________
	______________________
	______________________

B. *After expanding the support for the items above, do the same for the three best items in your own list for Topic 2.*

DRAFTING A PARAGRAPH

Because you have spent a good deal of time creating a list for the topic, refining it, and expanding the items to make them more convincing, you should use the list in writing your paragraph. The list can help you in two ways: First and most imporant, the most convincing items form an *outline* of the major ideas you will present in your paragraph or essay. Second, you can use most of the words and phrases in your list to write the sentences that will form your paragraph or essay. The difference between your list and your paragraph, of course, is that your list did not necessarily consist of complete sentences, while your paragraph, especially your final draft, should include *only* complete sentences.

What is a **draft**? Writers—and teachers—often refer to "drafts" when they talk about writing. Webster's defines a draft as "a rough or preliminary sketch of a piece of writing"—that is, a *first version* or first attempt at a piece of writing. This concept suggests something important about the writing process: a finished piece of writing is achieved only through a long series of steps, usually including several drafts.

Gwen's First Draft

I like the neighborhood I'm living in now for a number of different reasons. The best thing about my neighborhood is the neighbors. The people who live on my street are all friendly and make a special effort to show their concern for each other. People are always putting their neighbors' trash cans away or taking care of their pets when people go on vacation. Another point in this neighborhood's favor is the school. For parents, the quality of the school is often the most important aspect of a neighborhood. In our school there is a lot of parent participation in school activities like PTA meetings and fund-raising drives. Also, for the last three years, the test scores of seniors in the school have increased more than in any other school in our district. That's probably due to the quality of the teachers in the school.

WRITING ASSIGNMENT 1

Write a first draft using the expanded items from your list for Topic 2 in Exercise 2. Be sure to write enough to fully describe or explain each of the best three items in your list.

CORRECTNESS: PROCESS AND PRODUCT

Up to this point we have not dealt much with the idea of correctness in writing. In fact, we urged you not to worry about the *form* of the items that made up your list, but instead to concentrate on getting the *ideas* down as you thought of them. In other words, the value of your list depended upon how *useful* the thoughts were, not upon how correctly they were written down. Throughout much of this book we will deal with the issue of correctness in writing. However, correctness is something you should be concerned about only as you approach the final stages of your writing. Your ideas—like any writer's ideas—are generally more important than how correctly they are expressed. But if your ideas are *not* correctly expressed, they will not be as convincing as they could be.

The difference between ideas and how correctly they are expressed can be thought of as the difference between the writing process and the writing product. When we speak of the **writing process**, we are referring to the series of steps that writers take to prepare a finished piece of writing, like creating a list, sorting through it, and expanding the best of the items. There is no magic formula to these steps—no one book or one teacher can tell you exactly what the steps of the writing process should be. Finding what works best for you is a process of discovering your particular strengths.

The **writing product** is the finished piece of writing that results from the process. The key work here is "finished." Just when is a piece of writing truly finished? No doubt in the past you have handed in a completed composition to a teacher only to have it returned to be rewritten. The composition had been finished in your mind but not in the mind of your instructor. Throughout this book we will be exploring the meaning of the word "finished" as it applies to the writing product. As you practice more and master more skills, you will find that your own standard of what a finished product is will become more demanding. But be aware that even a paragraph that is perfect in terms of correctness will not be very effective if the ideas are not convincing. It is the blend of content and correctness that makes a piece of writing truly convincing and effective.

2 / Learn the sentence

As you work through this chapter and learn about the basic elements of correct sentences, apply what you learn to the rough draft you wrote in Chapter 1, testing each of your sentences and rewriting them if necessary.

Every complete sentence meets at least three requirements:

1. It has a *verb*.
2. It has a *subject*.
3. It expresses a *complete thought*.

UNDERSTAND VERBS

Action Verbs

Every sentence must have at least one verb. One kind of verb is the **action word** in the sentence:

The meadowlark *sings*.
The truck *races* down the street.

In these two sentences, the words "sings" and "races" are the verbs. In the first sentence, "sings" describes an action of the meadowlark. In the second sentence, "races" describes an action of the truck. Both of these words show the action in the sentence.

PRACTICE EXERCISES

EXERCISE 1

Write!

In this exercise, make a sentence out of each group of words by adding a verb.

Example:
The tree swayed in the gentle breeze.

1. The waves ______________________.
2. The wind ______________________.
3. The cars ______________________.
4. A child in the house ______________________
______________________.
5. The neighbor's Siamese cat ______________________
______________________.
6. The space shuttle ______________________.
7. A three-alarm fire ______________________.
8. A rickety old desk ______________________.
9. Tuesday's weather ______________________.
10. Our refrigerator ______________________.

EXERCISE 2

Write!

Next, write five short sentences of your own and underline the verb in each sentence. You may use sentences from the rough draft you wrote in Chapter 1 if you want to, but make sure they have verbs.

1. ______________________
____
____
2. ______________________
____
____

3. ______________________________

____

____

4. ______________________________

____

____

5. ______________________________

____

____

*EXERCISE 3 *Underline the action verb in each sentence. To find the action verb, find the word that describes the main activity or motion taking place in the sentence.*

1. The last snowstorm broke all the old records for storms in the city.
2. The city workers prepared for the storm late at night.
3. The road crews loaded rock salt into their trucks.
4. They also mounted the snow plows onto the front of the trucks.
5. The storm struck in the hours before dawn.
6. The road crews went out on the roads immediately.
7. They spread rock salt on all the major highways.
8. In the meantime, the fierce wind blew the snow into tremendous drifts.
9. The drifts stranded cars in driveways, in parking lots, and on major highways.
10. By the afternoon, over two feet of snow covered everything in the city.

---

*An asterisk (*) next to the word EXERCISE indicates that the answers to this exercise appear in the Answer Key, which begins on p. 325.

Linking Verbs

Another kind of verb is called a **linking verb**. This is a verb that tells something about the subject of the sentence; it tells what the subject *is* or how it *appears*.†

The restaurant *is* a wonderful place.
Swimming *looks* like an easy exercise.

In these sentences, the verbs "is" and "looks" link the subject to the rest of the sentence, where a further description of the subject is provided.

Think of linking verbs as *connectors* that join the subject of a sentence with a word or phrase that *describes* or *renames* the subject. (This part of the sentence if called the *subject complement* because it completes the description of the subject.) The following examples show how linking verbs connect the parts of a sentence:

(=)
The lamp *is* an antique.

In this example, the linking verb "is" connects "lamp" with a phrase that describes the lamp: "an antique." Look at another example.

(=)
The house *looks* ready to collapse.

Here, the linking verb "looks" connects "house" to a phrase that shows the condition of the house: "ready to collapse." Let's look at one more example.

(=)
She *is* a born leader.

The linking verb in this sentence connects "she" to a phrase that describes or *renames* "she": "a born leader."

It is usually easy to find action verbs, since they describe the main activity taking place in a sentence. It is sometimes more difficult to find the linking verbs, since they work as connectors and do not show any action. You should memorize the most common linking verbs.

†More information about subjects will be given on pp. 23–27.

Common Linking Verbs	
is	seems
am	looks
are	appears
was	were

PRACTICE EXERCISES

EXERCISE 4 *Using the subjects provided in Exercise 1, write a* linking verb *and a word or phrase that renames or describes the subject.*

Write!

Example:

The tree is older than my grandfather.

1. The waves ______________________________.
2. The wind ______________________________.
3. The cars ______________________________.
4. A child in the house ______________________________ ______________________________.
5. The neighbor's Siamese cat ______________________________ ______________________________.
6. The space shuttle ______________________________ ______________________________.
7. A three-alarm fire ______________________________.
8. A rickety old desk ______________________________.
9. Tuesday's weather ______________________________.
10. Our refrigerator ______________________________.

EXERCISE 5

Write!

Next, write five short sentences of your own, using linking verbs as connectors. After writing each sentence, go back and underline the linking verb.

1. ______________________________

2. ______________________________

3. ______________________________

4. ______________________________

5. ______________________________

*EXERCISE 6

Underline the linking verb in each sentence.

1. Not all dictionaries are the same.
2. There are many different kinds on the market.
3. The most obvious difference among dictionaries is their size.
4. The smaller paperback dictionaries seem complete.
5. But the full-sized, hardback dictionaries usually are more thorough.
6. Another difference among dictionaries is their dates of publication.

7. This is an important feature of any reference book.

8. Dictionaries are often out of date.

9. An up-to-date dictionary is a more accurate record of the language.

10. These changes are important to a student or a writer.

Words that Look like Verbs

Some words that are verb forms cannot be considered true verbs because they do not function as the main verb in a sentence.

Infinitives: "to" + verb

Any time a verb is preceded by the word "to," the verb is in its **infinitive** form. Verbs in their infinitive form ("to" + verb) can never be considered the main verb in a sentence. So, in the sentence

I wanted to go to the mountains.

the verb is "wanted." Even though "to go" expresses some action, it cannot be considered the main verb in the sentence. Now look at the following.

To sleep for the rest of my life.

"To sleep" cannot be the main verb of a sentence because it is in the infinitive form. No other word here describes an activity or connects a subject to a description of some kind, so there is no true verb. (*Note*: Since every sentence must have a true verb, this cannot be a sentence.)

Present Participles: verb + "-ing"

Any verb that ends with -ing is in its **present participle** form and must also have a helping verb* before it can be considered the main verb in a sentence. So, in the sentence

Susan was driving across the country.

*See page 23 for further discussion of helping verbs.

the complete verb is "was driving." The verb in this sentence consists of two words: "was" and "driving." If the helping verb "was" is left out, the -ing verb cannot be considered a true verb and this would no longer be a sentence.

Susan driving across the country.

Is there a true verb in this phrase? Even though "driving" looks like a verb, it cannot function as the main verb of a sentence; a helping verb must be added.

Susan *was driving* across the country.

Any of the following words may be used as *helping verbs* with *-ing* verbs.

Helping Verb	***Example***
am	I am going to the game.
are	We are going to the game.
is	He is going to the game.
was	I was going to the game.
were	They were going to the game.

PRACTICE EXERCISES

EXERCISE 7

Write!

Return to the rough draft you wrote at the end of Chapter 1. Check each sentence and circle any infinitives ("to" + verb: to sing) or participles (verb + -ing: singing). For each sentence that contains an infinitive or a participle, check to make sure there is a true verb.

EXERCISE 8

Underline the main verb in each sentence below. Remember that verbs preceded by "to" and verbs ending in -ing *without a helper cannot be considered true verbs.*

1. The investigative reporter was trying to discover the truth.
2. She believed the local government to be corrupt.
3. While doing a routine story a month ago, she discovered evidence of illegal contributions.
4. To get inside information, she made friends with the mayor's secretary.

5. By working day and night, she gradually began to learn some of the facts.
6. To begin with, the mayor's staff was running the city.
7. While holding the title of mayor, the mayor himself was only a puppet.
8. Also, the mayor's staff was giving important contracts to a few construction companies.
9. To get the contracts, the companies were making secret contributions.
10. The reporter wrote a story to expose the corrupt city government.
11. The editors of the paper refused to print the story.
12. They ordered the reporter to find more evidence to support her story.
13. Trying not to get discouraged, the reporter went back to work.
14. She tried to talk to other secretaries and office workers in the mayor's office.
15. She also called some people in the construction companies.
16. Everyone refused to talk to her.
17. Ready to give up at last, the reporter finally was rewarded.
18. An accountant for one of the construction companies was willing to talk to her.
19. During the interview, the accountant gave the reporter some evidence.
20. Using the accountant's statement as support, the reporter wrote the story.

REVIEW EXERCISES

Now review what you have learned about verbs so far. In Exercises 9 and 10, the sentence may contain either action verbs or linking verbs. Underline the verb in each sentence.

*EXERCISE 9

1. Automobiles are a tremendous pain.
2. They always break down for one reason or another.
3. One day they seem just fine.
4. The engine runs smoothly.
5. The next day the car is an absolute mess.
6. Nothing is working right.
7. It seems like a different car.
8. Auto mechanics welcome me to their garages.
9. I am their best customer.
10. Cars are man's worst invention.

*EXERCISE 10

1. There are many things wrong with the environment.
2. A great number of streams and rivers, for example, are polluted.
3. The air in our major cities is often filthy with fumes from city traffic.
4. But not everything in the environment is in such bad shape.
5. Many more people are now interested in the environment.
6. Powerful organizations represent the interest of the environmentalists.
7. Because of the efforts of these organizations, the government now protects many natural areas.
8. Also, the government stops industries from dumping wastes into streams and rivers.
9. Many states require vehicles to pass clean air standards as part of an inspection.
10. With all this new interest in the environment, there is good reason to hope for improvement.

EXERCISE 11

Write!

Now try writing some sentences of your own. Write ten sentences explaining your ideas about cars or the environment and then underline the verb in each sentence. The sentences in this exercise do not have to be related to each other.

1. ______________________________

2. ______________________________

3. ______________________________

4. ______________________________

5. ______________________________

6. ______________________________

7. ______________________________

8. ______________________________

9. ______________________________

10. ______________________________

Compound Verbs

It is possible to have more than one verb in a sentence. For example:

The dog barked and ran after the stranger.

In this sentence, two actions took place: "barked" and "ran."

It is also possible to have more than one linking verb in a sentence:

The house was old but looked warm and inviting.

In this sentence, two words link the describing phrases "old" and "warm and inviting" to the subject word "house." The linking verbs are "was" and "looked."

These verbs are called **compound verbs** because more than one verb is showing the action of the same subject. In the first example, "barked" and "ran" both show what the dog did; and in the second sentence, "was" and "looked" both connect "house" to phrases that describe the house's condition. Furthermore, "compound" can mean more than just two. A sentence may contain any number of verbs showing the action of one subject. For example:

The boat rocked, pitched, and crashed in the pounding surf.

In this sentence there are three verbs, all telling what the boat did: "rocked," "pitched," and "crashed."

PRACTICE EXERCISES

EXERCISE 12 *Return once more to the rough draft you wrote at the end of Chapter 1 and determine how many of your sentences have compound verbs.*

EXERCISE 13 **Write!** *Return to the sentences you wrote for Exercise 1 in this chapter. Add a second or third verb to at least five of the sentences you wrote. Do any of the sentences already have compound verbs?*

EXERCISE 14 *In this exercise underline the verb or verbs in each sentence. The verbs may be either action verbs or linking verbs.*

1. I do a number of different things before a major exam.
2. The night before the test, I read and study my notes.

3. I usually go to bed early and try to get plenty of sleep.
4. In the morning, I rise early and take a shower to wake myself up.
5. Then I cook and eat a big nutritious breakfast.
6. After breakfast, I again review my notes and memorize any important facts or dates.
7. While driving to school, I relax and listen to the radio.
8. It is important to forget about the exam for a while.
9. After arriving at school, I read over my notes and give myself a final quiz.
10. Finally, I go to class and maintain a positive attitude.

Main Verbs and Helping Verbs

So far you have worked with several different kinds of verbs: action verbs and linking verbs, either of which can be compound verbs. All of these verbs are called **main verbs**. Every sentence has at least one main verb, but very often the main verb is "helped" by another verb.

The plant has grown three inches.

In this sentence, "grown" is the main verb, but it is helped by the word "has," so "has" is called a **helping verb**. The following list includes the helping verbs most often used. Some of these are the same as the helping verbs, listed earlier, that are used with *-ing* verbs.

Common Helping Verbs

am	has	can	could	has been	do
are	have	may	might	have been	does
is	had	will	would	had been	did
was		shall	should		
were		must			

You will learn more about helping verbs in Chapter 7. The important point to remember right now is that the helping verb plus the main verb make up the **complete verb** in a sentence. For example, the complete verb in the sentence

The paint has dripped onto the floor.

is "has dripped." The complete verb consists of the helping verb ("has") and the main verb ("dripped"). Some other examples are provided below.

Sentence	***Complete Verb***
He has gone to that college before.	"has gone"
I am writing a letter to the mayor.	"am writing"
She is sailing for Bermuda next week.	"is sailing"
We were planning a great celebration.	"were planning"
He does write letters occasionally.	"does write"
The house could have been sold earlier.	"could have been sold"
We might watch the football game.	"might watch"
Frank should attend more regularly.	"should attend"

Whenever you look for the verb in a sentence, always look for the complete verb by checking to see if the main verb has a helper.

Note that a describing word that comes between the helping verb and the main verb is not considered a part of the complete verb; these words are *adverbs*.

She did not accept my invitation.

Helping Verb: "did"
Describing Word: "not"
(adverb)
Main Verb: "accept"
Complete Verb: "did accept"

We were really hoping to see you there.

Helping Verb: "were"
Describing Word: "really"
(adverb):
Main Verb: "hoping"
Complete Verb: "were hoping"

Most words that end in *-ly* are adverbs and are used as describing words with verbs. They are *never* used by themselves as verbs.

PRACTICE EXERCISES

EXERCISE 15 *Return to the sentences you wrote for Exercise 11 in this chapter and check to see if you underlined the* complete *verb in each sentence.*

*EXERCISE 16 *In this exercise, underline the complete verb in each sentence. The complete verb may be one, two, or more words in the sentence.*

1. I have lived in this city all my life.
2. It has changed a great deal over the years.
3. At one time the downtown area was a fashionable place to live.
4. Only the very rich could afford to live there.
5, The area had a lot of expensive shops and stores.
6. Since then, great changes have taken place.
7. Most of the wealthy people have moved into the suburbs.
8. The expensive shops moved, along with their customers.
9. Now these people come into the city only to work.
10. In the evening, they rush back to their suburban homes.

REVIEW EXERCISES

Now check your total understanding of verbs. The following review exercises are all paragraphs. In each exercise, underline the complete verb or verbs in each sentence. The verb in each sentence may be any one or more of the types you studied in this chapter.

*EXERCISE 17 The 55-mile-per-hour speed limit is a controversial topic. Many people oppose the law for a variety of reasons. Some people consider the highways to be just as safe at higher speeds. Other people support the 55-mile-per-hour law. According to them, reduced speeds on the highways conserve fuel. In addition, reduced speeds save lives. The number of highway fatalities under the law is much lower. But there is one major problem with the law. It is very difficult to enforce. Too many drivers still race along at 65 or 70 miles per hour.

EXERCISE 18

There are too many sports shows on television. Every weekend all the major networks show nothing but sports programs. The average weekend sports schedule on TV runs from noon to early evening. I watch and enjoy an occasional baseball or football game myself. But I object to football games on every channel. The most ridiculous television sports shows are the new ''celebrity sports'' programs. These programs are presented in between the regular sports seasons. These shows feature television and movie actors competing in ''special sports.'' Most times the ''special sports'' embarrass the actors. In my opinion, these shows embarrass the networks as well as the actors.

EXERCISE 19

Write!

Now make up your own review exercise. Write ten sentences about what you think of the 55-mile-per-hour speed limit, or sports on television, or both. The sentences can be a simple listing of your ideas about these topics. If you have more to write about either of these topics than just ten sentences, then write more. After you finish writing all of your sentences, underline the complete verb, just as you did in the other review exercises.

1. ______________________________

____

2. ______________________________

____

3. ______________________________

____

4. ______________________________

____

5. ______________________________

____

6. ______________________________

____

7. ______________________________

____

8. ______________________________

____

9. ______________________________

____

10. ______________________________

____

UNDERSTAND SUBJECTS

Nouns and Pronouns

Along with a verb, every sentence must also have a subject. The **subject** of a sentence is the person, place, thing, action, or idea about which the verb in the sentence says something. For example:

The plant grows quickly.

This sentence is about the "plant." Therefore, "plant" is the subject of the sentence.

The best way to find the subject of a sentence is to locate the verb and then ask "who" or "what" of the verb. That's why we reviewed the different types of verbs first. Look again at the same sentence.

The *plant* grows quickly.

Verb: ''grows''
Question: Who or what grows quickly?
Answer: ''The plant''; so ''plant'' is the subject of the verb ''grows.''

The subject can also be a person:

The *girl* races down the street.

Verb: ''races''
Question: Who or what races?
Answer: ''The girl''; so girl is the subject of the verb ''races.''

The subject can also be a place:

Chicago is the Windy City.

Verb: ''is''
Question: Who or what is the Windy City?
Answer: ''Chicago''; so ''Chicago'' is the subject of the verb ''is.''

The subject can also be an action:

Swimming looks like an easy exercise.

Verb: ''looks''
Question: Who or what looks like an easy exercise?
Answer: ''Swimming''; so ''swimming'' is the subject of the verb ''looks.''

The subjects in the above sentences are called **nouns** because they *name* particular persons, places, things, or actions. But the subject of a sentence may also be a pronoun. A **pronoun** is a word that takes the place of a noun. There are eight pronouns that may be used as subjects in a sentence.

The Pronouns

Singular (One)	*Plural (More Than One)*
I	we
you	you
he, she, it	they

You should memorize these pronouns in order to recognize them easily.

Notice in the following examples how these pronouns take the place of nouns as the subject of a sentence.

Noun: *Jesse* will fly to London tonight.
Pronoun: *I* will fly to London tonight.

Noun: *Erika* will go with the family.
Pronoun: *You* will go with the family.

Noun: *Elaine* was a lawyer.
Pronoun: *She* was a lawyer.

Noun: *Emily* invested her fortune in the stock market.
Pronoun: *She* invested her fortune in the stock market.

Noun: The *forest* looked dark and frightening.
Pronoun: *It* looked dark and frightening.

Noun: *Morris* and *I* volunteered for the job.
Pronoun: *We* volunteered for the job.

Noun: *Daniel* and *Martha* are welcome here.
Pronoun: *You* are welcome here.

Noun: The *firemen* responded to the alarm.
Pronoun: *They* responded to the alarm.

Another type of pronoun that is used as a subject is called a **demonstrative pronoun**.

Demonstrative Pronouns

Singular	*Plural*
this	these
that	those

Noun: The *movie* is fantastic!
Pronoun: *This* is fantastic!

Noun: The country *landscape* is the most beautiful painting you have done.
Pronoun: *That* is the most beautiful painting you have done.

Noun: The corn *chips* are stale and leathery.
Pronoun: *These* are stale and leathery.

Noun: The *books* on the table belong to Helen.
Pronoun: *Those* belong to Helen.

Note in the examples above that the sentences using demonstrative pronouns usually must refer to a previous sentence in order for the reader to understand what noun the pronoun refers to.

Simple Subjects and Complete Subjects

The **simple subject** is the one word that answers the question of "who or what is or does something?"

The tomato plant grows quickly.

Verb: "grows"
Question: Who or what grows quickly?
Answer: "plant"; so "plant" is the simple subject of the verb "grows"

The **complete subject** includes the article ("the," "this," "those," "these," "that," "a," "an") and any describing words that belong with the simple subject.

The tomato plant grows quickly.

Verb: "grows"
Question: Who or what grows quickly?
Answer: "The tomato plant"; so "The tomato plant" is the complete subject of the verb "grows."

Here are some other examples.

Sentence: The beautiful yellow house is sold.
Complete Subject: The beautiful yellow house
Simple Subject: house

Sentence: Passing a chemistry exam is a great challenge.
Complete Subject: Passing a chemistry exam
Simple Subject: Passing

Sentence: To arrive on time is almost impossible.
Complete Subject: To arrive on time
Simple Subject: To arrive (In this case the simple subject is two words: "to" and "arrive".)

Sentence: The blue and white sweater with the hole under the arm is in the bottom drawer.
Complete Subject: The blue and white sweater with the hole under the arm
Simple Subject: sweater

PRACTICE EXERCISES

EXERCISE 20

Write!

Now you know enough about subjects to be able to recognize them in sentences. Return to the sentences you wrote for Exercise 19 in this chapter and underline the simple subject in each sentence. The subject may be either a noun or a pronoun. To find the subject in your sentence, remember to locate the verb and then ask "who" or "what."

EXERCISE 21

Write!

In this exercise, a verb has been provided for you. Write a subject that makes sense with each verb, and then add details or description to the part of the sentence containing the verb. Remember that your subject may be either a noun or a pronoun.

Example:

________________ frightened ________________________

1. ____ shattered
____ .

2. ____ flew
____ .

3. ______________________________________ looked like
____ .

4. _____________________________________ seemed to be
____ .

5. ____ grew into
____ .

Locating the Subject

Remember that you cannot identify a subject by its location in the sentence. Many sentences begin with the subject, but this is not true for all sentences. The first part of a sentence will often describe the subject before it appears. For example:

Leaning way over the side of the boat, he gazed into the deep water.

What is the subject of this sentence? Is it "leaning"? What did "leaning" do? Is it "the boat"? What did "the boat" do? The best way to locate the subject is to find the verb first.

> *Verb*: "gazed"
> *Question*: Who or what gazed into the deep water?
> *Answer*: "he"; so "he" is the subject of the verb "gazed."

A subject, like a verb, may consist of more than one word. This is especially true when the subject of a sentence is an action or an idea. For example:

> Winning an Olympic medal required tremendous dedication.

> *Verb*: "required"
> *Question*: Who or what required tremendous dedication?
> *Answer*: "Winning an Olympic medal"; so "winning an Olympic medal" is the subject of the verb "required."

Always find the verb first when you are looking for the subject of a sentence.

PRACTICE EXERCISES

*EXERCISE 22 *Underline the simple subject in each sentence. Remember that the subject may not always be in the beginning of the sentence. Note: There may be more than one subject and more than one verb in some of the following sentences.*

1. Henry's divorce was caused by many different factors.
2. For one thing, money was always a problem.
3. Although Henry worked hard, his job did not pay too well.
4. Henry's desire for independence was another reason.
5. Every once in a while, he just liked to go for a walk or drive by himself.
6. Henry's wife could not understand why he wanted to be alone.
7. Another important factor leading to the divorce was Henry's father.
8. While trying to be helpful, he always told Henry's wife how to do everything.

9. Henry's fondness for playing poker two times a week was the final reason.

10. In the end, all the problems and disagreements finally caused them to decide on a divorce.

EXERCISE 23

Write!

Write five to ten sentences about divorce. You may write about what you think causes it, what happens as a result of it, or about any other aspect of divorce. The sentences can be a simple listing of your ideas about this subject. After writing each sentence, underline the simple subject or subjects.

1. ______________________________

2. ______________________________

3. ______________________________

4. ______________________________

5. ______________________________

6. ______________________________

7. ______________________________

8. ______________________________

9. ______________________________

10. ____

____

Delayed Subjects

In most of your writing you will want to include as much specific detail as possible. In doing this, you will often write a sentence in which the subject comes near the middle or the end. This is particularly true of sentences that begin with the words "there" and "here."

There were four horses in the pasture.

Verb: "were"
Question: Who or what were in the pasture?
Answer: "horses"; so "horses" is the subject of the verb "were."

Here is my favorite house.

Verb: "is"
Question: Who or what is here?
Answer: "house"; so "house" is the subject of the verb "is."

There are too many cars on the road.

Verb: "are"
Question: Who or what are on the road?
Answer: "cars"; so "cars" is the subject of the verb "are."

Subjects can also be delayed when the sentence begins with a **prepositional phrase**. The phrase may appear in any part of the sentence.

Behind the couch was a thick collection of dust.
The store *in the middle of the block* sells great pastries.
We hope to take our vacation *at the same time next year*.

Prepositional phrases are always introduced by **prepositions**, many of which are included in the following list.

Prepositions

after, as, at, behind, beneath, between, by, for
from, in, like, near, next to, of, on, over,
through, to, towards, under, up, with

It is easy to think that the noun in a prepositional phrase is the subject, but you can avoid this mistake by following the questioning process.

In the barn was an old Model T.

Verb: "was"
Question: Who or what was in the barn?
Answer: "Model T"; so "Model T" is the subject of the verb "was."

Next to the refrigerator is the new dishwasher.

Verb: "is"
Question: Who or what is next to the refrigerator?
Answer: "dishwasher"; so "dishwasher" is the subject of the verb "is."

PRACTICE EXERCISES

EXERCISE 24 *Underline the simple subject in each sentence. Remember that the subject may not always be in the beginning of the sentence.*

1. There is nothing more frustrating than doing laundry at a laundromat.
2. In the first place, you must get a ton of change together.
3. At the laundromat there are never enough washing machines.
4. And, of course, on every other dryer is the sign: "Out of Order."
5. At the end of the ordeal comes the time for even more fun: ironing.

EXERCISE 25 **Write!** *Complete the five sentences begun below. After writing each sentence, underline the simple subject. If you use more than one subject in a sentence, underline all of them.*

1. Towards the end of the day ______________________________

____.

2. In the corner of the bedroom was __________________________

____.

3. In the trunk of the old Chevy is ______________________________

____.

4. At the end of the street there are ______________________________

____.

5. Over here behind the dictionary is ______________________________

____.

Plural Subjects

Subjects may also be **plural**, which means "more than one." Most plural nouns have *-s* or *-es* as an ending to indicate they are plural. For example:

one girl—two girls	one bus—two buses
one town—two towns	one city—two cities

Some subjects, however, form their plurals by changing a vowel or by adding an ending other than *-s* or *-es*. For example:

one man—two men (vowel changes from *a* to *e*)
one woman—two women (vowel changes from *a* to *e*)
one child—two children (ending *-ren* added)

Also, remember that the subject pronouns may be singular or plural. These words, too, form their plurals by ways other than adding *-s* or *-es* (see p. 28).

Compound Subjects

Just as a sentence may have more than one verb, it may also have more than one subject. This happens when a sentence is about more than one person, place, thing, or action. For example:

Fred and Ethel went to the party.

Verb: "went"
Question: Who or what went to the party?
Answer: "Fred" and "Ethel"; so "Fred" and "Ethel" are the subjects of the verb "went."

Here the sentence is not just about Fred and not just about Ethel; it is about *both* Fred and Ethel. These kinds of subjects are called **compound subjects**.

PRACTICE EXERCISE

EXERCISE 26 *Return to the sentences you wrote for Exercise 21. For each sentence, indicate whether the subject is singular, plural, or compound. If none of the subjects is plural or compound, rewrite so that at least two sentences have plural subjects and at least two have compound subjects.*

Understood Subjects

In some sentences, the subject may not be stated. This is especially true in sentences that give instructions. For example:

Go to the store and buy a loaf of bread.

Verb: "go"
Question: Who or what go to the store?
Answer: Not stated.

As you can see, the subject of the verb "go" in the example sentence is not directly stated. Instead, the subject is *understood*.

(You) Go to the store and buy a loaf of bread.

The subject of the sentence is "You," and it does not always have to appear in the sentence. Any time a sentence gives instructions without naming a subject, check to see if the sentence is telling "you," the reader, to do something. If it is, then the subject is the **understood you**.

PRACTICE EXERCISE

EXERCISE 27 *In the following exercise, underline the simple subject in each of the sentences. If the subject is understood, write "you" in the space above the sentence.*

Anyone can make a good impression in an interview by following a few simple steps. First, prepare for the interview the day before. Do this by selecting your clothes, keeping the employer's expectations in mind. Next, go to bed early the night before the interview. Getting plenty of sleep is important. In the morning, eat a good breakfast. Your mind will not function at its best on an empty stomach. You should allow extra time to get to the interview. Arriving half an hour early is better than being one minute late. Finally, try to relax during the interview.

REVIEW EXERCISES

EXERCISE 28 *Now check your total understanding of subjects. For this exercise, return to the sentences you wrote for Exercise 25 and underline the simple subject in each sentence. The subject may be any of the types you studied in this chapter. Remember, the best way to locate a subject is to find the verb first, then ask "who" or "what."*

*EXERCISE 29 *Underline the simple subject of each sentence in the following paragraph.*

Enrolling for the fall semester at college was an interesting experience. According to the instructions in the college bulletin, I was eligible for mail-in registration. I mailed in my form, feeling proud of myself for beating the long registration lines. But problems developed during my first day of classes. In my second class of the day, my math instructor told me to take a more advanced math course. In order to do that, I had to go to the registrar's office to get a new class card. During my hour-long wait in the line, I wondered about the value of mailing in my form. When I finally reached the registrar's desk, all of the math courses were closed. The clerk gave me a special form to get me into one of the closed courses. For the rest of the day, I wandered around the campus trying to get the dean and the vice-president to sign my form.

EXERCISE 30 *Underline the simple subject of each sentence in the following paragraph.*

One very successful enterprise in America today is the pet food industry. More Americans own pets now than ever before. This can be explained by a number of factors. For one thing, people feel a greater need for protection because of high crime rates in most cities. Another reason for the rising number of pets is loneliness. For more and more people, an animal is a companion. All of these pets must eat. As a matter of fact, most American pets eat better than many people do in other countries. People in America often look upon their pets as human. For this reason, they spend a lot of money on them, making the pet food industry a very profitable business.

EXERCISE 31

Write!

Write five to ten sentences listing the ideas you have about pets and explaining why you think people devote so much time to animals. After writing all of your sentences, underline the subject or subjects.

1. ______________________________

____

2. ______________________________

____

3. ______________________________

____

4. ______________________________

____

5. ______________________________

____

6. ____

____

7. ____

____

8. ____

____

9. ____

____

10. ____

____

PRODUCE A COMPLETE THOUGHT

In addition to having a verb and a subject, every sentence *must express a complete thought*. This means that a sentence must provide the reader with complete information and not leave out any essential elements. For example:

Shirley takes a bus to the airport.

In this sentence, the reader learns all there is to know: who is involved (Shirley), and what she does (takes a bus to the airport). Now look at this example:

If Shirley takes a bus to the airport.

Does this give a complete thought? The reader still knows who is involved (Shirley), and what she does (takes a bus to the airport), but there is an additional element in this sentence—the word "if."

The word "if" makes this sentence incomplete because it creates a condition. After reading this sentence, a reader would ask, "What will happen?" There is no answer to that question, so the sentence is incomplete. Several such words create a condition; when they are placed in front of a sentence, they make the thought incomplete. In order to be complete, a sentence that states a condition must also state the possible result of that condition. For example, to make the above sentence complete, the "if" condition must be described.

CONDITION	RESULT
If Shirley takes a bus to the airport,	she will miss her plane.

Now the sentence expresses a complete thought because it shows the possible results of the condition introduced by "if."

You will learn more about producing a complete thought in the next chapter. For now, it will be enough to practice recognizing complete and incomplete thoughts.

PRACTICE EXERCISE

*EXERCISE 32 *In the following exercise, place an "X" next to the number of any sentence that does* not *express a complete thought. Remember, if a sentence presents a condition but does not show the possible results of that condition, the thought is not complete.*

____ 1. My uncles hang wallpaper for a living.

____ 2. If the car does not stop at the intersection.

____ 3. Because the choir rehearses every Sunday night.

____ 4. The lights on the Christmas tree are blinking.

____ 5. Since the print on the pages is too small to read.

____ 6. When I feel lost and alone.

____ 7. Although my courses require strict attention.

____ 8. Some of the people in my apartment house are weird.

____ 9. Until he is able to pay the rent.

____10. If the policeman falls asleep in his car.

WRITING ASSIGNMENT 2

Write a paragraph on any one of the topics listed below. Remember what you learned about the writing process in Chapter 1:

- Make sure you *understand the topic.*
- *List* all of the thoughts you have about the topic.
- *Select* the most convincing items from your list and arrange them into an order.
- *Expand the ideas* you will be using for support.
- *Write the rough draft.*

When you finish writing your rough draft, read it again to make sure that each sentence has at least one main verb and one subject.

Topics

1. Name a favorite hobby, sport, or activity and explain why you enjoy it.
2. Explain all of the different steps you went through during college registration and indicate whether you thought the process was efficient or not.
3. Name the qualities that you look for in a good car and explain why each one is important.

CHAPTER REVIEW

In this chapter you learned that every sentence must have a complete verb and a subject, and that it must express a complete thought.

The verb is the word that completes the message of a sentence. The verb may show action, or it may connect the subject with a word or phrase that describes the subject. Infinitives ("to" + verb) and participles (verb + "ing") are verb forms, but they cannot function as true verbs in a sentence. Thus, it is essential that every sentence have at least one *action* or *linking* verb. Of course, many sentences that you write will contain more than one verb.

The subject is the word the sentence is about. It is the word about which the verb says something, so the best way to locate the subject in a sentence is to find the verb first and then to ask "who" or "what." Subjects, like verbs, come in various forms: they may be nouns (words that name something), pronouns (words that refer to nouns), single words, or long phrases. Also like verbs, subjects may be located in the beginning, middle, or towards the end of a sentence. In the case of sentences which give instructions or commands, the subject may be understood (["you"] Take the trash out.) rather than stated directly. Because your writing contains many ideas, most of your sentences will contain more than one subject.

Some groups of words, even though they contain both a verb and a subject, still do not express a complete thought. This happens when a sentence is introduced by a word that creates a condition ("If" we go today). The result of the condition must be included to make the sentence complete (If we go today, we will need a babysitter.).

SUPPLEMENTAL EXERCISES

Use the exercises below for additional practice in locating verbs and subjects.

*EXERCISE 33 *Underline the action verb in each sentence.*

1. Freda goes into the downtown part of the city at least once a week.
2. She likes the excitement and the variety.
3. The clothing shops always sell things at lower prices.
4. Also, the shops offer the latest styles before any of the suburban stores.
5. For these reasons, Freda buys all of her clothes downtown.
6. She also enjoys the different movies and theaters downtown.
7. The movie theaters always show the latest movies.
8. The people in the city amuse Freda more than anything else.

9. On almost every corner she sees something strange or funny.

10. The most interesting people come downtown.

*EXERCISE 34 *Underline the linking verb in each sentence.*

1. Registration for classes was on Tuesday.
2. It seemed too early for the end of summer.
3. I was with all my friends in the long registration lines.
4. We were happy to see each other again.
5. Many of us were in the same classes last semester.
6. Bruce was in my French class with me.
7. He looked very healthy after the long summer off from school.
8. Marlene and Tom were concerned about their schedules.
9. My classes are all in the morning.
10. Registration seemed to go very quickly this semester.

EXERCISE 35 *Underline the verb or verbs in each sentence. The verbs may be either action or linking verbs.*

1. My car coughs and sputters in the morning.
2. I talk to it and encourage it to run smoothly.
3. Sometimes the car responds and gives me no trouble.
4. Other times it is stubborn and refuses to start.
5. At such moments, I become unreasonable.
6. Instead, I scream and curse.
7. I pound my fists against the steering wheel and stamp my feet on the floorboards.
8. These actions have no effect.

9. I finally open the hood and tinker with the carburetor.

10. Sometimes I succeed and get the car to start.

In Exercises 36 and 37, underline the simple subject in each sentence. The subject may be either a noun or a pronoun.

EXERCISE 36

1. Fred did not enjoy his trip to college.
2. The bus ride took over twelve hours.
3. The bus seemed to stop at every small town.
4. Falling asleep was impossible.
5. Hartford was the biggest city along the way.
6. The driver stopped at a restaurant there.
7. Fred did not want anything to eat.
8. His stomach was unsettled from the long ride.
9. He ate an antacid tablet while sitting in the bus.
10. His stomach gradually began to feel a little better.

EXERCISE 37

1. The trip started again after half an hour.
2. The girl sitting beside Fred put down her magazine.
3. She looked at Fred and smiled.
4. Fred smiled back and introduced himself.
5. He told her he was on his way to college.
6. Soon they were having a nice conversation.
7. Most of their conversation was about movies.
8. A movie they both enjoyed was *Beverly Hills Cop*.
9. It was the most exciting movie of the summer.
10. At the next stop, the girl said good-bye and got off the bus.

*EXERCISE 38 *Underline the simple subject in each sentence and indicate whether the subject is singular or plural.*

1. People go to college for many different reasons.
2. For one thing, college offers opportunities.
3. Many different programs are available.
4. Some students go to college to learn about new ideas.
5. They want to increase their knowledge.
6. Other students are more interested in getting a good job.
7. These students take courses to train for a specific occupation.
8. Going to college is a way to occupy time for some people.
9. These students have not yet decided what careers they want to pursue.
10. A college should be able to serve all the different needs of its students.

In Exercises 39 and 40, circle *the complete verb and then* underline *the simple subject in each sentence. Remember to find the verb* before *you look for the subject.* Note: *Some sentences may have more than one pair of subjects and verbs.*

*EXERCISE 39 Many students have a great fear of writing courses. To them, a writing class is a strange and mysterious place. In it, they will be asked to perform complicated tricks with words and sentences. Of course these fears are unnecessary. A writing course, like most other college courses, presents the student with a clear set of objectives. Most of the students in such a course can complete it successfully. Basic writing students must remember that writing is not a mysterious process. Writing requires more time and practice than many other college activities. If a student is willing to devote the time and energy, he can become a good writer. Writing, like most worthwhile things in life, does not come easily for many people.

EXERCISE 40

Tapes are better than records for several reasons. First of all, tapes produce better sound than records. Also, tapes are more convenient. Three or four albums may be included on one reel of tape, thus taking up less storage space. Next, tapes cannot be broken as easily as records. Unless something goes wrong with the tape recorder, tapes will last for many years. Also, tapes may be used in more places. With a cassette tape recorder, tapes can be played in the car or just about anywhere. Finally, owning tapes is much less expensive.

3 / Identify and correct sentence fragments

FIND AND CORRECT BY ADDING OR COMBINING

In the last chapter you learned to recognize correct sentences by making sure each sentence met the three requirements of all correct sentences: (1) it must have a complete verb; (2) it must have a subject; (3) it must express a complete thought.

In this chapter, you will apply this knowledge. First, you will practice recognizing sentences as either correct or incorrect by checking each sentence for the three requirements. Then, after you have located the incorrect sentences, you will learn how to correct them by adding what is missing, or by combining a fragment with a correct sentence.

Complete Verb

As you know, every correct sentence has at least one verb:

The meadowlark *sings*.

Now consider the following:

The meadowlark

Is this a fragment or a sentence? You can check it by looking for the three requirements:

Does it have a verb? No.
Does it have a subject? Yes: "meadowlark."
Does it express a complete thought? No.

If the answer to any one of these questions is "no," then the group of words is a **sentence fragment**. It is a sentence fragment because it does not tell you anything about the meadowlark. What did the meadowlark do? You cannot say because the *verb* is missing.

The easiest way to correct a sentence fragment is to add whatever is missing from the sentence. To correct the example above, we simply add a verb:

The meadowlark *sings.*

Now test the sentence again:

Does it have a verb? Yes: "sings."
Does it have a subject? Yes: "meadowlark."
Does it express a complete thought? Yes: "The meadowlark sings."

Always ask these three questions when you are trying to decide whether a group of words is a sentence or a sentence fragment. If you find that a requirement is missing, add what is needed to correct the sentence fragment.

PRACTICE EXERCISES

In Exercises 1 and 2, decide whether each group of words is a correct sentence or a sentence fragment by checking for the three requirements. Correct any sentence fragments you find by adding whatever is missing.

Example:

The streets of the city were crowded with shoppers.

EXERCISE 1

Write!

1. Last week Sheila and I.
2. A wonderful time in the morning.
3. Breakfast in the fancy New York restaurant.
4. After breakfast we walked through the city streets.
5. The shop windows along Fifth Avenue.

6. The colorful street vendors on every corner.
7. A hamburger and potato chips for lunch.
8. A matinee on Broadway.
9. We both thought the show was terrific.
10. A party at a friend's house.

EXERCISE 2

Write!

1. On the way to the airport.
2. My first real vacation in five years.
3. I left the house two hours ahead of time.
4. Between two exits on the expressway.
5. Traffic at a dead stop.
6. Two miles ahead, a big accident.
7. A tractor trailer, a pickup truck, and three cars.
8. It took the police an hour to clean everything up.
9. Finally at the airport.
10. The last passenger on the jet.

Words that look like verbs

Remember the two kinds of words that look like verbs:

1. *to* + verb: To sleep for the rest of my life.
2. verb + *-ing*: Susan driving across the country.

Remember that neither of these types of verbs can be considered the "true verb" in a sentence. It is especially important to remember these two types when you are checking to see if a group of words is a sentence or a sentence fragment. For example:

To sleep for the rest of my life.

Check this group of words by looking for the three requirements:

> *Does it have a verb?* No: (''To sleep'' cannot be the verb.)
> *Does it have a subject?* No.
> *Does it express a complete thought?* No.

In this case, the group of words is missing both a verb and a subject, so you add both parts:

> *I wanted* to sleep for the rest of my life.

Now it has a verb (''wanted''), and it has a subject (''I''), and it expresses a complete thought.

Check this group of words to see if it is a sentence or a fragment:

> Susan driving across the country.
>
> *Does it have a verb?* No. (''driving'' cannot be the verb because verbs ending in *-ing* must always have a helping verb.)
> *Does it have a subject?* Yes: ''Susan.''
> *Does it express a complete thought?* No.

Now correct the sentence fragment by adding what is missing:

> Susan *was* driving across the country.

Now the sentence has a verb (''driving''), and it has a subject (''Susan''), and it expresses a complete thought.

Another way to correct fragments of this type is to combine them with other sentences. This is usually possible in paragraphs, since all of the sentences in a paragraph relate to each other. For example:

> My sister and I had a wonderful time at the party. Singing and dancing all night long.

You can see that the second group of words is a fragment. You can correct it by adding a subject and a helping verb:

> S V
> *We were* singing and dancing all night long.

But you can also correct it by combining it with the preceding sentence:

> My sister and I had a wonderful time at the party, singing and dancing all night long.

This kind of correction is also possible with fragments caused by verbs beginning with "to." For example:

My sister exercises every morning. To keep herself in shape.

You can correct the fragment by adding a subject and a verb.

S V
She does this to keep herself in shape.

Or you can combine the fragment with the sentence.

My sister exercises every morning to keep herself in shape.

It is usually better to combine both of these types of fragments with correct sentences. If you combine fragments with sentences, your writing will have more details and will be more interesting to read.

Notice how the fragments in the following paragraph have been combined with correct sentences to form longer, more interesting sentences.

He ran to the corner, frantically waving his arms. The bus driver saw him out of the corner of his eye. Grumbling under his breath, the driver pulled over to pick him up. Feeling a tremendous sense of relief, the young man saw the bus coming toward him. Riding into the city, feeling relaxed and comfortable, he knew he would get there on time.

PRACTICE EXERCISES

EXERCISE 3

Write!

Check the paragraph you wrote for Writing Assignment 2 to see if it has any sentence fragments of the type discussed in this section. If it does, correct the fragments or combine them with correct sentences.

*EXERCISE 4

Locate and correct any sentence fragments in the following groups of sentences. Try to make corrections by combining fragments with correct sentences.

1. Yelling "Geronimo!" My brother jumped from the tree limb into the creek.

2. She awoke the next morning to find that it had snowed. She made her way to the bus stop. Slipping and sliding on the ice.

3. The passion-pink Oldsmobile cruised along the avenue. Whenever they saw a girl, the teenagers in the car leaned out the windows. To attract her attention.

4. To ride in the car with him. We had to hold on and brace our feet against the floor. He was the worst driver I have ever known.

5. He carefully moved the coffee pot out of the way. To avoid knocking it over. Then he reached for the butter and spilled the orange juice.

6. Mildred's husband brought home a painting to give to her. She was very excited and surprised. Thanking him again and again.

7. That was one party I will never forget. All of my friends were there, having a wonderful time. To start the evening off right. Ralph did his imitation of a duck.

8. I can never get in the bathroom because they take half of the morning playing in the bathtub. Leaving only after I pound on the door.

9. My baby is very proud of his vocal chords. Sometimes he spends the entire morning rocking back and forth in his playpen. Singing along with the songs on the radio.

10. My two daughters always dress up like grown-ups. Each of them goes searching in my jewelry box for a pair of my earrings. They love to get all dressed up. Pretending they are in a fashion show.

*EXERCISE 5 *Now locate and correct any fragments you find in the following paragraph. Try to make the corrections by combining fragments with correct sentences.*

I stumbled to the bathroom to take a refreshing shower. Singing and wasting time. After I had showered, I lay across the bed wondering if I should wear what I had already pressed. I finally made up my mind. To wear my blue jeans instead. I spent the next 15 minutes looking for the right shirt. Pulling out every drawer in my bureau. When I finally got dressed, I realized that I was running out of time. To get to school on time. I would have to skip breakfast. I got an apple out of the refrigerator and ran out to the bus stop. Biting into it as I ran.

Fragments with Relative Pronouns

Another kind of fragment is introduced by one of the following words:

who which that

These words are called **relative pronouns**. Recall from Chapter 2 that a pronoun is a word that takes the place of a noun. A relative pronoun is a special kind of pronoun that introduces a description which *relates* back to a noun. For example:

The man who has a red beard is my father.

In this sentence, the relative pronoun "who" introduces the words "who has a red beard." These words *describe* the noun "man." They *relate back* to the word "man."

Now look at the following group of words:

The student who earns the highest grade.

Groups of words introduced by one of the relative pronouns ("who," "which," or "that") are *describing* words; they describe the noun they follow in the sentence. In this example, "who earns the highest grade" describes "the student." But the describing words do not complete the sentence. What about the student? The group of words does not tell you what the student *did* because there is no verb. The verb "earns" is part of the group of words that describes the student; it is *not* the main verb in the sentence.

SUBJECT DESCRIPTION OF SUBJECT VERB?
Fragment: The student who earns the highest grade

To correct this kind of fragment, simply add the part that is missing: a verb

SUBJECT DESCRIPTION OF SUBJECT VERB
Sentence: The student who earns the highest grade *will win*.

The same is true of the other relative pronouns, "which" and "that."

SUBJECT DESCRIPTION OF SUBJECT VERB?
Fragment: The house that I would like to own

SUBJECT DESCRIPTION OF SUBJECT VERB
Sentence: The house that I would like to own *is* on Baker Street.

SUBJECT DESCRIPTION OF SUBJECT VERB?
Fragment: The plant, which is a kind of cactus

SUBJECT DESCRIPTION OF SUBJECT VERB
Sentence: The plant, which is a kind of cactus, bloomed today.

Remember: (1) Groups of words introduced by the relative pronouns "who," "which," and "that" usually describe the subject of the sentence. (2) To correct this kind of fragment, simply complete the sentence by adding a verb.

PRACTICE EXERCISES

EXERCISE 6 **Write!** *Return again to the paragraph you wrote for Writing Assignment 2. Underline all of the relative pronouns you used and check to make sure that every sentence that includes a relative pronoun has a main verb. Correct any fragments that you find.*

EXERCISE 7 *Identify and correct any sentence fragments by adding what is missing.*

1. My favorite television show, which comes on once a week.
2. The actor who makes the show interesting.
3. The star of the show, who is a woman.
4. The one thing that makes the show entertaining.

5. Some other shows that I like.

6. Comedies, which are my favorite kind of shows.

7. Police stories, which are often violent.

8. The crimes that are solved by the detectives.

9. The chase scenes, which are the best part.

10. My favorite actor, who plays a detective.

Review

So far in this chapter, you have learned to identify fragments that lack verbs. These kinds of fragments may be in several different forms:

1. The fragment with no verb at all:

SUBJECT VERB?
The meadowlark

2. The fragment with a verb preceded by "to":

SUBJECT VERB?
I to sleep for the rest of my life.

3. The fragment with an *-ing* verb:

SUBJECT VERB?
Susan driving across the country.

4. The fragment with a relative pronoun:

SUBJECT DESCRIPTION OF SUBJECT VERB?
The student who earns the highest grade.

You have also learned two ways to correct these kinds of fragments:

1. Add a verb to the fragment:

The meadowlark *sings*.
I *want* to sleep for the rest of my life.
Susan *was* driving across the country.
The student who earns the highest grade *will win*.

2. Combine the fragment with a correct sentence:

CORRECT SENTENCE
My sister and I had a wonderful time at the party,

FRAGMENT
singing and dancing all night long.

CORRECT SENTENCE FRAGMENT
My sister exercises every morning to keep herself in shape.

Subject

As you know, every correct sentence has at least one subject. This is the word that tells who or what the sentence is about.

The meadowlark sings all day long.

If you remove the subject from the sentence, the result is another kind of sentence fragment:

Sings all day long.

This is a fragment because it does not tell you who or what sings. If you test it, you will find that it does not meet the three requirements:

Does it have a verb? Yes: "sings."
Does it have a subject? No.
Does it express a complete thought? No.

You can correct this kind of fragment the same way you corrected fragments in the last section: by adding what is missing:

The *meadowlark* sings all day long.

Now test the sentence again:

Does it have a verb? Yes: "sings."
Does it have a subject? Yes: "meadowlark."
Does it express a complete thought? Yes: "The meadowlark sings all day long."

Notice that the process for finding and correcting fragments has not changed. First you test the sentence by seeing if it meets the three requirements, and then you add whatever is missing to correct any sentence fragments.

PRACTICE EXERCISES

EXERCISE 8

Write!

In this exercise, a subject has been provided. For each subject, add a verb to complete the sentence.

Example:

The old floorboards creak during the night.

1. Our new kitten ______________________________ .
2. My favorite car ______________________________ .
3. My last day off ______________________________ .
4. The meal of steak and eggs ______________________________ .
5. The telephone call ______________________________ .
6. His parents ______________________________ .
7. The boss with the bad temper ______________________________ .
8. Her back yard ______________________________ .
9. The trees in the park ______________________________ .

10. The cars parked in the street ______________________________

____.

EXERCISE 9 *Decide whether each group of words is a correct sentence or a sentence fragment by checking for the three requirements. Correct any sentence fragments you find by adding whatever is missing.*

1. Americans are spending more and more time in recreation.
2. In the past, only visited parks during summer vacations.
3. Now are providing year-round recreation.
4. Not only are traveling, but enjoy other forms of recreation as well.
5. Spend weekends golfing, canoeing, hiking, and biking.
6. Most communities are now conscious of this need for recreation.
7. They plan their communities so that they will offer recreation opportunities.
8. Build man-made ponds and lakes for boating and ice skating.
9. Often establish nature centers in nearby parks.
10. Set aside some city streets only for jogging and bicycle riding.

Review

In this section of the chapter, you learned to identify and correct sentence fragments that lack subjects. First you test the sentence by seeing if it meets the three requirements:

SUBJECT? VERB
Sings all day long.

and then you add whatever is missing to correct the fragment:

SUBJECT
The *meadowlark* sings all day long.

WRITING ASSIGNMENT 3

Now take time to apply what you know about sentences to your own writing. Write a paragraph on any one of the topics listed below. Remember the following points.

- Make sure you *understand the topic*.
- *List* all of the thoughts you have about the topic.
- *Select* the most convincing items from your list and arrange them into an order.
- *Expand the ideas* you will be using for support.
- *Write the rough draft*.

When you finish writing your rough draft, read it again to locate and correct any sentence fragments.

Topics

1. Name the one thing that you find most annoying in your everyday life and explain how it annoys you.
2. Name the one thing that you find most pleasing in your everyday life and explain how it pleases you.
3. Describe a process that you go through every day. It could be the way you get up in the morning, the way you drive to school or work, or the way you prepare your meals. Be sure to give all of the steps involved in the process.

Complete Thought

As you know, the third requirement of every sentence is that it must express a complete thought. The cause of most sentence fragments is the fact that they do not express a complete thought.

The meadowlark sings.

Is this a sentence?

Verb:	"sings"
Subject:	"meadowlark"
Complete thought:	"The meadowlark sings."

After you have completed your tests, you find that that is a sentence. Now try this one:

When the meadowlark sings.

Verb:	"sings"
Subject:	"meadowlark"
Complete thought:	No!

This group of words still has a verb and a subject, but now it is a sentence fragment because it no longer expresses a complete thought. The word "when" at the beginning of the sentence creates a condition: "When the meadowlark sings . . . "—what happens? There must be a statement that explains what happens as a result of the condition.

CONDITION RESULT
When the meadowlark sings, the other birds listen.

Now the condition created by "when" is completely stated, so the sentence expresses a complete thought. *Remember: A group of words can have a verb and a subject and still be a sentence fragment.*

Conditional words

The group of words listed below all create fragments when they are put in front of sentences. These words are called *subordinating conjunctions*, but we can also think of them as **conditional words**, since, like "if," they create a condition that makes the sentence incomplete.

*Category**	*Word*	*Example*
TIME	before	Before the ship sails, ____________
	after	After my income tax check arrives, ____________
	since	Since she graduated from college, ____________
	until	Until he learns how to drive, ____________
	while	While we watch the basketball game, ____________
	when	When the Senator goes to Washington, ____________
	whenever	Whenever my wife goes on a diet, ____________
	as	As Bob left his house in the morning, ____________
	just as	Just as the jet touched down on the runway, ____________
EXPLANATION	because	Because there was nothing else to do, ____________
	since	Since the price of coffee kept increasing, ____________

*A complete definition for each of these words will be provided later in this section.

CONDITION	if	If she stays out too late, ________________
		________________________________
	unless	Unless a new source of energy is developed, ________________
OPPOSITION	although	Although the weatherman predicted rain,
		________________________________
	though	Though I wanted to spend the day at the beach, ________________

The word "even" in front of any of these words also creates a condition:

Even before the ship sails, ________________________________

Even if she stays out too late, ______________________________

Even though I wanted to spend the day at the beach, ________________

If you place any conditional word at the beginning of a sentence, you will find that a fragment results. Each of these words creates some kind of condition or question, and the possible results of that condition must be explained before the sentence can be considered complete.

Place any of the words in the list in front of the sentences that follow, and notice how they create an incomplete thought.

1. a. All of us go to the game

   b. ______ all of us go to the game.

2. a. Susan wants to build a bookcase.

   b. ______ Susan wants to build a bookcase.

3. a. The entire class learned the lesson

   b. ______ the entire class learned the lesson

4. a. Claire loves to drive her new car.

   b. ______ Claire loves to drive her new car

5. a. The jet had only one good engine.
   b. ______ the jet had only one good engine

Sentence fragments of this kind can be corrected by following the same general procedure we have been using. For example, to correct fragments that were missing verbs, you added a verb. To correct fragments that were missing subjects, you added a subject. So, to correct a fragment that is missing a complete thought because it starts with a conditional word, you add a complete thought:

FRAGMENT + SENTENCE
When the meadowlark sings, the other birds listen.

Any group of words that expresses an incomplete thought may be corrected in this way.

When to use a comma

When you add a complete thought to a fragment, it is sometimes necessary to use a comma. The following rule should be used: *If the conditional word comes at the beginning of the sentence, put a comma between the fragment and the sentence*:

When the meadowlark sings, the other birds listen.

If the conditional word comes in the middle of the sentence, do not use a comma.

The other birds listen *when* the meadowlark sings.

Now return to the five example fragments above and correct them by adding a complete thought. Use a comma if one is necessary.

PRACTICE EXERCISES

EXERCISE 10 **Write!** *Return to the paragraph you wrote for Writing Assignment 2. Underline all of the conditional words you used and check to make sure that none of them has created a sentence fragment. Correct any fragments that you find.*

*EXERCISE 11 *Correct any fragments you find by adding the missing part. Wherever possible, correct the fragments by adding them to a complete thought.*

Example:
My neighbor had a party last night/ because he just got a big raise in salary. It was a great party with a lot of food, music, and interesting people.

1. Last week I finally did something I have always wanted to do. I took my girlfriend down to the lake and went out in a rowboat. Even though neither of us really knew how to row a boat.

2. When we got out onto the lake. I really started to enjoy the experience. There was a nice breeze out on the water, the sun was shining, and the boat was rocking with a soothing, gentle motion.

3. I was thoroughly delighted with the afternoon. Until the boat overturned. Neither Cheryl nor I really knew how it happened. One minute we were in the boat, rowing along very happily. The next minute Cheryl leaned too far over the side, and we were both in the water.

4. Although the water was deep in that part of the lake. Cheryl and I held onto the boat and were able to stay afloat. We were both frightened at first, but then we started to laugh at our situation.

5. We were in the water a long time. Before another boat came along and picked us up. The man who rented us the boat was pretty angry, and we were both soaking wet when we got in my car, but Cheryl and I had a good time anyway.

EXERCISE 12 *Now try identifying and correcting fragments in a paragraph. Correct any fragments you find by adding the missing part. Wherever possible, correct the fragments by adding them to a complete thought.*

My friend Irv has more energy than anyone I've ever met. Even though he labors all day at work as a carpenter. He jogs around the neighborhood as soon as he gets home. After he is finished eating his supper. Irv goes into his recreation room and does exercises for half an hour. As if that is not enough exercise, he dashes off to the tennis courts at night. When there is nothing good on television. If Irv is not doing something active every minute of the day. He thinks he is being lazy. The more things he does, the more energy he gets to go out and do more things. Irv just never seems to get tired. Although that much activity would be more than enough to wear me out.

How to use conditional words in sentences

Each conditional word has its own special meaning and presents its own special condition. It is important to recognize conditional words when you see them so you can avoid writing sentence fragments. But these words are also very useful in creating interesting sentences. The following list explains how each word is used in a sentence and what kind of condition it creates. It is not necessary to memorize these words, but you should refer back to them when necessary.

CONDITIONAL WORDS OF TIME These words create time limitations on the sentence; what happens in the main part of the sentence depends on the time word used in the other part.

before = "in advance"; "earlier than"
Before the children cross the street, they look both ways.
Before I eat dinner, I usually read the newspaper.

after = "behind"; "later than"
After the student passed the test, he breathed a sigh of relief.

since = "from an earlier time until now"
Since the beginning of winter, I have been waiting for spring.

until = "up to a particular time or event"
Until she gives the money back, I will not speak to her.

while = "during a certain time"
While the children fought, he removed his leather belt.

when = "at a certain time"
When the rooster crows, the sun is rising.

whenever = "at any time"
Whenever you leave the house, lock all the doors and windows.

as = "at the same time"
As he swung the bat, the ball curved sharply.

just as = "at the same time"
Just as he swung the bat the ball curved sharply.

CONDITIONAL WORDS OF EXPLANATION These words create conditions in which the conditional part of the sentence gives a reason for what happens in the main part.

because = "for a certain reason"
Because you borrowed the money, you must pay it back.

since = "for a certain reason"
Since you borrowed the money, you must pay it back.

WORDS OF CONDITION These words create possible conditions, and the main part of the sentence explains what will happen under those conditions.

if = "according to a certain condition"
If you pay the money, I will fix your car.

unless = "except for a certain condition"
Unless it rains today, I will lie out in the sun.

CONDITIONAL WORDS OF OPPOSITION These words create conditions in which one part of the sentence is the opposite of the other.

although = "in spite of the fact that a certain thing is so"
Although he may be reliable, I still don't trust him.

though = "in spite of the fact that a certain thing is so"
Though he may be reliable, I still don't trust him.

The word "**even**" used in front of any of these words adds emphasis to the condition. For example:

If you go to the movie, I will not stay home. (This sentence states a condition, a "deal.")
Even if you go to the movie, I will not stay home. (Now the condition is more strict; there is almost no way out of the condition.)

PRACTICE EXERCISES

EXERCISE 13

Write!

Write a different sentence for each of the conditional words listed below. After you finish writing each sentence, check it to make sure that it is not a fragment and that it is punctuated correctly.

1. before: ______________________________

____

2. after: ______________________________

____

3. since: ______________________________

____

4. while: ______________________________

____

5. even before: ______________________________

____

6. when: ______________________________

____

7. whenever: ______________________________

____

8. as: ______________________________

____

9. just as: ______________________________

____

10. because: ______________________________

____

*EXERCISE 14

In the following sentences, fill in the spaces with one of the conditional words. Make sure that the conditional word you use has the appropriate meaning to fit into the sentence. A number of different conditional words may make sense when placed in the blank spaces. You may refer back to the list on the preceding pages.

1. I have to pay the rent ______________ I can pay the electric bill.
2. ______________ the dog ran away, he felt sad and alone.
3. ______________ the dishes have been washed, the children may watch television.
4. ______________ the Mayor does not resign, he will probably be impreached.
5. I am going to the conference in Dallas ______________ my company is paying for it.
6. ______________ what you say may be true, I still believe my team will win.
7. Maria did all her English homework ______________ she watched television.
8. ______________ Albert stepped off the curb, a car splashed water all over him.
9. I refuse to talk to you any more ______________ you go out with me tonight!
10. ______________ my car is fixed in time, I can drive to the beach for the weekend.

EXERCISE 15 *Now do the same thing in the following paragraph. Be sure to use a conditional word that is appropriate to the meaning of the sentence.*

I hate shopping at the supermarket ______________ everything always seems to go wrong for me. First of all, ______________ I arrive, all the shopping carts are gone. If I am lucky enough to find a cart for myself, it usually has only three wheels. ________________________ supermarkets have millions and millions of items in stock, they are always out of what I need. ________________________ I need brown shoelaces, they have only black ones. When I want a small can of peas, they have only the jumbo size. Finally, five of the six cashiers who are in the store always seem to go on a coffee break ________________________ I reach the checkout counters.

Phrases as fragments

The fragments you have studied up to this point have been missing either a verb, a subject, or a complete thought. The last type of fragment is probably the easiest to recognize because it does not meet any of the three requirements of a sentence. These fragments are **phrases**, groups of words that may have a verb or a subject but do not have *both*.

Including London, Paris, and Rome.
Especially George.
And the day before, too.
With a lot of chocolate syrup.
For example, a Cadillac.
Also some scrambled eggs.

As you can see, these groups of words are only *parts* of sentences; they have no verb or subject and do not express a complete thought. You probably would not write this kind of fragment by itself, but you might write one in combination with another sentence.

I want to go to many different places. Including London, Paris, and Rome.
A lot of my friends are crazy. Especially George.
Linda had a miserable day yesterday. And the day before, too.
He loves pecan crunch ice cream. With a lot of chocolate syrup.
There are a lot of different things I want. For example, a Cadillac.
I had a big steak for breakfast this morning. Also some scrambled eggs.

Now the fragments make a little more sense because you can see that they add to the sentences that come before them. But they are still not correct because they do not have the three requirements of a sentence: a verb, a subject, and a complete thought.

You can correct this kind of fragment by combining it with the preceding sentence.

> I want to go to many different places, including London, Paris, and Rome.
> A lot of my friends are crazy, especially George.
> Linda had a miserable day yesterday and the day before, too.
> He loves pecan crunch ice cream with a lot of chocolate syrup.

Or you can correct it by adding the missing parts.

> There are a lot of different things I want. For example,
> S V
> I want a Cadillac.

> S
> I had a big steak for breakfast this morning. I also
> V
> had some scrambled eggs.

This kind of fragment is useful because it adds details and examples to sentences and makes them more interesting. But it must be combined with a correct sentence or made into a complete sentence by adding a verb and a subject. Fragments like these are often introduced by one of the following words:

especially	with
including	for example
and	also

PRACTICE EXERCISE

EXERCISE 16 *In the following sentence groups, correct any fragments you find either by combining them with correct sentences or by adding a verb and a subject to them.*

1. I watched the Late Late Show on television last night. It's unusual for me to stay up that late. Especially on a Wednesday night.

2. The movie was about a criminal who was terrorizing an entire city. He did this by stealing people's pets. And holding them for ransom.
3. The local police department did everything it could to catch the criminal. They even put out several decoys, hoping to catch the petnapper in the act. For example, a trained police dog.
4. No matter what the police did, they couldn't catch the criminal. Finally they contacted the FBI to ask for help. With their unusual problem. The FBI could not decide whether to help with the case or not since only animals were being kidnapped.
5. I thought I had the mystery all figured out. I was sure I knew how the movie was going to end. Including who was kidnapping all the pets. Unfortunately, I'll never know if I was right or wrong because I fell asleep before the movie ended.

Review

In this part of the chapter, you learned to identify and correct sentence fragments that do not express a complete thought. The two most common fragments of this type are those introduced by one of the conditional words:

When the meadowlark sings.

or parts of sentences that add details or examples:

Especially George.

The best way to correct these fragments is to combine them with complete sentences or to add a complete thought to them.

FRAGMENT + SENTENCE
When the meadowlark sings, the other birds listen.

SENTENCE + FRAGMENT
A lot of my friends are crazy, especially George.

REVIEW EXERCISE

EXERCISE 17 *This exercise contains all the types of fragments you have learned in this chapter. Correct any fragments you find by adding what is missing.*

1. The scientist who invented the atom bomb.
2. Nancy and Virginia planning on going to Florida over spring break.
3. If it keeps on snowing.
4. To drive on the expressway during rush hour.
5. Since Fred and I studied for the exam.
6. The young lady wearing the tweed suit.
7. The part of my vacation that I enjoyed the most.
8. Hoping to hear from you very soon.
9. When you get to the corner candy store.
10. To be in the army for over twenty years.
11. Including the money she spent for groceries.
12. Although one of my girlfriends is no longer speaking to me.
13. Your invitation, which arrived only yesterday.
14. As I was watching the movie last night.
15. To spend my weekends doing anything at all.
16. Letting their dogs do their business on my lawn.
17. The teenager who ran through the neighborhood late last night.
18. Because she is interested in getting a good job.
19. Since I decided to make my own supper.
20. If you are sure that you can drink that much without getting sick.

FIND AND CORRECT FRAGMENTS IN PARAGRAPHS

In the first part of this chapter, you learned how to identify and correct the most common kinds of sentence fragments. You have probably found it pretty easy to find and correct the fragments in the sentence exercises, but more difficult to correct the fragments in the sentence group and paragraph exercises and in your own writing.

Most of the writing you do will be in paragraphs and groups of paragraphs. For this reason, it is most important that you learn to correct your paragraphs. Finding and correcting fragments in paragraphs is different from finding and correcting them in isolated sentences in two ways. (1) Fragments in paragraphs are harder to find; and (2) fragments in paragraphs are easier to correct. When you do find fragments in a paragraph, they are easier to correct because *they can almost always be combined with another sentence.* This is true of the exercise paragraphs in this book, and of your own paragraphs. Thus, your main task when you write your own paragraphs will be to *find* the fragments. Most of these fragments contain useful information and should be combined with correct sentences.

Here is an example of a paragraph that contains some sentence fragments. Underline the fragments.

> Last week my brother and I went to see a Broadway show. <u>Although I didn't think the show was very good. It was still an interesting experience.</u> After the show we went for a long walk. <u>And had dinner at a fancy restaurant.</u> When dinner was over, we started on the long trip home. <u>Hoping that we could go back to New York again some time.</u>

Here is the same paragraph, but the fragments have been corrected by combining them with correct sentences.

> Last week my brother and I went to see a Broadway show. Although I didn't think the show was very good, it was still an interesting experience. After the show we went for a long walk and had dinner at a fancy restaurant. When dinner was over, we started on the long trip home, hoping that we could go back to New York again some time.

Notice that none of the details in the paragraph has been eliminated. Instead, they remain in the paragraph as parts of correct sentences. Take a look at what happens if you simply eliminate all the fragments from the paragraph.

> Last week my brother and I went to see a Broadway show. It was an interesting experience. After the show we went for a long walk. When dinner was over, we started on the long trip home.

If you simply remove the fragments instead of combining them with sentences, the paragraph is stripped of several important details and no longer makes sense or is as interesting as it was. *Always try to use the fragments you write by combining them with correct sentences.*

PRACTICE EXERCISE

EXERCISE 18 *Correct any sentence fragments you find in the following paragraph. Wherever possible, correct the fragments by combining them with correct sentences.*

> I used to sleepwalk. When I was younger. I also talked in my sleep. I could never remember doing these things, but my brother would always tell me the next morning. Some of the things I did in my sleep were pretty funny. One time I wandered around in the back yard late at night. Dressed only in my underwear. A week after that my father found me in the kitchen at two o'clock in the morning. Smiling and eating a bowl of Cheerios. On other occasions, I was found sleeping in the bathtub. Or under the bed. Although I don't walk in my sleep any more. Sometimes I still talk in my sleep. Some day I am going to have a tape recorder going so I can hear what I have to say during the night.

It is sometimes difficult to locate fragments in a paragraph because they are "hiding" among the rest of the sentences. Many times, when you read over a paragraph that contains fragments, your mind automatically combines the fragments with other sentences, so you cannot "hear" the fragments. If you find this is happening to you, you must try to separate each sentence in the paragraph. There are three ways you can do this.

1. Read each sentence in the paragraph *out loud*, making sure to stop at the end of each sentence. You may not always be able to read your work out loud, but try

it when it is possible. It will make it easier for you to "hear" where each sentence ends.

2. Read each sentence in the paragraph *from the last to the first*. This technique will force you to see where each sentence begins and ends, and your mind will not be able to combine automatically.
3. The best method to start with, since it is the most mechanical, is to *rewrite each sentence in the paragraph, one at a time*. Do this *after* you have written your paragraph. On a separate piece of paper, write out the sentence, then *stop*! Examine that sentence to see if it is correct. If it is, fold the paper over to get the first sentence out of your sight and then write out the second sentence from beginning to end and examine it by itself. If it is correct, fold the paper over again and start on the third. Do this for every sentence in the paragraph. This technique allows you to examine each sentence *by itself* and eliminates the distractions that other sentences may provide. You will probably find it a dull and mechanical process, but after you master this procedure, you will be able to isolate and check each sentence mentally, without writing each one out.

With the paragraph below, we will see how this third technique works.

Bill is a tall, slender man who has a very pleasant personality. I have often seen him say hello to the people he meets on the street, whether he knows them or not. He is always easy to talk with because he is rarely in a bad or unpleasant mood. He has never failed to offer me, and many other people, a ride home from school. Even if we do not live along the way. Someday, maybe I'll get him to tell me how he can remain so pleasant all the time. He must have something special going for him.

Here is the above paragraph broken down into sentences for proofreading.

OK 1. Bill is a tall, slender man who has a very pleasant personality.
OK 2. I have often seen him say hello to the people he meets on the street, whether he knows them or not.
OK 3. He is always easy to talk with because he is rarely in a bad or unpleasant mood.
OK 4. He has never failed to offer me, and many other people, a ride home from school.
fragment 5. Even if we do not live along the way.
OK 6. Someday, maybe I'll get him to tell me how he can remain so pleasant all the time.
OK 7. He must have something special going for him.

In this example, the student found that every sentence was correct except for number 5, which was a fragment because of the conditional phrase "even if." Now that the student has located the fragment, he or she can correct it by simply adding it onto the correct sentence with which it would make the most sense. How would you correct the fragment?

PRACTICE EXERCISES

In Exercises 19 and 20, identify and correct any sentence fragments by combining wherever possible. If you have difficulty locating the fragments in these paragraphs, use one of the three techniques described for locating sentence fragments in a paragraph.

*EXERCISE 19

There are several reasons why I decided to major in physical education. To begin with, I have always enjoyed sports. While baseball is my best sport. I have played almost every sport there is, and I do well in most of them. Another reason is that a career teaching physical education would keep me in great shape. For the rest of my life. In addition, I like working with children, and I am sure I would get along well with them and they would be able to learn from me. Finally, my friend, who teaches physical education in high school. Has told me all about the requirements of his job. And the benefits that he receives. His advice to me was that if I wanted a secure and rewarding job. I should major in physical education.

EXERCISE 20

There are many advantages to early morning classes. Even though it may be difficult to get yourself out of bed in the morning. First, attending all of your classes in the morning frees you for the rest of the day. To do whatever you want. Also, whether you believe it or not. Your mind is generally more alert and active early in the morning. This applies not only to you but also to your instructor. When he meets a class at two in the afternoon. He is probably seeing his third class of the day. It is always to the student's advantage to have a class before the instructor has been tired out by a full day of teaching. So, although your eyelids may be heavy. You know you're getting the best out of your teacher.

WRITING ASSIGNMENT 4

Now write a paragraph applying everything you have learned about fragments to your own writing. For this assignment, write a paragraph on one of the topics listed below. Remember the following points.

- Make sure you *understand the topic*.
- *List* all of the thoughts you have about the topic.
- *Select* the most convincing items from your list and arrange them into an order.
- *Expand the ideas* you will be using for support.
- *Write the rough draft*.

When you finish writing your paragraph, rewrite each sentence, one at a time, on a separate piece of paper according to the instructions on p. 76. After you have found and corrected any sentence fragments in your paragraph, copy it over again in regular paragraph form. This will be your "final draft."

Topics

1. What is the best time of day for classes? Write a paragraph presenting your opinion on this, and support it with good reasons. (See Exercise 20.)
2. Write a paragraph naming the curriculum you are in and explaining why you chose that particular curriculum. (See Exercise 19.)

SUPPLEMENTAL EXERCISES

Use Exercises 21–23 below for additional practice in identifying and correcting sentence fragments. Add whatever is missing to make a complete thought (not every group of words, however, may be a fragment). Make sure to punctuate correctly, according to the rule for commas you have learned.

EXERCISE 21

1. Financial difficulties have caused marital problems.
2. A couple who gets married at a young age.
3. One thing that always presents difficulties.
4. Two young people who are not aware of the cost of living.
5. Rent for an apartment, which is a necessity.
6. A husband or wife who has not had enough education to make a lot of money.
7. The expenses that a family has.
8. A couple who thinks that their love will feed them.
9. Marriage, which is becoming more and more expensive.
10. People who have had a divorce.

EXERCISE 22

1. Henry has owned more cars than anyone I know.
2. Bought a run-down '56 Chevy first.
3. Worked on the engine every weekend.
4. Learned a lot about fixing cars.
5. The next car was a five-year-old Ford.
6. Ran all right, but had been in an accident.
7. Good for learning how to repair dents.
8. After that, bought a station wagon.

9. Was happy with that for only a little while.

10. In all, has owned seven or eight different cars.

EXERCISE 23

1. If the job situation does not improve.

2. Because I am interested in this matter.

3. All the carpets have been cleaned.

4. Although he is an excellent typist.

5. Since we all enjoy the shows on television.

6. Unless my uncle gives me some money.

7. Before you can complete the project.

8. Even before I ever knew her name.

9. While I do not enjoy sports, I do like the outdoors.

10. When you are finished reading that magazine.

The paragraphs in Exercises 24 to 26 contain a number of sentence fragments. Wherever possible, correct the fragments by combining them with correct sentences.

*EXERCISE 24

Since I have changed my curriculum to Law Enforcement. There have been some amazing consequences. First of all, I am now interested in my classes. I could never get interested when I was in Business Administration. As a matter of fact, I have done a lot of extra reading about law enforcement. In my spare time. My father is a policeman and, as I expected, he is more concerned with my schoolwork now. Last week he really surprised me. When he invited me to ride with him in his patrol car. My grades have also changed since the change in curriculum. Improving from a "D" to a "B" average. Most of the students in the Law Enforcement curriculum are getting good grades in their courses. Because they are interested in them.

EXERCISE 25 Smoking should not be permitted. In public places like restaurants and theaters. There are several reasons for this. First of all, it is a fire hazard. Another reason is the danger of contracting a disease. From the nicotine in cigarettes. Although almost everyone is well aware that smoking is a dangerous habit. Many people still do not believe that their habit can hurt others who do not smoke. Recent studies show that the amount of smoke a nonsmoker inhales just by being in a room with a smoker is at a dangerous level. Because of these studies. It seems only reasonable to expect that public places would establish separate areas for smokers and nonsmokers.

EXERCISE 26 It was well past the time my daughter should have been home after school. When she did finally come in. She had a scared look on her face. I wanted to know why she was late, because I was very strict about my children being home on time after school. Her story was that one of the girls in the school was constantly picking on her, and this girl and her friends were waiting to fight her. Hoping to avoid a fight. She had decided to take the long way home. I was furious. I told her that she must never let anyone inconvenience her in any way. Because she had the right to walk the street like the rest of the children. I also told her that she must fight the girl, whatever way she could. I told her to fight to win. And never run away again. I never heard anything more about this particular girl again until my daughter was a grown woman with a child of her own. My daughter has often thanked me for making her stand up for her rights. I can say now that I am thankful also, because she continues to exercise this determination. In everything she attempts to do.

4 / Combine sentences

You learned in Chapter 3 that it is always better to combine fragments with sentences than it is to eliminate them. Your sentences become more interesting when you add details or examples to them. In this chapter, you will learn how to identify and use three different types of sentences: the simple sentence, the compound sentence, and the complex sentence.

LEARN THE DIFFERENCE BETWEEN PHRASES AND CLAUSES

As you learned in Chapter 2, every complete sentence has a verb and a subject and expresses a complete thought. Other terms used to describe the main parts of sentences are phrase and clause. If you understand these terms and the concepts they name, you will then be able to identify and correctly use the different *types* of sentences.

Now that you know how to identify verbs and subjects in your sentences, you can easily determine whether a group of words is a phrase or a clause. The following chart shows the difference between **phrases** and **clauses**.

Does the group of words have a		*Then*
Verb?	Yes ⟶	Check for a subject
	No ⟶	It is a *PHRASE*
Subject?	Yes ⟶	Check for a verb
	No ⟶	It is a *PHRASE*
Verb and Subject?	Yes ⟶	It is a *CLAUSE*
	No ⟶	It is a *PHRASE*

PRACTICE EXERCISE

EXERCISE 1 *In this exercise, identify each group of words as either a phrase or a clause. If it is a phrase, indicate what part is missing.**

1. the woman in the Toyota

   phrase? ____ *clause?* ____

   missing part ____________________

2. the cat scampered up the tree

   phrase? ____ *clause?* ____

   missing part ____________________

3. the woman driving the Toyota

   phrase? ____ *clause?* ____

   missing part ____________________

4. taking a leisurely stroll

   phrase? ____ *clause?* ____

   missing part ____________________

5. received a card from my friend

   phrase? ____ *clause?* ____

   missing part ____________________

As you can see from the exercise and the chart, any group of words that does not have *both* a subject and a verb is a **phrase**. A phrase may have a subject OR a verb, but it will not have both.

A **clause**, on the other hand, *does* have both a subject and a verb. Clauses consist of *subject-verb sets*. The subject-verb set in number 2 in the exercise is ''cat scampered.'' Any time you find a subject-verb set within a group of words, you have a clause.

*Here are the correct answers to Exercise 1:
(1) phrase, no verb; (2) sentence; (3) phrase, no verb; (4) phrase, no subject, incomplete verb; (5) phrase, no subject.

As you will see in the following sections, whether a sentence is considered simple, compound, or complex depends upon the number and type of *clauses* it contains.

PRACTICE EXERCISES

EXERCISE 2

Write!

In this exercise, indicate whether each group of words below is a phrase or a clause. First, decide whether each group of words has a subject-verb set. *If the group of words is a phrase, add a clause to it. If the group of words is a clause, expand the clause by adding a phrase to it. See the following examples.*

Examples:

at the races phrase ✓ clause ____

Rewrite: We had a great time at the races.

____

the door slammed *phrase* ____ *clause* ✓

Rewrite: The door slammed, scaring everyone in the room.

1. bought a new record *phrase* ____ *clause* ____

   Rewrite: ____________________

   ____________________.

2. Bob and his sister *phrase* ____ *clause* ____

   Rewrite: ____________________

   ____________________.

3. their parents gave *phrase* ____ *clause* ____

   Rewrite: ____________________

   ____________________.

4. with the new jacket *phrase* ____ *clause* ____

   Rewrite: ____

   ____.

5. the puppy whines *phrase* ____ *clause* ____

   Rewrite: ____

   ____

EXERCISE 3 *Return to the paragraph you wrote for Writing Assignment 4. Underline the* subject-verb sets *in each sentence. You may find more than one set in some sentences because these sentences have more than one clause.*

LEARN THE SIMPLE SENTENCE

The following is an example of a simple sentence.

> The leaves turned scarlet.

Is a simple sentence a phrase or a clause? You are correct if you answered "clause" because this sentence has the subject-verb set "leaves turned." This sentence, like all simple sentences, consists of one **independent clause**. A clause is called "independent" because it expresses a complete thought and can therefore stand alone as a sentence. *All simple sentences are independent clauses.*

Now look at this sentence.

> The leaves on the maple tree turned scarlet.

Is this still a simple sentence? You are correct if you answered "yes" because the sentence still has only a single subject-verb set: "leaves turned." What would you call the additional element—"on the maple tree"—that was added to the sentence? This, of course, is a *phrase* because it contains neither a subject nor a verb. A sentence remains a simple sentence as long as it has only one subject-verb set, or independent clause, no matter how many phrases are added to it. For example, this is still a simple sentence:

> The leaves on the old maple tree turned scarlet before spinning gracefully to the forest floor.

There is only one independent clause here, so it is still a simple sentence. An infinite number of phrases could be added to this sentence and it would remain a simple sentence as long as it had only one independent clause. Obviously, then, the *length* of a sentence does not determine the *type* of sentence.

PRACTICE EXERCISES

EXERCISE 4 *Return to Writing Assignment 4 and count the number of* simple sentences *in your paragraph.*

*EXERCISE 5 *Underline the* clause (subject-verb set) *in each simple sentence below.*

1. My friend Curt believes in UFO's.
2. He has read all the books about them.
3. He watches every movie and television show on UFO's.
4. He often drives around at night looking for them.
5. Curt considers himself an expert on the subject.
6. Curt's dream is to take a ride in a UFO someday.
7. According to Curt, UFO's bring visitors from outer space.
8. They fly near Earth to investigate our planet.
9. The visitors want to learn about our way of life.
10. In Curt's opinion, it is foolish to deny the existence of UFO's.

Now look at these examples:

Bruce studied for the test and passed it with ease.
Veronica and Desmond took the train to Florida.

How many independent clauses does each of these sentences have? What kind of sentences are they?

Even though the first sentence has more than one verb, "studied" and "passed," both verbs have the same subject, "Bruce," so the sentence has *one* subject-verb set, or *one* independent clause. The second sentence has more than one subject, "Veronica" and "Desmond," but both subjects have the same verb, "took." Thus, this sentence, like the first, has *one* subject-verb set, or *one* independent clause. Because both of these sentences consist of a single independent clause, both are simple sentences.

PRACTICE EXERCISE

*EXERCISE 6 *Underline the* clause *in each sentence below and indicate how many subjects and verbs are in each one.*

1. My brothers and I have always wanted to write a book.
2. To begin with, all four of us would like to make a lot of money.
3. We decided to try writing a best seller.
4. At first, Jack and Chet wanted to write a murder mystery.
5. Vince and I, however, disagreed with that idea.
6. Murder mysteries are too common and do not sell very well.
7. The next idea was a spy thriller.
8. Vince, Jack, and Chet all liked that idea.
9. However, I disagreed and argued with all of them.
10. All of us are still trying to think of a good idea for the book.

LEARN THE COMPOUND SENTENCE

The following is an example of a compound sentence.

An architect designed the house, but we built it.

How many clauses are in a compound sentence? You are correct if you answered "two" because this sentence has two subject-verb sets, "architect designed" and "we built." Also notice that both clauses could stand alone as sentences:

An architect designed the house.
We built it.

This indicates that each of the two clauses is an independent clause; each expresses a complete thought and can stand alone as a sentence.

Now we can define a **compound sentence** as a sentence that contains *more than one independent clause*. That is, a compound sentence consists of two or more simple sentences joined together. The reason for combining independent clauses into a compound sentence is to join two closely related ideas to produce a more interesting sentence. Your writing will be easier to read if you combine related ideas rather than present them separately in short, choppy sentences.

There are several ways of combining independent clauses to form compound sentences. The first, most commonly used, method is to join the two clauses with a **coordinating conjunction**. For the sake of convenience, however, we will use the term "connecting word" in our discussion of coordinating conjunctions because it explains exactly what these words do: they *connect* one independent clause to another and show the relationship between them. What is the connecting word in this compound sentence?

An architect designed the house, but we built it.

The connecting word is "but," which joins the two clauses and indicates that the second clause means something opposite or contrary to the meaning of the first clause.

How to Use Connecting Words

Each of the following connecting words has a specific meaning when it is used in a compound sentence.

Connecting Words				
and	but	for	so	or

and indicates that the second idea is *in addition to* the first; it is something added on.

The truck raced through the intersection, *and* the policeman started after it.

but indicates that the second idea presents *an opposite point*; "but" is similar in meaning to "although" and "however."

> Frank wanted to go to a movie, *but* I wanted to go bowling.

for indicates that the second idea *gives a reason* for the first; "for" is similar in meaning to "because."

> The painting had cost a lot of money, *for* it was both famous and old.

so indicates that the second idea is a *consequence* of the first; "so" is similar in meaning to "therefore."

> All of the students were falling asleep, *so* the instructor leaped onto his desk.

or indicates that the second idea presents an *alternative* or *choice* to the first; "or" is similar in meaning to "instead."

> We could go to see the ships come in, *or* we could stay home and play cards.

Note: No matter which connecting word is used, it is always preceded by a *comma* in a compound sentence.

PRACTICE EXERCISES

EXERCISE 7 *In this exercise, fill in the blanks with the connecting word that would make the most sense.*

1. Last week I went horseback riding, ______________________ I discovered that it is not as easy as it looks.
2. Veterans deserve their educational benefits, ______________________ they earned them by serving their country.
3. You can spend the money to get the car fixed, ______________________ you can sell the car and buy a new one.

4. The house is finished, ________________ we will not move in for another month.

5. Yesterday my boss was in a nasty mood, ________________ I just tried to stay out of his way.

6. Bob and Sharon are coming to the sale, ________________ they will probably not buy anything.

7. All of my assignments were due this week, ________________ I have three major exams.

8. Maxine didn't go to the party, ________________ she thought Ed would be there.

9. Another new disaster movie is coming out, ________________ I'm not going to waste any of my money on it.

10. Bill and Judy bought some land up in the mountains, ________________ now they are designing their house.

EXERCISE 8 *Now do the same thing in the following paragraph. Be sure to use the appropriate connecting word in each space.*

Reggie was tired of all the snow and cold weather, ________________ he decided to go to Florida for the Easter vacation. Reggie asked Steve to go with him, ________________ Steve had already made plans to go somewhere else. In Florida, the weather was sunny and mild, ________________ Reggie spent every day basking in the sun. In the evenings he went to one of the nightclubs, ________________ he went for a stroll along the beach. After a week, Reggie took a plane back to New York, ________________ his money had begun to run out.

EXERCISE 9

Write!

In this exercise you are given the beginning of a sentence. Make a simple sentence out of five of the groups of words and a compound sentence out of the other five.

1. The cat cannot ____________________

____

2. The typewriter needs ____________________

____

3. The box is ____________________

____

4. My father cut the grass ____________________

____

5. I have to wash my car ____________________

____

6. Sharon bought ____________________

____

7. The branches of the trees were swaying ____________________

____

8. The chemical company was ____________________

____

9. She kissed him ____________________

____

10. The car's headlights must be fixed ____________________

____

How to punctuate connecting words

THE COMMA As we pointed out earlier, when a compound sentence is formed with a connecting word, *a comma comes before the connecting word* to separate the independent clauses.

Why is a comma *not* used in the following sentence?

We went to the computer store but decided not to buy anything.

There is a connecting word (''but'') in this sentence, but the sentence does not require a comma because there is only one independent clause. Although the sentence has two verbs, ''went'' and ''decided,'' both of the verbs belong to the same subject, ''We,'' so there is only one subject-verb set. Remember that a comma is required before a connecting word when the connecting word is used in a *compound sentence*, not in a simple sentence.

PRACTICE EXERCISE

EXERCISE 10 *Return to the sentences you wrote for Exercise 9 and check to see if you punctuated them correctly. Remember that connecting words that join compound subjects or compound verbs do not require a comma.*

THE SEMICOLON The second way that independent clauses can be joined to form a compound sentence is with a **semicolon**.

An architect designed the house; we built it.

Notice that the essential ingredients of a compound sentence are still here: two or more independent clauses. But now, instead of a connecting word, the clauses are joined by a semicolon. Used in this way, the semicolon functions as a kind of *equals sign*, indicating that the two (or more) independent clauses are equal to each other in importance or emphasis.

independent clause	=	independent clause
clause 1	;	clause 2

It is especially important to remember the following two points about the semicolon:

- When a semicolon is used in a compound sentence, a connecting word is *not necessary*.
- Use a semicolon *only* between independent clauses.

PRACTICE EXERCISE

*EXERCISE 11 *The following paragraph contains simple sentences and compound sentences that use both connecting words and semicolons. Correct any punctuation that is incorrect and add any punctuation that is missing.*

An architect designed the house but we built it ourselves. That was our first mistake. My wife, and I should have known better, but we were feeling ambitious. We began by hiring a contractor to pour the cement, and lay the foundation. From that point forward we relied on friends, and relatives to help us erect the house. Some of the people knew something about carpentry, or plumbing but most of them had little or no real experience. We spent a week getting the first wall up and then a gust of wind came along, and knocked it back down onto the ground. At this point some of the crew were ready to give up, but my wife, and I wanted to keep trying. We persuaded everyone to stick with it, and give it one more try. We eventually got the house built but it required far more time, and money than expected.

How to Use Introductory Words

The third method of joining independent clauses in a compound sentence also uses a semicolon, but this method also adds emphasis to the relationship between the clauses. The words that signify these relationships are called *conjunctive adverbs*, but they are referred to here as **introductory words** because they usually *introduce* the second clause of a compound sentence. Look at the following introductory words and examples of their use in compound sentences.

Introductory Words			
therefore	however	in addition	otherwise
thus	consequently	then	

therefore = "for that reason"

thus = "for that reason"

consequently = "for that reason;" all of these introductory words are similar in meaning to "so"

> I found several major defects in the house; *therefore*, I decided not to buy it.
> The terrorists were clearly in control of the situation; *thus*, the police chief decided to give them what they wanted.
> Everyone but Sharon had the flu; *consequently*, she had to cook dinner and wash the dishes by herself.

however = "in spite of the fact;" similar to "but"

> She really wanted to go out to dinner; *however*, she had to study for the test.

in addition = "also;" similar to "and"

> The candidate is a successful businessman and a respected member of the community; *in addition*, he is a colonel in the Army Reserves.

otherwise = "or else"

> The problem of industrial pollution must be solved; *otherwise*, our world will no longer be a fit place in which to live.

then = "next" or "afterwards"

> At first we thought we would go to the museum; *then*, we changed our minds and went to a movie instead.

Notice that each of these introductory words is always followed by a comma. These words can also be used in simple sentences.

> The sun was shining and there was a warm breeze blowing. Therefore, Linda decided to do the spring cleaning.

All of these introductory words are used *to introduce* independent clauses; they are *not* connecting words. Thus, you must always use a semicolon or a period to separate the two independent clauses.

> INCORRECT: She went to bed early the night before the exam,
> however, she still felt sleepy when she got up.

CORRECT: She went to bed early the night before the exam; however, she still felt sleepy when she got up.

CORRECT: She went to bed early the night before the exam. However, she still felt sleepy when she got up.

PRACTICE EXERCISES

*EXERCISE 12 *Fill in the blanks below with the introductory word that best fits the meaning of the sentence.*

1. My father has worked hard all his life; ______________________, he is entitled to a full pension.
2. Many people don't bother to read the directions when they buy a new product; ______________________, they get upset when it doesn't work.
3. Swimming is always a lot of fun; ______________________, it is great exercise.
4. The President vetoed the bill; ______________________, Congress voted the bill into law anyway.
5. First, decide exactly what it is you want to say; ______________________, say it with conviction!
6. The car needed four new tires and an engine overhaul; ______________________, I decided to sell it.
7. Every society must have rules and regulations; ______________________, people would not be able to live together.
8. From the time I started school my parents encouraged me to go to college; ______________________, when I decided to become a carpenter, they were upset.

9. They have three dogs in their apartment; ______________________, they are seriously considering buying a pair of kittens.

10. The boat leaks and the motor won't start; ______________________, I'm not even thinking about going water skiing.

EXERCISE 13

Write!

In this exercise, you are given only the first independent clause. Add one of the introductory words and a second independent clause to go along with it. Be sure to punctuate the finished sentence correctly.

1. Henry never paid back the money he borrowed from me ____________

____

2. The Senator decided not to run for reelection ____________

____

3. Bob and Sharon need the money for a new house ____________

____

4. I must get my car inspected this week ____________

____

5. Vanessa has done some silly things in the past ____________

____

6. The cat found a way into the chicken coop ____________

____

7. Maxine got A's in three of her midterm exams ____________

____

8. The traffic light stopped working during the morning rush hour ____________

____

9. He planted the tomato seeds in early March ____________

____

10. She couldn't decide what she wanted to wear to the dance ____________
____

LEARN THE COMPLEX SENTENCE

The following is an example of a **complex sentence**.

When the meadowlark sings, the other birds listen.

How many clauses does the complex sentence have? How is the complex sentence different from the simple and compound sentences you have studied in this chapter?

You are correct if you said that the **complex sentence** contains two clauses, because there are two different subject-verb sets, "meadowlark sings" and "birds listen." But does that make this a compound sentence? No, because both of the clauses are *not independent*.

Independent and Dependent Clauses

You learned in Chapter 3 that conditional words make a sentence incomplete; in other words, the presence of a conditional word (subordinator) makes a clause **dependent**. We refer to clauses of this type as dependent because they must be combined with other clauses in order to express a complete thought; that is, they *depend* upon other clauses. Let's break the above sentence into its two clauses to see an example of this.

Dependent Clauses: When the meadowlark sings
Independent Clause: the other birds listen

As you can see, when the sentence is divided into its two clauses, the dependent clause cannot function as a sentence on its own; it is a *sentence fragment*. The independent clause, however, does express a complete thought by itself; it can function as a complete sentence. Remember that all clauses *always* have *both* a subject and a verb, so the only difference between an independent clause and a dependent clause is *the presence of a conditional word*. If we removed the conditional word from the dependent clause above,

the meadowlark sings

the result would be an independent clause. *Only the conditional word makes a clause dependent.*

The following chart illustrates how to determine whether a group of words is a dependent or independent clause.

Does the clause have a		*Then*
conditional word (subordinator)?	Yes ⟶	It is *DEPENDENT*
	No ⟶	It is *INDEPENDENT*

PRACTICE EXERCISE

*EXERCISE 14 *Underline the independent clause and circle the dependent clause of each complex sentence below.*

1. Although I don't look like the outdoor type, camping is my favorite leisure activity.
2. I love camping because I enjoy nature.
3. When I go camping, I get a chance to hike in the woods and observe nature.
4. It brings me special pleasure when I see a wild animal or bird in the woods.
5. While I am in the woods, I feel a closer relationship with nature.
6. Being in the woods gives me the feeling that I am getting away from all the troubles of the world.
7. I also like camping because it requires me to be self-sufficient.
8. Though I take along some modern equipment, I try to keep the whole experience as basic as possible.
9. I don't take a tent along since that would only block out the stars at night.
10. If I didn't go camping once in a while, I would probably go crazy in a very short time.

Now that you know how to identify both independent and dependent clauses, you can identify all three types of sentences. Look at the following chart.

If the sentence has	*Then*
one independent clause	⟶ it is a SIMPLE SENTENCE
two or more independent clauses	⟶ it is a COMPOUND SENTENCE
one independent clause and one or more dependent clauses	⟶ it is a COMPLEX SENTENCE

Remember that all independent clauses can stand alone as complete sentences. All dependent clauses and all phrases cannot stand alone and are therefore sentence fragments. Now that you know some of the terminology of sentences, you will recognize that *all sentence fragments are either phrases or dependent clauses*.

PRACTICE EXERCISE

*EXERCISE 15 *Identify each sentence below as either simple or complex. If the sentence is complex, underline the independent clause and circle the dependent clause.*

1. I enjoy *Time* magazine for several reasons.
2. First of all, it keeps me up to date on the news.
3. Even if I don't read the newspaper every day, I can still be aware by reading *Time*.
4. *Time* is also good because it has so many different sections.
5. There are sections reporting on everything from sports to psychology.
6. Each of these sections is a thorough treatment of the important developments in that field.
7. My favorite section of the magazine is the "American Notes" section.
8. The section consists of four or five paragraphs that report on some minor event.

9. I like this section because the reports often describe something particularly ridiculous.

10. When all parts of the magazine are considered, *Time* is clearly superior to the other weekly news magazines.

How to Punctuate Complex Sentences

As you learned in Chapter 3, some complex sentences require a comma. When the dependent clause comes *first* in the sentence, put a comma between the dependent and the independent clauses.

DEPENDENT CLAUSE — INDEPENDENT
When I work on Saturdays, I get paid time-and-a-half.

When the dependent clause comes *second* in the sentence, a comma is not required.

INDEPENDENT CLAUSE — DEPENDENT
I get paid time-and-a-half when I work on Saturdays.

PRACTICE EXERCISES

*EXERCISE 16 *In the sentences below, insert a comma wherever one is required.*

1. Reading and writing are taken for granted in America.
2. Since the television is so convenient people rely on it for their entertainment.
3. When they want to relax people turn on the television instead of reading a book.
4. They don't read newspapers because they can watch the news on television.
5. Although it is not used as much as television the radio is another substitute for reading.

6. Some people listen to music on a radio for hours instead of reading a good book.
7. Since the telephone was invented people do much less writing than they did before.
8. When people want to communicate with their friends they simply call them on the phone.
9. It is always easier to speak to someone on the phone than it is to sit down and compose a letter.
10. Since the modern conveniences have made life easier for us far more people are growing up without learning to enjoy reading and writing.

EXERCISE 17

Write!

In this exercise, create your own complex sentences. Beside each number below, a conditional word is placed either at the beginning or in the middle of the sentence. Write a sentence using the word and punctuate the sentence correctly.

1. If ______________________________
______________________________ .
2. ______________________________
because ______________________________ .
3. While ______________________________
______________________________ .
4. As ______________________________
______________________________ .
5. ______________________________
since ______________________________ .
6. Before ______________________________
______________________________ .

7. ______________________________

even if ______________________________ .

8. After ______________________________

______________________________ .

9. When ______________________________

______________________________ .

10. Until ______________________________

______________________________ .

How to Recognize Conditional and Connecting Words

Conditional Words		*Connecting Words*
after	since	and
although	though	but
as	unless	for
because	until	or
before	when	so
if	whenever	
just as	while	

You may have noticed in some of the exercises that you could use a conditional word instead of a connecting word to connect two clauses. It is important for you to remember the difference between conditional words and connecting words.

When a *conditional word* is placed at the beginning of a clause, it makes the clause dependent.

Independent Clause: The train pulled out of the station.

CONDITIONAL WORD
/
Dependent Clause: *When* the train pulled out of the station

As you know, a dependent clause is a sentence fragment. To correct it, an independent clause must be added to the dependent clause. The result is a **complex sentence**.

DEPENDENT CLAUSE
/
Complex Sentence: When the train pulled out of the station,

INDEPENDENT CLAUSE
/
Jim waved good-bye to his sister.

A *connecting word* is placed *between* independent clauses to connect them. A connecting word does not make one clause dependent upon the other. Instead, it establishes an equal relationship between the clauses. The result is a **compound sentence**.

INDEPENDENT CLAUSE CONNECTING WORD
/ /
Compound Sentence: There was a brisk wind blowing, and

INDEPENDENT CLAUSE
/
the leaves were starting to fall to the ground.

PRACTICE EXERCISE

EXERCISE 18 *Fill in the blanks with a connecting word or a conditional word. Be sure to punctuate the finished sentence correctly and label the sentence as* complex *or* compound.

Example: It would be a great job to have because ______ the supervisor is a friend of mine.

Sentence type: complex ______

1. The sky became dark with threatening clouds ______ it had not yet started to rain. *Sentence type:* ______
2. The President cancelled his news conference ______ he had a sore throat. *Sentence type:* ______
3. ______ the sea was calm, many of the people on the boat became seasick. *Sentence type:* ______

4. The table is made out of oak ______________________ the china closet is made out of mahogany. *Sentence type:* ______________________

5. Mr. Grant could probably be a professional baseball player __________ he were a little taller. *Sentence type:* ______________________

CHAPTER REVIEW

In Chapter 4, you learned how to use and identify the three kinds of sentences: simple, compound, and complex.

The *simple sentence* consists of one independent clause, or subject-verb set. It expresses only one complete thought.

> He ran to the store.

The *compound sentence* consists of two or more independent clauses, or subject-verb sets, joined by a comma and a connecting word or by a semicolon without a connecting word.

> He ran to the store, but he walked back home.
> He ran to the store; he walked back home.

Emphasis may be added to a compound sentence by using one of the *introductory words*.

The *complex sentence* consists of one independent clause (simple sentence) combined with one dependent clause (fragment).

> Because he was hungry, he ran to the store.

When the dependent clause comes first, put a comma between the two clauses:

> Because he was hungry, he ran to the store.

When the independent clause comes first, a comma is not required.

> He ran to the store because he was hungry.

Remember the important differences between conditional, connecting, and introductory words. If you use one of these words or phrases with the wrong punctuation, you may create a sentence fragment. The important points about these words are summarized on the following page:

CONNECTING WORDS

Word	*Use*	*Function*	*Punctuation*
and but for or nor so yet	compound sentence	to join 2 or more independent clauses	Comma comes before the connecting word when the connecting word joins 2 or more independent clauses.

Example:
The train pulled out of the station, *and* Jim waved goodbye to his sister.

INTRODUCTORY WORDS

Word	*Use*	*Function*	*Punctuation*
consequently however in addition otherwise therefore thus then	simple & compound sentences	to introduce an independent clause and emphasize its relationship to a preceding idea	When used in a compound sentence, place a semicolon after the first independent clause and a comma after the introductory word. When used at the beginning of a simple sentence, place a comma after the introductory word.

Example:

Compound Sentence:	The summit meeting was a great success; therefore, the President's popularity increased.
Two Simple Sentences:	The summit meeting was a great success. Therefore, the President's popularity increased.

CONDITIONAL WORDS

optional

Word		*Use*	*Function*	*Punctuation*
after although as because before if just as	since though unless until when whenever while	complex sentence	to make one clause dependent on another	If dependent clause comes first in complex sentence, use a comma between the dependent and independent clauses. If independent clause comes first, no comma is needed.

Example:
When the train pulled out of the station, Jim waved goodbye to his sister.

WRITING ASSIGNMENT 5

Write a paragraph applying everything you have learned about the different kinds of sentences. Remember the following points.

- Make sure you *understand the topic*.
- *List* all of the thoughts you have about the topic.
- *Select* the most convincing items from your list and arrange them into an order.
- *Expand the ideas* you will be using for support.
- *Write the rough draft*.

When you finish writing your paragraph, rewrite each sentence, one at a time, on a separate piece of paper according to the instructions in Chapter 3, p. 76. After you have found and corrected any sentence fragments in your paragraph, copy it over again in regular paragraph form; this will be your "final draft."

Topics

1. Write a paragraph that tells about a large project you tried to do once. Explain how the project succeeded or failed. (See Exercise 11.)
2. Write a paragraph that names your favorite magazine, newspaper, or television program. Provide at least three specific reasons that explain why this is your favorite publication or program. (See Exercise 15.)

SUPPLEMENTAL EXERCISES

Use the exercises below for additional practice in recognizing and punctuating the different types of sentences.

*EXERCISE 19 *Identify each of the following sentences as simple (S), complex (CX), or compound (CP).*

___ 1. My favorite pet is a goldfish.

___ 2. It is definitely the easiest pet to care for.

___ 3. While a dog or cat requires a paper or a litter pan, a goldfish requires almost nothing at all.

___ 4. Cleaning out the tank once in a while is the only necessity.

___ 5. When you have a goldfish for a pet, you never get your socks dirty when walking to the bathroom at night.

___ 6. A fish is considerate of its owner, and it is a loyal pet too.

___ 7. A goldfish will never run away from you.

___ 8. Most dogs are gone as soon as someone opens the door.

___ 9. Everyone has been kept awake sometime in his life by howling dogs or screaming cats, but I have yet to hear my goldfish make a sound.

___10. In conclusion, a goldfish is by far the most convenient pet since it requires the least amount of work.

EXERCISE 20 *In this exercise, each number is followed by two simple sentences. Combine the two sentences into one simple, complex, or compound sentence; be sure to punctuate the finished sentence correctly.*

1. I enjoy going to parties. They provide a refreshing change.
2. I like to meet new people. Parties give me an opportunity to do this.
3. Also, I love to dance. There is always plenty of dancing at a good party.

4. Sometimes people are reluctant to dance at the beginning of a party. They usually ''loosen up'' after a little while.
5. It is also fun to dress up for a party. I get tired of dressing the same way day after day.

*EXERCISE 21 *The following paragraph contains simple, complex, and compound sentences. Check to see if each sentence is punctuated correctly, and add a comma wherever it is needed.*

I would much rather watch a football game on television than go to the stadium. Although seeing a game live has some attractions I prefer the comfort of my living room. When I am at home I can sit wherever I want and be perfectly comfortable. The television gives me the best seat in the house for every play and I don't have to worry about people standing up in front of me. Some people love to be in a crowd but I can see no advantage to it. Finally, if I happen to miss an important play on the television I can always see it later on instant replay. There is no instant replay when you watch the game at the stadium.

EXERCISE 22 *Complete the following sentences. Be sure that the part you add connects logically with the other part, and punctuate each sentence correctly.*

Write!

1. Although Bruce would prefer to drive ______________________________

____

2. The school was only six years old however ______________________

____

3. ____

when she heard her husband come in the front door.

4. Smoking is a very dangerous habit but __________________________

____

5. ______________________________

otherwise I won't have enough money to take a vacation.

6. Both of us want to go to the wedding for ______________________________

____

7. If he passes his driving test this time ______________________________

____

8. ______________________________

therefore he was awarded the grand prize.

9. ______________________________

as the ship set sail for the Bahamas.

10. The govenor promised to lower taxes and ______________________________

____

____

5 / Identify and correct errors in combination

In Chapter 4 you learned to recognize the correct form of simple, compound, and complex sentences. In this chapter you will apply this knowledge by identifying and correcting sentences that are incorrectly combined.

FIND THE RUN-ON SENTENCE AND THE COMMA SPLICE

Sentences that are run together with nothing to connect them are difficult to understand.

> Most new cars cost at least $10,000 the cost of insurance is also high.

This is actually two sentences even though they are punctuated as one.

> *Sentence 1:* Most new cars cost at least $10,000.
>
> *Sentence 2:* The cost of insurance is also high.

When two sentences are run together with nothing to separate them, the result is a **run-on sentence**.

Two sentences separated by only a comma are still difficult to understand.

> Most new cars cost at least $10,000, the cost of insurance is also high.

When two sentences are separated by only a comma, the result is a **comma splice**. (''Splice'' means ''join together,'' so a comma splice is the joining together of two sentences with a comma.)

One way to find a run-on sentence or a comma splice is to read the sentence aloud and ''hear'' where the two sentences come together; there is a natural tendency to pause at the end of the first sentence. This procedure will allow you to spot the place where the sentences run together.

If you cannot hear where two sentences run together, check each sentence for its three requirements. Notice that the example sentences above meet the three requirements of a sentence.

S V
Sentence 1: Most new cars cost at least $10,000.

S V
Sentence 2: The cost of insurance is also high.

Recall from Chapter 4 that when two independent clauses are combined, they form a compound sentence. In a compound sentence, the two independent clauses are joined by a comma and a connecting word or by a semicolon. *Run-on sentences and comma splices are actually compound sentences that are incorrectly joined.* Therefore, a good way to find run-on sentences and comma splices is to look for compound sentences and make sure they are correctly joined. Look at the following examples:

S V S V
The cat jumped onto the table the lamp fell to the floor with a crash.

In this sentence, there are two independent clauses, so it could be a compound sentence. But the comma and connecting word are missing, so it is a run-on sentence.

S V S V
The cat jumped onto the table, the lamp fell to the floor with a crash.

Now the same sentence has a comma, but the connecting word is still missing, so it is a comma splice.

Remember: Run-on sentences and comma splices are compound sentences that are incorrectly joined. If a sentence has one or more dependent clauses and one or more independent clauses, it is a complex sentence, and a connecting word is not needed.

INDEPENDENT CLAUSE CONNECTING WORD
Compound Sentence: The wallpaper is faded, but
INDEPENDENT CLAUSE
the paint is in good condition.

DEPENDENT CLAUSE
/
Complex Sentence: Although the wallpaper is faded,

INDEPENDENT CLAUSE
/
the paint is in good condition.

PRACTICE EXERCISES

EXERCISE 1 *Return to the paragraph you wrote for Writing Assignment 5. In each compound sentence you find, underline the place where the two independent clauses are joined.* Are any of these sentences run-on sentences or comma splices?

*EXERCISE 2 *Identify any run-on sentences or comma splices by checking each sentence below to see if it is correctly combined. In each run-on sentence or comma splice, underline the place where the two sentences are incorrectly joined.*

1. In the past two years I have held two full-time summer jobs.
2. These jobs may seem very different they are actually very much alike.
3. Two years ago I had the job of selling fruit juice on the Wildwood boardwalk last summer I pumped gas and changed tires in a gas station.
4. In Wildwood I had the problem of supporting myself in a rented apartment with two of my friends, with the gas station job I had the problem of supporting myself with two of my parents.
5. I can't decide which summer was worse they both had their disadvantages.
6. The work I did in both jobs was pretty easy, I didn't mind it too much.
7. I had the duty of locking up at night in both of the jobs that meant I had to work until two o'clock in the morning.
8. The people I worked with at both jobs were friendly, I liked the people at the fruit juice job a bit more.

9. Both jobs kept my social life to a minimum not many girls want to go out on a date which starts at two in the morning.

10. I usually managed to get one or two days off each week, I tried to do all my socializing on those days.

EXERCISE 3 *Identify any run-on sentences or comma splices you find in the following paragraph. Underline the place where the two sentences come together.*

There is an art to taking tests. Many people have difficulty with tests because they get too nervous this is not necessary. Nervousness can be overcome, the student must first be aware of a few simple points. First, a student who is doing well in class has nothing to fear from a test. For a well-prepared student, only a "trick test" would prove difficult very few teachers give trick tests. A second point to remember is that one test is rarely used as the only measure of a student's performance. A good test-taker is a student who begins to study well in advance of the test date, he or she doesn't wait until the last minute. Another good habit to form for test taking is getting to bed early the night before. A student should plan to get at least eight hours of sleep when morning comes the student will be fresh and alert.

ADD THE MISSING PART

Once you have identified a run-on sentence or a comma splice, the easiest way to eliminate it is to make a correct compound sentence out of it.

Add a Comma and a Connecting Word

Look at the following examples:

Run-on Sentence:
The cat jumped onto the table the lamp fell to the floor with a crash.

This sentence is a run-on because it is missing a comma and a connecting word. To correct it, simply add a comma and a connecting word between the two independent clauses.

Correct Compound Sentence:
The cat jumped onto the table, *and* the lamp fell to the floor with a crash.

Now it is a correct compound sentence. Look at the next example:

Comma Splice:
Byron wanted to sue the company, his lawyer advised him not to.

This sentence is a comma splice because only a comma joins the two independent clauses; a connecting word is missing. To correct it, simply add a logical connecting word to join the two independent clauses.

Correct Compound Sentence:
Byron wanted to sue the company, *but* his lawyer advised him not to.

Add a Semicolon

Recall from Chapter 4 that you can use a semicolon in a compound sentence instead of a comma and a connecting word.

Run-on Sentence:
The couple strolled down the street everyone could tell they were in love.
Correct Compound Sentence:
The couple strolled down the street; everyone could tell they were in love.

Make Two Sentences

When the two independent clauses in a run-on sentence or a comma splice are not closely related, it is better to make two sentences by placing a period after the first sentence and starting the second one with a capital letter.

Run-on Sentence:
Charlotte will graduate from college in May her brother is in his third year of medical school.
Two Correct Sentences:
Charlotte will graduate from college in May. Her brother is in his third year of medical school.

Whenever the two independent clauses are closely related, it is better to correct the run-on sentence or the comma splice by making it into a correct compound sentence.

Remember: To find run-on sentences and comma splices, check each of your sentences to see if it is correctly combined. To correct run-on sentences: (1) add a comma and a connecting word (*and, but, for, or, so*), or (2) add a semicolon, or (3) make two sentences. To correct comma splices: (1) add a connecting word *(and, but, for, or, so),* or (2) add a semicolon, or (3) make two sentences.

Now go back to Exercises 1, 2, and 3 in this chapter and correct the run-on sentences and comma splices you identified in each exercise.

PRACTICE EXERCISES

*EXERCISE 4 *Identify and correct any run-on sentences or comma splices in the following groups of sentences. You may correct the errors by making two sentences or by making a compound sentence.*

1. Many people believe that small cars are more dangerous than larger ones. Research on this subject has shown that small cars are actually involved in fewer accidents than large cars. There are many reasons for this one of them is that larger cars are more difficult to maneuver.

2. There are still plenty of con artists around. Most of them now make their money selling land the property actually belongs to someone else. By the time the police are informed of the swindles, the con artists are usually in a different state.

3. Sometimes I really enjoy being alone. I take long walks through the city streets, I stay out for hours. When I do this, I can usually straighten out any problems that I have, and I often get some really useful ideas.

4. It is surprising how many different customs there are regarding office doors. In America, for example, a closed office door means that private business is being conducted. When the door is open, the occupant is en-

gaged in his or her normal work routine this is not the case in some European countries.

5. Riding a horse is almost as easy as driving a car. You pull the reins to the left to make the horse turn left and pull right to make him go right. When you want the horse to stop, pull back on the reins, to go forward you loosen up on the reins.

EXERCISE 5 *Identify and correct any run-on sentences or comma splices in the following paragraph. You may correct the errors by making two sentences or by making a compound sentence.*

Wildlife photography is quite different from other kinds of photography before I started taking wildlife pictures, I had done a lot of photography work. However, taking pictures of animals and birds demands a whole new approach. First of all, special equipment is required, extremely powerful lenses are necessary for detailed wildlife pictures. Another difference is the cooperation of the subject I have had lots of good pictures run away from me just before I pressed the shutter button. This is what makes wildlife photography so different, it requires a tremendous amount of patience and dedication. I have spent hours and hours waiting for a bird or animal to get just a little closer. Finally, the wildlife photographer has to know when to take the picture this may sound silly, but it is really very important. Patience is necessary, but it can also be a disadvantage if the animal gets away before his picture has been taken. A good photographer waits patiently but then shoots quickly when the time is right. When the animal has already run off, it is too late to worry if the camera settings were correct.

WRITING ASSIGNMENT 6

Write a paragraph applying everything you have learned about sentences up to this point. Remember the following points:

- Make sure you *understand the topic*.
- *List* all of the thoughts you have about the topic.
- *Select* the most convincing items from your list and arrange them into an order.
- *Expand the ideas* you will be using for support.
- *Write the rough draft*.

When you finish writing your paragraph, rewrite each sentence, one at a time, on a separate piece of paper according to the instructions on p. 76 of Chapter 3. Identify and correct any sentence fragments, run-on sentences, or comma splices in your paragraph, and then write the sentences on a new piece of paper in regular paragraph form.

Topics

1. Write a paragraph describing one or two jobs you have had in the past or the kind of job you would like to have. (See Exercise 1.)
2. Write a paragraph describing how you prepare to take a major exam. (See Exercise 3.)

PROOFREAD PARAGRAPHS FOR ERRORS IN COMBINATION

As is the case with sentence fragments, it is usually more difficult to find run-on sentences and comma splices in paragraphs than it is to find them in single sentences. To make it easier to locate the run-on sentences and comma splices, isolate the sentences in a paragraph according to the techniques described in Chapter 3. To correct the errors after you have found them, simply add whatever is missing.

PRACTICE EXERCISE

Identify and correct any run-on sentences or comma splices in the following paragraph. You may correct the errors by making two sentences or by making a compound sentence.

*EXERCISE 6

Enjoying a baseball game on television is a matter of careful planning. First, check the television schedule to make sure of the starting time missing an opening pitch is always a disaster. Next, be certain that you have an adequate supply of food and beverages on hand this should include chilled beverages, luncheon meats, and snacks. After preparing a few sandwiches, the next step is to send the children off to a movie, preferably a double feature. If possible, convince your wife that she should visit her sister, you may have to promise to take her to dinner in return for this favor. At last, alone with your tube, set up your TV tray your beverage should be exactly one arm's length away when resting on the tray. With your refreshments conveniently situated in front of you, you are ready for an afternoon of bliss, now just hope that the game doesn't get rained out.

CHAPTER REVIEW

In this chapter you learned to find and correct run-on sentences and comma splices.

First, to find run-on sentences and comma splices, check each sentence to make sure it is correctly combined. Remember that two or more independent clauses must be joined by a comma and a connecting word, or by a semicolon.

Next, to correct run-on sentences and comma splices, simply add whatever is needed to produce a correct compound sentence, or make two sentences. There are three ways to correct run-on sentences and comma splices:

1. Add a comma and a connecting word between the independent clauses.
2. Place a semicolon between the independent clauses.
3. Make two sentences out of the independent clauses.

SUPPLEMENTAL EXERCISES

Use the exercises below for additional practice in finding and correcting run-on sentences and comma splices.

*EXERCISE 7 *Identify any run-on sentences or comma splices in these sentence groups. Underline the place where the two sentences come together.*

1. Student newspapers are a good idea. Students who work on the paper gain valuable practical experience they also get plenty of writing practice.
2. The South has produced more of America's greatest leaders than any of the other areas in the country. The most influential statesmen have been Southerners, many of our famous generals came from the South, too.
3. The national wildlife refuge system has been successful in maintaining the populations of waterfowl. The brant, or sea goose, was once considered threatened it is now increasing in numbers in the East.
4. Languages are considered "alive" because they undergo frequent changes. If the population using a language stops using a word, that

word will eventually disappear from the language, on the other hand, new words are added to the language as they become necessary.

5. The advantages of small-town life are often overlooked small-town people are usually more concerned about their community than city dwellers.

In Exercises 8–10, identify and correct any run-on sentences or comma splices. You may correct the errors by making two sentences or by making a compound sentence.

*EXERCISE 8

The two kittens I have are named Hamlet and Horatio. Hamlet is two months older than Horatio he is not as frisky. Horatio always seems happier than Hamlet, but I think Hamlet is smarter than Horatio. Hamlet often gets very moody and refuses to eat or do anything Horatio is always trying to be Hamlet's buddy. He is the most playful kitten I've ever seen.

Hamlet's father, a cat named Hamlet Senior, was a pedigreed Persian who was a grand champion he was the most beautiful cat of his time. Hamlet Senior was bigger and more colorful than his son. Unfortunately, he died earlier than most cats die a neighbor of mine, who had one of the ugliest alley cats I've ever seen, put some poison out under the hemlock tree in my back yard and Hamlet Senior ate it. The man who put out the poison is the worst neighbor anyone could ever have. I'm going to get my revenge some day right now, I'm just trying to figure out how I should do it.

EXERCISE 9

Aptitude tests are often used in the business world, an aptitude test evaluates an individual's abilities. The results of the test indicate, for example, whether a person is likely to be more successful as an architect or as an auto mechanic this is a valuable service for most large companies. A company which has a long training program cannot afford to let into the program someone who cannot succeed in it this would simply cost too much money. Companies also use aptitude tests to evaluate the management potential of their employees. Although there are no right or wrong answers to the test, it can indicate whether or not an individual will make a good manager. Each company has its own way of interpreting the answers on the test, according to the qualities that company looks for in a manager. Some people try to respond to the questions with the "right" answers, this is not a good idea. When a person does this, the results of the test become meaningless it is always better to answer the questions honestly.

*EXERCISE 10 There are two major problems in my life, I have no trouble identifying them. Their names are Scooby and Dooby they are my wife's long-haired cats. I specify that they are long-haired cats because it is their long hair that is slowly but surely driving me crazy. Every time I find one of their hairs, I either start sneezing or get furious because it has found its way into my mouth. My wife is entirely innocent in this matter Scooby and Dooby are the culprits. What they do is shed their long hairs in every conceivable location throughout the house. When I am drying my face with a towel, for example, I somehow end up with one of Scooby's hairs in my mouth. When I sit down to enjoy a breakfast of bacon and eggs, there in the middle of the yolk appears a hair from the hide of Dooby. Their hairs find their way onto my sweaters and my slacks, and on the living room furniture. Once I even found one long strand in the pocket of my raincoat. My wife takes great pains to clean up after them, she cannot follow them around the house with a vacuum cleaner in her hand. I must also admit that Scooby and Dooby themselves are probably not dropping their hairs deliberately there remains only one clear solution. I must alert my wife to the extent of the problem and insist that she either spend her entire day picking up cat hairs or trade Scooby and Dooby in for a pair of short-haired models.

PART ONE REVIEW

In Chapters 2–5, you learned the requirements of a correct sentence; how to combine short sentences to produce longer, more interesting sentences; and how to identify and correct the major sentence errors, including the sentence fragment, the run-on sentence, and the comma splice.

The exercises in this review will require you to identify and correct all three types of errors in sentences, sentence groups, and paragraphs. The exercises will also require you to punctuate all sentences correctly, using a comma or a semicolon wherever it is required. If you have difficulty with any of these exercises, return to the section in the appropriate chapter for an explanation of the material.

REVIEW EXERCISES

EXERCISE 1

Write!

In the following exercise, correct any sentence fragments by adding whatever is missing. Be sure to punctuate the finished sentence correctly.

1. Last week while walking along Market Street ____________________

2. The raging wind and the freezing air ____________________

3. For example, my favorite meat ____________________

4. My aunt, who is wealthy and famous ________________________

____

5. In order to take full advantage of the offer ________________________

____

6. Doing twenty deep knee bends each night ________________________

____

7. Although I got the check in the mail last week ________________________

____

8. A tall, distinguished-looking gentleman with a gray beard ____________

____

9. Since we all agree on that particular point ________________________

____

10. The group that I want to see more than any other ________________

____

EXERCISE 2

Write!

In the following exercise, create a complex or compound sentence by using the simple sentence that is provided plus the conditional word or connecting word. Be sure to punctuate the finished sentence correctly.

Example:
(but) He had cleaned the apartment on Tuesday.

He had cleaned the apartment on Tuesday, but it was cluttered by Thursday

Example:

(while) My car ran out of gas.

While I was on my way to work, my car ran out of gas.

(although) 1. He received his college diploma. ________________________

____

(*and*) 2. Fred and Linda went out to a nightclub on Friday. ______________________

____

(*however*) 3. Diane decided to move to Baltimore. ______________________

____

(*since*) 4. There was still some snow on the ground in April. ______________________

____

(*or*) 5. The police could stake out the suspect's house. ______________________

____

(*but*) 6. Susan was always looking for a new job. ______________________

____

(*therefore*) 7. I have done all the homework and studied for all the tests. __________

____

(*if*) 8. The gang on the corner did not move out of the way. ______________________

____

(*so*) 9. My mother's birthday is next week. ______________________

____

(*when*) 10. Theresa became furious with the paper boy. ______________________

____

EXERCISE 3 *In the following exercise, correct any run-on sentences or comma splices by adding what is missing. Be sure to use a logical connecting word and punctuate the finished sentence correctly. You may make two sentences or make a compound sentence.*

1. Last week I went to a party almost all of my friends were there.
2. The occasion for the party was the arrival of spring.
3. It had been a long cold winter, people were overjoyed just to feel a warm breeze again.

4. I arrived at the party right on time everyone else was already there.
5. The host, Larry, had provided all the ingredients for a good party there were a lot of guests, colorful decorations, and lively music.
6. There was also a tremendous amount of food, I stuffed myself until I could hardly walk.
7. My favorite food was the stuffed mushrooms everyone said I must have eaten two dozen of them.
8. After everyone had something to eat, they all started to dance and have a good time.
9. I couldn't dance until all of my food digested, I just sat back and watched everyone else.
10. The party continued through most of the night almost everyone stayed until Larry fell asleep with a smile on his face.

*EXERCISE 4 *In the following exercise, correct any sentence fragments, run-on sentences, or comma splices. Wherever possible, correct the errors by combining. Be sure to punctuate the finished sentences correctly.*

1. The reason I wanted to go to college was to get a better education so I could get a better job. When I graduate.
2. I want to marry Susan however I don't want to marry her right away.
3. There is not much difference between a Democrat and a Republican president. Although they may represent different political parties. Both men are politicians and both face the same kinds of problems.
4. Litter is a major problem in this country people throw trash in the street as if it will all magically disappear. Unless some action is taken to punish the litterbug, the trash in our streets will continue to accumulate.

5. My favorite sport is basketball. It is a fast and exciting game, with some kind of action taking place every minute. Players always running, jumping, and shooting.
6. Most students find it hard to believe, but eight o'clock classes are actually better for them. The brain is much more alert at eight in the morning, students often do their best work at this time.
7. There may be a shortage of oil in this country, but there is certainly no shortage of oil spills. The different countries of the world must start inspecting oil tankers. To prevent the disaster of a major spill.
8. In this day and age there are books that tell you how to do almost everything. The latest of the ''how-to'' books is a series describing how to do your own legal work with one of these books you can be your own lawyer when you file for divorce.
9. By the time the delivery man finally brought the pizza. All of us had filled up on potato chips and pretzels. Cindy put the pizza in the refrigerator, saying that she would eat it for breakfast the next day.
10. The thing I like most about Sunday is the Sunday paper. I love to relax in the living room with the huge Sunday edition, I go through every page of the paper from the news to the book reviews.

*EXERCISE 5 *In the following exercise, correct any sentence fragments, run-on sentences, or comma splices. Wherever possible, correct the errors by combining. Be sure to punctuate the finished sentences correctly.*

One very successful enterprise in America today is the pet food industry more Americans own pets now than ever before. This can be explained by a number of factors. For one thing, people feel a greater need for protection. Because of high crime rates in most cities. Another reason for the rising number of pets is loneliness. For people who are all alone. An animal is often a companion. All of these pets must eat, as a matter of fact, most American pets eat better than many people do in other countries. People in America often look upon their pets as human they spend a lot of money on them. This makes the pet food industry a very profitable business.

EXERCISE 6 *Identify and correct any sentence fragments, run-on sentences, or comma splices you find in the following paragraph. Wherever possible, make your corrections by combining sentences. Be sure to punctuate the finished sentences correctly.*

Fast Food

Although the "fast-food" restaurants are relatively new to America. They are the fastest-growing of all the restaurant types. There are many varieties, I have found a convenient way to classify them. All the fast-food restaurants can be classified into three types. According to the type of service a customer receives. In the first type. The counter is staffed by two waitresses one of these is just learning the job. If you are lucky enough to order the type of food that is available. You can obtain your food shortly before your lunch hour is over. At the other extreme is the restaurant which is overstaffed. There are usually more waitresses crowded around the counter than there are customers. As soon as anyone wanders within fifteen feet of the counter. He is swamped with requests for his order. Before he is completely sure he has ordered what he wants. The customer has his lunch in his hands and is being thanked and wished a pleasant day. Somewhere in the middle of these two extremes is the third type of restaurant. This is one which is adequately staffed a customer usually has time to decide between the regular and the super burgers before he is asked for his order. The item he orders is usually available, he has ample time to suffer through his dry hamburger and greasy French fries.

EXERCISE 7 *Identify and correct any sentence fragments, run-on sentences, or comma splices you find in the following paragraph. Wherever possible, make your corrections by combining sentences. Be sure to punctuate the finished sentences correctly.*

Going to College

It took me a long time to decide what I wanted to do when I got out of high school. I thought about going to college for a while, I wasn't sure that I was ready for it. Before long, I found I was running out of money I decided to look for work and think about college some other time. I applied for a lot of jobs I managed to get a job as a typist at Bell Telephone Company. After three weeks on the job. I knew everything there was to know about it. The job was so boring that I had trouble staying awake I finally decided to apply to a college. When I sent in the required forms. I met with a counselor and set up a schedule for some tests. The testing, which took most of the day. It covered reading, writing, mathematics, and science. They were the most difficult tests I have ever taken, all the other students taking the tests said the same thing. The last step signing up for classes. Now, I'm very happy with the classes I have this semester, I'm not worried at all about passing them.

EXERCISE 8 *Identify and correct any sentence fragments, run-on sentences, or comma splices you find in the following paragraphs. Wherever possible, make your corrections by combining sentences. Be sure to punctuate the finished sentences correctly.*

Birding

Many people believe that bird watching is a hobby that died out in the beginning of the twentieth century. Those who still enjoy this hobby know that this is not true more people are involved in bird watching now than ever before. Those interested in birds refer to the hobby as "birding" rather than "bird watching." People who go birding are called "birders." The enjoyment of birding comes through keeping a complete list of the different kinds of birds. Which the birder can identify. There is also enjoyment in just being outside observing nature.

Although many birders have tried. No one has been able to see and identify all of the different kinds of birds in North America. There are over seven hundred different kinds of birds on this continent half of these can be seen on the East Coast. Birding has become an increasingly appealing hobby in America, it will not be long before someone manages to see and identify all of the North American species.

WRITING ASSIGNMENT 7

Write a paragraph applying everything you have learned up to this point about sentences.

When you finish, rewrite each sentence, one at a time, on a separate piece of paper according to the instructions p. 76 of Chapter 3. Identify and correct any sentence fragments, run-on sentences, or comma splices, and then write the sentences on a new piece of paper in regular paragraph form.

Remember the following points:

- Make sure you *understand the topic*.
- *List* all of the thoughts you have about the topic.
- *Select* the most convincing items from your list and arrange them into an order.
- *Expand the ideas* you will be using for support.
- *Write the rough draft.*

Topics

1. Write a paragraph naming a problem in your life and explaining how you plan to solve it. This could include poor performance in school, not enough money, a troublesome friend, nagging parents or in-laws, etc. (See Exercise 10.)
2. Write a paragraph describing a party you have been to recently. Try to describe the party by using enough details and examples to "show" the reader what it was like. (See Review Exercise 3.)
3. Write a paragraph giving the reasons you decided to come to college. (See Review Exercise 7.)

6 / Verbs: Learn the principal parts

In this chapter, you will learn to recognize the tense, or time, indicated by all verbs, and you will learn when to use each of the principal parts of a verb. You will also learn how to use active verbs to express yourself clearly and directly. Finally, you will learn how to check the consistency of the verb tenses in your writing.

USE THE CORRECT FORM OF THE VERB

The Principal Parts

Verbs have three parts called **principal** (or **main**) **parts**. These are the *present*, the *simple past*, and the *past participle*.

The Present Tense Look at the following sentences:

Sentence 1: George hugs the baby.
Sentence 2: Linda seems happy.

Within what time period does George hug the baby in Sentence 1? You are correct if you said "now." In this sentence, the action—hugging—is taking place in the **present**. When does Linda seem happy in Sentence 2? In this case, there is no action, because "seems" is a linking verb. But the statement about Linda refers to her *now*, at this moment in time. Notice that in both sentences the action or the statement could also refer to a time period that is indefinite. For example, Sentence 1 could mean that George hugs the baby every afternoon at 5:30 as soon as he gets home from work. Sentence 2 could mean that Linda seems happy whenever she is reading a good book. Both of these meanings are slightly different from actions described or statements being made *now*; instead, they signify actions that *continue*, or make statements that apply *indefinitely*. Both uses of the present tense, however, clearly show that the statement does *not* refer to any time in the *past*.

The Simple Past Tense Now look at these sentences:

Sentence 3: George hugged the baby.
Sentence 4: Linda seemed happy.

Now when does George hug the baby? You are correct if you said ''yesterday,'' ''a moment ago,'' ''a year ago,'' or at any *definite* time in the *past*. In Sentence 4, Linda was happy only at a very particular moment in the past. Neither sentence tells us exactly when George hugged the baby or Linda seemed happy, but both sentences could be expanded to indicate a specific time in the past.

George hugged the baby before putting her to bed.
Linda seemed happy when she hung up the telephone.

Now both sentences refer to specific moments in the past time, so the verbs are in the **simple past tense**.

The Past Participle Now look at these sentences:

Sentence 5A: George has hugged the baby often.
Sentence 5B: George had hugged the baby before, but never with so much emotion.

Sentence 6A: Linda has seemed happy lately.
Sentence 6B: Linda had seemed happy before the accident.

When is the action taking place in Sentence 5A? As you can see, it is no longer occurring in the simple present or in the simple past. Using a present tense helping verb (''has'') with the past participle form of the main verb (''hugged''), changes the time period of the action. Now the sentence indicates that George hugged the baby at some time in the past *and continues to do so into the present time*. This tense is called the **present perfect**.

In Sentence 5B, a past tense helping verb (''had'') is used with the past participle form of the main verb (''hugged'') to form the **past perfect tense**. This tense indicates that an action took place in the *distant* past. Notice in Sentences 6A and 6B how these verb forms are used with the linking verb "seem" to change the meaning of the sentences.

This is one use of the past participle: to form the perfect tenses. The following figure illustrates the relationship of the present, past, and perfect tenses to each other. The left side of the time line indicates the most distant point in the past, and the right side of the line indicates the future.

Time Line

PAST PERFECT   PAST   PRESENT   PRESENT PERFECT   FUTURE

→

One other use of the past participle form has nothing to do with time. Look at this sentence:

Sentence 7: The baby was hugged by George.

How is this sentence different from the others you have looked at? In this case, the use of the participle with the helping verb "was" forms the **passive voice**. As you can see if you compare Sentence 7 with Sentence 3, the passive voice focuses attention on the person *receiving* the action rather than on the person *doing* the action. You will learn more about active and passive voice later in this chapter.

Every verb in English has these three principal parts: the present, the simple past, and the past participle. Knowing how to use them effectively will help you to achieve the exact meaning you intend when you write.

Regular Verbs

In the list below, you will notice that both the simple past and the past participle are formed by adding *-ed* to the present tense form. Verbs that form their principal parts in this way are called **regular verbs**.

Present	***Past***	***Past Participle (used with helping verbs)***
hug	hugged	hugged
seem	seemed	seemed
call	called	called
spell	spelled	spelled

Other verbs, however, form the simple past tense and the past participle by changing the spelling entirely from one principal part to another. These are called **irregular verbs**.

Irregular Verbs

There are many different types of irregular verbs, and the past and past participle parts may be formed in many different ways. You have been using these verbs in your speech and writing all of your life, and you have used most of them correctly. Let us review the forms of these irregular verbs so you can check your use of them when you write. The list below contains many of the irregular verbs that you are likely to use in your everyday speech or writing. As you read through the list, cover the *Simple Past* and *Past Participle* columns to see if you can spell these forms of the verb correctly on your own. Put a check mark next to the number of any verb that you misspell or that is new to you. This will help you learn the correct forms. Be sure to review the forms of any verb you did not know.

Common Irregular Verbs

	Present	*Simple Past*	*Past Participle*
1.	beat	beat	beaten
2.	become	became	become
3.	begin	began	begun
4.	break	broke	broken
5.	bring	brought	brought
6.	buy	bought	bought
7.	choose	chose	chosen
8.	come	came	come
9.	cry	cried	cried
10.	do	did	done
11.	drink	drank	drunk
12.	drive	drove	driven
13.	eat	ate	eaten
14.	fall	fell	fallen
15.	feel	felt	felt
16.	find	found	found
17.	fly	flew	flown
18.	freeze	froze	frozen
19.	give	gave	given
20.	go	went	gone
21.	grow	grew	grown
22.	hurt	hurt	hurt
23.	keep	kept	kept
24.	know	knew	known
25.	lead	led	led

	Present	Simple Past	Past Participle
26.	lose	lost	lost
27.	make	made	made
28.	meet	met	met
29.	ride	rode	ridden
30.	run	ran	run
31.	say	said	said
32.	see	saw	seen
33.	shoot	shot	shot
34.	sing	sang	sung
35.	sit	sat	sat
36.	slide	slid	slid
37.	speak	spoke	spoken
38.	spend	spent	spent
39.	stand	stood	stood
40.	steal	stole	stolen
41.	sweep	swept	swept
42.	swim	swam	swum
43.	swing	swung	swung
44.	take	took	taken
45.	teach	taught	taught
46.	tell	told	told
47.	think	thought	thought
48.	throw	threw	thrown
49.	understand	understood	understood
50.	win	won	won

PRACTICE EXERCISES

EXERCISE 1 *Return to the writing assignments you have completed so far in the book. For each assignment, identify the tense in which the paragraph is written. If you used more than one tense in the paragraph, identify the tense the paragraph begins with.*

Writing Assignment 1: Verb Tense: ____________________

Writing Assignment 2: Verb Tense: ____________________

Writing Assignment 3: Verb Tense: ____________________

Writing Assignment 4: Verb Tense: ____________________

Writing Assignment 5: Verb Tense: ____________________

Writing Assignment 6: Verb Tense: ______________________

Writing Assignment 7: Verb Tense: ______________________

EXERCISE 2

Write!

In this exercise, write a sentence using the past tense or past participle form of each of the verbs you checked on the list. If you spelled all of the verbs correctly, write ten sentences using the ten verbs you found the most difficult to spell correctly.

1. ____
____

2. ____
____

3. ____
____

4. ____
____

5. ____
____

6. ____
____

7. ____
____

8. ____
____

9. ____
____

10. ____
____

USE THE DICTIONARY TO FIND PRINCIPAL PARTS

The list of Common Irregular Verbs on pages 136–137 contains only 50 verbs, but there are about 200 different irregular verbs in English. You could memorize the principal parts of all these verbs, but it is easier to check the spelling of each principal part as you proofread your writing. For example, if you wrote the sentence, "The other day Fred brung me a new record," you would probably recognize that "brung" is not the correct past tense form of the verb "bring." You could find the correct past tense form in a dictionary.

Most dictionaries list the principal parts of all irregular verbs. To find the principal parts in a dictionary, follow these steps:

1. Look up the present tense form in the dictionary. (The present tense form is the first principal part.)
2. When you find the word in the dictionary, *make sure it is a verb*. Some words, like "fly," can be either a verb ("The birds fly") or a noun ("The fly landed on my plate"). If the word is a verb, it will be followed by one of the following abbreviations: *v, vb, vi, vt.*
3. The principal parts are shown in heavy print after the *v, vb, vi,* or *vt*. Most dictionaries follow the same format when they present this information.
   a. The first entry in heavy print is the simple past tense form.
   b. The second entry in heavy print is the past participle form.
   c. The *-ing* form in heavy print is the *progressive* form; this is never used as the simple past or past participle.
   d. If the entry gives a choice for one of the parts ("shrank" or "shrunk"), either form is correct, but the first is usually used.

fall (fôl) *vi.* **fell, fall'en, fall'ing** [ME. *fallen* < OE. *feallan*, to fall, akin to G. *fallen* < IE. base ***phol-**, to fall] **I.** to come down by the force of gravity; drop; descend; specif., **1.** to come down because detached, pushed, dropped, etc.; move down and land forcibly [apples *fall* from the tree] **2.** to come down suddenly from a standing or sitting position; tumble; topple; become prostrate **3.** to be wounded or killed in battle **4.** to come down in ruins; collapse [the building *fell*] **5.** to hang down [hair *falling* about her shoulders] **6.** to strike; hit [the arrow *fell* wide of its mark] **II.** to pass to a position, condition, etc. regarded as lower; specif., **1.** to take a downward direction [land *falling* away to the sea] **2.** to become lower in amount, number, degree, intensity, value, etc.; drop; abate [prices *fell*] **3.** to lose power; be overthrown [the government has *fallen*] **4.** to lose status, reputation, dignity, etc. **5.** to yield to temptation; do wrong; sin; specif. in earlier use (esp. of women), to lose chastity **6.** to be captured or conquered **7.** to take on a look of disappointment or dejection [his face *fell*] **8.** to become lower in pitch or volume [her voice *fell*] **III.** to happen as if by dropping; specif., **1.** to take place; occur [the meeting *fell* on a Friday] **2.** to come by lot, distribution, inheritance, etc. [the estate *falls* to the son] **3.** to pass into a specified condition; become [to *fall* ill] **4.** to come at a specified place [the accent *falls* on the third syllable] **5.** to be directed by chance [his eye *fell* on a misspelled word] **6.** to be spoken in an involuntary way [the news *fell* from his lips] **7.** to be born: said of animals **8.** to be divided (*into*) [to *fall* into two classes] —*vt.* [Dial.] to fell (a tree, etc.) —*n.* [< the *v.*] **1.** a dropping; descending; coming

4. If the verb you look up is a *regular* verb, there will be no entries in heavy print. This is because all regular verbs form the past tense form and the past participle form the same way: by adding *-ed* to the present tense form. So, if the verb you look up has *v, vb, vi,* or *vt* after it, but no principal parts are listed, simply add *-ed* to form the past tense and the past participle.

> **look** (look) *vi.* [ME. *loken* < OE. *locian,* akin to OS. *lōkōn,* OHG. *luogen* (G. dial. *lugen*), to spy after, look for] **1.** to make use of the sense of sight; see **2.** *a)* to direct one's eyes in order to see *b)* to direct one's attention mentally upon something **3.** to try to see or find something; search **4.** to appear to be; seem [to *look* sick] **5.** to be facing or turned in a specified direction **6.** to expect (followed by an infinitive) —*vt.* **1.** to direct one's eyes on [to *look* someone in the face] **2.** to express by one's looks, or appearance [to *look* one's disgust] **3.** [Rare] to bring to a certain condition by looking **4.** to appear as having attained (some age) [to *look* one's years] —*n.* **1.** the act of looking; glance **2.** outward impression; appearance; aspect [the *look* of a beggar] **3.** [Colloq.] *a)* [*usually pl.*] appearance; the way something seems to be [from the *looks* of things] *b)* [*pl.*] personal appearance, esp. of a pleasing nature [to have *looks* and youth] —*interj.* **1.** see! **2.** pay attention! —**it looks like 1.** it seems that there will be **2.** [Colloq.] it seems as if —**look after** to take care of; watch over —**look alive** (or **sharp**) [Colloq.] to be alert; act or move quickly: usually in the imperative —**look back** to recall the past; recollect —**look down on** (or **upon**) **1.** to regard as an inferior **2.** to regard with contempt; despise —**look for 1.** to search or hunt for **2.** to expect; anticipate —**look forward to** to anticipate, esp. eagerly —**look in** (**on**) to pay a brief visit (to) —**look into** to examine carefully; investigate —**look on 1.** to be an observer or spectator **2.** to consider; regard —**look (like)**

5. If there is only one principal part given, this is the past tense form, and it means that the past participle form is exactly the same as the past tense. For example, if you look up the verb "bring," the entry reads: "bring *vt* brought, bringing." This entry indicates to you that both the past tense and the past participle forms are "brought." (Remember: The *-ing* form is never used as the simple past tense or past participle.)

> **think**[1] (thiŋk) *vt.* **thought, think'ing** [< ME. *thenchen,* to think, confused with *thinchen,* to seem < OE. *thencan,* to think, caus. of *thyncan,* to seem: for IE. base see THANK] **1.** to form or have in the mind; conceive [*thinking* good thoughts] **2.** to hold in one's opinion; judge; consider [many *think* her charming] **3.** to believe; surmise; expect [they *think* they can come] **4.** to determine, resolve, work out, etc. by reasoning [*think* what your next move should be] **5.** [Now Rare] to purpose; intend [*thinking* to do right] **6.** *a)* to bring to mind; form an idea of [*think* what the future holds] *b)* to recall; recollect [*think* what joy was ours] **7.** to have the mind turned steadily toward; have constantly in mind [*think* success] —*vi.* **1.** to use the mind for arriving at conclusions, making decisions, drawing inferences, etc.; reflect; reason [learn to *think*] **2.** to have an opinion, belief, expectation, etc. [I just *think* so] **3.** to weigh something mentally; reflect [*think* before you act] **4.** to call to mind; recall; remember (with *of* or *about*) **5.** to have an opinion, judgment, etc. (with *of* or *about*) **6.** to allow oneself to consider (with *of* or *about*) **7.** to have regard for; consider the welfare of (with *of* or *about*) **8.** to discover or invent; conceive (*of*) —*n.* [Colloq.] the act of thinking [give it a good *think*] —*adj.* [Slang]

Whenever you are in doubt about the form of a verb, look up the word in the dictionary. There you will find whether the verb is regular or irregular. If it is irregular, you will learn how to spell the principal parts.

PRACTICE EXERCISE

*EXERCISE 3 *The following exercise will give you some practice in finding the principal parts of a verb in a dictionary. Look up each word and write the simple past tense and past participle forms in the appropriate place below.*

	Present	*Simple Past*	*Past Participle*
1.	do	______________	______________
2.	tear	______________	______________
3.	crawl	______________	______________
4.	set	______________	______________
5.	wear	______________	______________
6.	steer	______________	______________
7.	creep	______________	______________
8.	lay	______________	______________
9.	hope	______________	______________
10.	hop	______________	______________

LEARN THE DIFFERENCE BETWEEN ACTIVE AND PASSIVE VOICE

In most of the sentences you have seen so far in this book, the *subject* (actor) *does something* (verb) *to someone or something* (object) *that receives the action.* This way of writing a sentence is called **active voice**.

Active Voice:	**Actor**	**Action**	**Receiver**
	The clerk	lost	the report.

Sentences written in active voice tend to express ideas very effectively because the sentences remain simple and direct, and the sentences say exactly who did what. In other words, active voice sentences emphasize the subject of the sentence, the actor.

Sentences written in the **passive voice**, on the other hand, emphasize the *receiver* of the action (object) instead of the actor (subject).

Passive Voice:	**Receiver**	**Action**	**Actor**
	The report	was lost	by the clerk.

Although it is preferable to write in a straightforward style by using the active voice, sometimes the passive voice can be useful. For example, there are situations when you will want to emphasize the receiver of the action instead of the actor. Look at the following example:

Passive Voice: The old post office was destroyed by the blast.

In this case, the condition of the post office is more important than the cause of the damage ("the blast"), so the passive voice is appropriate.

As you can see in the above examples, the passive voice is formed by using the past participle form of a verb in combination with one of the forms of the helping verb "be."

EXERCISE 4

Write!

Return to the paragraph you wrote for Writing Assignment 7 and check to see if any of your sentences are written in passive voice. If you find any, try rewriting the sentences in active voice to see if they are more effective.

*EXERCISE 5

Rewrite the following passive voice *sentences in* active voice *to make them more effective.*

1. According to the company spokesman, the truth was concealed by the treasurer.

   Active: ______________________________

   ____

   ____

2. The ball was hit by the batter.

   Active: ______________________________

   ____

   ____

3. According to the child, the vase was broken by someone.

   Active: ______________________________

   ____

   ____

4. The national award was won by Gerald Finley.

   Active: ______________________________

   ____

   ____

5. The treaty was signed by the American president and the Soviet premier.

   Active: ______________________________

   ____

   ____

6. The meeting of the committee was held on Tuesday, January 4.

   Active: ______________________________

   ____

   ____

7. The boy was bitten by a squirrel.

   Active: ______________________________

   ____

   ____

8. The world's record in the Olympic event was broken by the youngest member of the Yugoslavian team.

   Active: ______________________________

   ____

   ____

9. He was tormented by his dreams of grandeur.

Active: ______________________________

____

____

10. The first offer was made by the professional football team in Miami.

Active: ______________________________

____

USE VERB TENSES CONSISTENTLY

When you write about something that happened in a particular time period (past or present), you must always be sure that you are using verbs that are in that same tense. For example:

Last week I *sold* three sets of encyclopedias, but I *earned* only fifty dollars.

In this sentence, the words "last week" indicate the time period, and the verbs in the sentence should be in the appropriate tense. "Sold" and "earned" are both in the past tense, so the verb tense in this sentence is *consistent*. Now look at this example.

Fred had a good time at the beach even though he gets a bad sunburn.

In this sentence, the first verb is in the past tense, but the second verb is in the present tense, so the verb tense in this sentence is *inconsistent*. The tenses must be corrected so they are both the same.

Fred had a good time at the beach even though he *got* a bad sunburn.

In most sentences that you write, the verb tense should remain consistent, but there are some situations in which the tense of one verb will be different from the tense of another.

PAST TENSE PRESENT TENSE

1. Yesterday I *felt* miserable, but today I *feel* fine.

PRESENT TENSE PRESENT TENSE
2. The old man *sits* on the park bench and *dreams* of

PAST TENSE
how he once *was* young.

In these sentences, the time period changes from one part of the sentence to another. This kind of time change is usually signaled by a word or phrase in the sentence. In Sentence 1, the first part of the sentence deals with "yesterday" (past), and the second part deals with "today" (present). In Sentence 2, the sentence starts out with what the old man is doing now (present tense), but the word "once" indicates that a past tense verb is needed in the second part of the sentence.

When you write your own sentences, you don't usually consciously decide what verb tense you are going to use. Most of the time the correct tense will come to you naturally. The best way for you to check to see if you are using verb tenses consistently is to finish writing and then go back and check the verbs in the sentence. To do this, first identify what verb tense the sentence starts with and then make sure you use that tense throughout the sentence group unless you change the time period within the sentence.

Verb tense must also be consistent in larger units, like the paragraph. If, for example, you begin a paragraph in the past tense, the rest of the paragraph should be in past tense unless there is a change in the time period. Often a writer will refer back in time to something that happened in the past, even though he or she started writing in the present tense. Read the following paragraph and notice how the verb tenses change:

> I think writing skills courses should meet at least two times a week. In previous semesters, nighttime writing skills courses were taught just once a week. The students in those classes did not learn as much about writing as the students in the daytime classes. There are several possible reasons for this. For one thing, one meeting a week does not give students enough time to practice their writing. Another reason may be that the evening classes meet for two and a half hours. When a class meets for that long, the students usually become tired more quickly. A final reason is that many teachers find it harder to teach a class which meets only once a week. I taught both types of classes last semester, and I noticed a big difference in student achievement. I always hated to teach that one long evening class each week.

Where does the first tense change occur? (Circle the first change in tense.) Does the tense change again? Where? (Circle any other changes.) Can you explain why the verb tenses change as they do in this paragraph?

The answer, of course, is that they change because the time periods change. The first sentence, for example, is an opinion being expressed now, in the *present tense*. The second sentence, however, deals with *previous semesters*, so it is written in the *past tense*. The tense of each sentence depends on whether the sentence refers to present or past time.

PRACTICE EXERCISES

*EXERCISE 6 *Read the following paragraph and check to see if the verb tenses are consistent. Correct any verbs that are not consistent.*

When I was a child, one of my favorite places was the neighborhood haunted house. Of course the house was not really haunted—it was just an old abandoned place that looked a little frightening to children. It became "haunted" when one of the local kids fell and broke his leg while playing in the house. From then on, it was dangerous to enter the place. Even so, most of the neighborhood kids use the place as their playground. We scare each other by jumping out of closets, use the house for a hideout when we play hookey from school, and use it as a meeting place for our gang. It was a sad day for the neighborhood children when the haunted house was demolished. The city had decided to build a playground on that spot.

EXERCISE 7 *In this paragraph it is correct to use more than one tense, depending on the time period of each sentence. Correct any verbs that are inconsistent.*

One kind of person whom I hate more than any other is a salesman. I know that is an unreasonable attitude to have, but I simply cannot feel any kindness towards salesmen. One reason for this is that salesmen are always successful with me. No matter what they are selling, if they are good enough, I end up buying it. A year or two ago an encyclopedia salesman came to my house. When I answered the door, I told him that I was not interested in buying encyclopedias. As a matter of fact, I had just bought a set recently. The salesman acts like he does not hear a word I said and asks if he can come in anyway. Like a fool, I let him in. It is not hard to guess what happens; before the salesman left the house that night, I bought another set of encyclopedias. That is not the only time I ever bought something I did not need. Now I just avoid salesmen of any type as much as I can, because if I let them start talking to me, I know I will end up buying something.

CHAPTER REVIEW

In this chapter, you learned that verbs have three principal parts: the present, the simple past, and the past participle (used with helping verbs). With regular verbs, the simple past and the past participle forms are produced by adding an *-ed* ending to the present tense form. However, with the irregular verbs, the simple past and the past participle forms are often spelled differently than the present tense. In addition, you learned how to find the principal parts of verbs in the dictionary.

You also learned that the tense of verbs in sentences and paragraphs should be consistent. That is, the verbs in any one sentence or paragraph should be in the same tense unless the time period of the sentence or paragraph changes. If the time period changes, a sentence or paragraph can be written in more than one tense. To check your own writing for verb tense consistency, first identify what tense you started with and then make sure that that tense is used throughout your writing unless the time period changes (from present to past, for example).

WRITING ASSIGNMENT 8

Write a paragraph on any of the topics listed below, applying everything you have learned up to this point about sentences and verb tenses. When you finish writing your paragraph, rewrite each sentence, one at a time, on a separate piece of paper according to the instructions on p. 76 of Chapter 3. Identify and correct any sentence fragments, run-on sentences, comma splices, or verb tense errors in your paragraph; then write the sentences on a new piece of paper in regular paragraph form.

Remember the following points:

- Make sure you *understand the topic*.
- *List* all of the thoughts you have about the topic.
- *Select* the most convincing items from your list and arrange them into an order.
- *Expand the ideas* you will be using for support.
- *Write the rough draft*.

Topics

1. Explain why you would or would not like to get married (or remarried). (See Exercise 11.)
2. Describe an experience you had that was different from the way you had imagined it would be. Try to show how what actually happened was different from what you thought would happen. (See Exercise 8.)
3. Name your favorite type of physical fitness exercise and explain why it is your favorite. (See Exercise 10.)

SUPPLEMENTAL EXERCISES

Use the exercises below for additional practice in identifying the correct principal parts of verbs and in using verb tenses consistently.

*EXERCISE 8 *In the following paragraph, some incorrect verb forms are used. Find the incorrect forms and correct them. If you do not know the correct forms of any of the verbs, look them up in a dictionary.*

The first time I ever went camping I discovered it was not exactly what I thought it would be like. I imagined that I would gather up a few bare necessities and march off into the depths of the forest. I pictured a long and interesting hike, after which I would quickly set up camp and sleep peacefully, surrounded by the sounds of the forest. Unfortunately, the trip did not turn out quite like this. I went with two friends of mine who sayed they knowed of a beautiful state park. To prepare for the trip, we went to a supermarket and buyed an enormous quantity of food and supplies. We load everything into Tony's station wagon, and we finally leaved. I got my first true picture of what "camping" was like as soon as we arrived. All camping in the state park was restricted to one area, so that's where we went. I could not believe what I saw. The camping area was swarming with people! Everywhere I looked there were camping trailers, screaming children, dogs, frisbees, barbecues, and beer cans. We squeezed our station wagon in between two trailers and tryed to set up "camp." That night, instead of falling asleep with the soothing sounds of the forest, I tossed and turned, keeped awake by a half dozen radios turned all the way up. The three of us spended the weekend dodging frisbees and trying to find some quiet solitude. We finally gave up and drived back to the city. We had find out what "roughing it" was all about.

*EXERCISE 9 *In some of the following sentence groups, the verb tense shifts from one tense to another. Identify tense or tenses used in the sentence groups, and indicate where the tense shifts.*

1. Linda was on the gymnastics team when she was in high school. She competed in every meet and was considered the best gymnast on the team. Her specialty was the uneven parallel bars. Even though Linda is married and has a baby, she is still in good physical condition.

   Tenses Used: ______________________

2. Not all college professors are absentminded, but I do know several who are. A chemistry professor I once knew walked all the way from his house to his office without his coat, and the temperature outside was only 10 degrees!

   Tenses Used: ______________________

3. It is difficult for a prime-time television show to stay on the air for more than one season. One reason for this may be that people get into a television viewing "rut." They watch the same shows, week after week, and they resent it when a new show is introduced as a replacement.

   Tenses Used: ______________________

4. People who say they read *Playboy* magazine for the "interesting articles" are probably lying. I said that too when I bought the magazine, but all I was really interested in were the pictures.

   Tenses Used: ______________________

5. When my uncle was younger, he smoked two or more packs of cigarettes a day. In between cigarettes he also smoked an occasional cigar. One day he got up in the morning, looked at an ash tray overflowing with

cigar and cigarette butts, and decided to stop smoking. He still does not smoke, but occasionally he chews tobacco.

Tenses Used: ______________________

*EXERCISE 10 *In the following paragraph, the verb tense is inconsistent in several places. Correct any verbs that are inconsistent.*

Jogging is a popular form of exercise nowadays. People of all types and from all parts of society get their exercise by jogging. For most, it is a convenient way to exercise. Very little equipment is necessary, and people can run anywhere there is a level surface. For people who lived near a park or woods, jogging was ideal because they got their exercise while they were in a pleasant outdoor setting. Jogging is an exercise for everyone, too. All types of people, whether they are athletic or not, can jog because each person determines his own limit and stops running when he wants to. As the exercise becomes more and more popular, a number of runners are writing books on the subject. The books offer advice on the different kinds of running shoes, the best time of day for jogging, and the amount of jogging that was required to lose weight.

EXERCISE 11 *In the following paragraph, it is correct to use more than one tense, depending on the time period of each sentence. Correct any verbs that are inconsistent.*

Everyone thinks that because I am a female I want to get married right away, but they could not be further from the truth. The last thing I want to do right now is get married. Being single is something I really enjoy; it gives me a chance to go out often and meet a lot of new people. I doubt that I would meet new people if I were married. Also, getting married would damage my chances of finding a good job. Every time I ever applied for a job, the employer asks me if I am married, because he thinks that if I am married I would have children sooner or later. Being a woman is enough of a disadvantage in the job market, and I do not intend to give a prospective employer anything else to find wrong with me. My final reason for staying single is what I have seen happen to my friends. Several of my friends who were always very active and happy change completely when they got married. All they want to do now is stay at home and watch television. They can have that kind of life; I intend to stay single.

---

7 / Verbs: Learn the present tense

In Chapter 6 you learned to recognize the tense of verbs in sentences, and you learned that verb tenses must be used consistently. In addition, you learned the three principal parts of verbs. In this chapter you will learn which present tense verbs must have an ending in order to "agree" with their subjects.

LEARN THE PRESENT TENSE ENDINGS

When a verb is in present tense, it may or may not end in *-s*, depending on the subject that goes with the verb. For example:

Present tense: I *park* my car in the driveway.
Present tense: He *parks* his car in the driveway.

Notice that both sentences are written in present tense, but one verb ends in *-s* and the other does not. This is because the subjects in the two sentences are different. In present tense, a verb must *agree* with its subject.

When the Subject Is a Pronoun

To learn whether or not a verb must have an *-s* ending in present tense, you must know what ending a verb takes with different kinds of subjects. To find this out, place the verb next to each of the subject pronouns. This process is known as **conjugation**. When a verb is conjugated, it is put beside the different subject pronouns in English. These pronouns represent the different kinds of subjects that might be used with the verb. Here is a conjugation of the verb "park" in present tense:

Singular		***Plural***	
I	park	we	park
you	park	you	park
he, she, it	parks	they	park

Notice that the verb ends in *-s* only when the subject is "he," "she," or "it." This is why the verb ended in *-s* in the sentence,

He parks his car in the driveway.

If the verb is in present tense and the subject is "he," "she," or "it," the verb must end in "-s." For example:

He goes to the store.	*We go* to the store.
She flies to Peru.	*You fly* to Peru.
It works occasionally.	*They work* occasionally.

PRACTICE EXERCISE

*EXERCISE 1 *The following sentences are written in present tense and have one of the subject pronouns as a subject. Circle the correct form of the verb. Remember, if the subject is "he," "she," or "it," the verb must end in -s.*

1. On Tuesdays, she (deposit, deposits) her check in the bank.
2. Although it (seem, seems) silly, I love to walk in the rain.
3. Of all the cars made today, I (prefer, prefers) the small economy models.
4. We (visit, visits) my aunt every summer when we go on vacation.
5. He (agree, agrees) to go along only if Charlotte goes too.
6. She (paint, paints) signs for a living.
7. They (intend, intends) to sue the bus company.
8. The road is poorly maintained, and it (cause, causes) many accidents.

9. You (jog, jogs) half a mile today while I watch.

10. I (find, finds) English a very difficult language to learn.

When the Subject Is a Noun

If you completed Exercise 2 correctly, you will notice that the verb ends in *-s* only when the subject is "he," "she," or "it." But not all sentences have pronouns for their subjects; most often the subject in a sentence is a noun.

When a noun is the subject of a present tense sentence, it is even easier to decide whether or not the verb ends in *-s*. If the subject is singular, add *-s* to the verb; if the subject is plural, do not add *-s* to the verb. For example:

SINGULAR ADD -s
/ /
The *boat* glide*s* through the water.

PLURAL NO -s
/ /
The *boats* glid*e* through the water.

This rule is really no different from the rule for pronouns since "he," "she," and "it" always represent singular nouns.

Now we can combine both rules for adding *-s* in the present tense: *If the subject is "he," "she," "it," or any singular noun, add "-s" to the verb.*

Remember, to find the subject of a sentence, find the verb first and then ask "who" or "what" of the verb. For example, in the first sentence above you would ask: "Who or what glides?" The answer is the subject: "The boat."

To make sure the endings are correct on present tense verbs, you should follow these steps.

Find the verb:	The boat *glides* through the water.
Find the subject:	The *boat* glides through the water. (Singular; add *-s*.)
Apply the rule:	The *boat* glide*s* through the water.

The Present Tense of "Be"

The verb "be" in present tense requires special attention. The forms of this verb are highly irregular, but the form used with the third person singular pronouns—"he," "she," and "it"—still ends in *-s*. Note in the following examples that each time a third person singular pronoun is the subject, the verb ends in *-s*.

S V
I am a bus driver.

S V
He is a bus driver.

S V
You are a good friend.

S V
She is a good friend.

S V
They are beautiful paintings.

S V
It is a beautiful painting.

Since the verb "be" is such an irregular verb, and such a commonly used verb, you should memorize the present tense forms.

Present Tense of "Be"

I am	we are
you are	you are
he, she, it *is*	they are

Of course, if the subject of the sentence is not a pronoun but a singular noun, the correct form of the verb will still be "is." See the following example:

Singular pronoun as subject: *He is* a bus driver.
Singular noun as subject: *Frank is* a bus driver.

If the subject of the sentence is a plural pronoun or a plural noun, the correct form of the verb will be "are." For example:

Plural pronoun as subject: *They are* beautiful people.
Plural noun as subject: *Ralph* and *Judy are* beautiful people.

PRACTICE EXERCISE

*EXERCISE 2 *In the following sentences, circle the correct form of the verb. The subject in each sentence may be either a pronoun or a noun.*

1. Fred (work, works) at two different jobs.
2. He (go, goes) to school in his free time.
3. During the week, he (pump, pumps) gas at the local gas station.
4. He also (check, checks) oil and does minor repairs.
5. On weekends, Fred (is, are) a waiter at a local restaurant.
6. Friday night (is, are) the busiest night of the week.
7. Most people (like, likes) to eat out on payday.
8. The five tables in the back of the dining room (is, are) Fred's responsibility.
9. In the evenings, Fred (attend, attends) college.
10. Although he is interested in his courses, he sometimes (has, have) trouble staying awake in his classes.

Present Tense Helping Verbs

As you learned in earlier chapters, many verbs often have helping verbs. When helping verbs are used to form the present perfect tense, the *-ing* form (the progressive), or the passive, the present tense helping verb must agree with the subject. In all of these cases, the helping verb will be either "have" or "be."

As with all other verbs in present tense, both of these helping verbs end in *-s* when used with "he," "she," "it," or any singular noun. The conjugations of these verbs show the *-s* ending with the pronouns "he," "she," and "it." ("Be" was conjugated on p. 156.)

Present Tense of "Have"

I have	we have
you have	you have
he, she, it *has*	they have

The following sentences show how the present tense helping verbs end in *-s* when the subject is singular; note that they *do not* end in *-s* when the subject becomes plural (*except* in passive constructions).

Present tense:	Barry *pays* the rent.
	George and Helen *pay* the rent.
Present perfect tense:	Barry *has* paid the rent.
	George and Helen *have* paid the rent.
Progressive:	Barry *is* paying the rent.
	George and Helen *are* paying the rent.
Passive:	The rent *is* paid by Barry.
	The rent *is* paid by George and Helen.

Can you explain why the helping verb remained the same in both passive voice sentences? It is because the subject of the sentence—"rent"—is singular, and it remains the subject of both sentences. Because the sentences are written in passive voice, the person or persons who do the action are not the subject of the sentence.

PRACTICE EXERCISE

*EXERCISE 3 *In the following paragraph, fill in the blank spaces with the correct present tense form of "be."*

My boss is against it, but I ____________ going to quit my job tomorrow. What do I need with the money? I ____________ going to go out and do all the things I have always wanted to do. Who ____________ going to blame me? I have this friend named Joe. He ____________ always on the move; he ____________ always having a good time. He knows lots of different people and they ____________ all a great group! They ______________________ all out of work, but that has not stopped them from planning lots of exciting trips. Now that I ______________________ joining the group, we ______________________ going to consider a trip to Paris. We may never go, but at least we ______________________ going to plan it.

EXERCISE 4 *For each of the following sentences, check to make sure the present tense form is correct. Next, rewrite the sentence in present perfect tense, in the present progressive tense, and in the passive voice.*

Example:

Present:	The bitter wind chills their bones.
Present Perfect:	The bitter wind has chilled their bones.
Present Progressive:	The bitter wind is chilling their bones.
Passive:	Their bones are chilled by the bitter wind.

1. *Present:* The bearded man paddles the canoe.

   Present Perfect: ____

   ____.

   Present Progressive: ____.

   ____.

   Passive: ____

   ____.

2. *Present:* Weeds invade my vegetable garden.

   Present Perfect: ____

   ____.

   Present Progressive: ____.

   ____.

   Passive: ____

   ____.

3. *Present:* His favorite store in the city holds a sale.

   Present Perfect: ______________________________

   ______________________________.

   Present Progressive: ______________________________.

   ______________________________.

   Passive: ______________________________

   ______________________________.

4. *Present:* The florist deliver the bouquet.

   Present Perfect: ______________________________

   ______________________________.

   Present Progressive: ______________________________.

   ______________________________.

   Passive: ______________________________

   ______________________________.

5. *Present:* The department store turn down the request for a credit card.

   Present Perfect: ______________________________

   ______________________________.

   Present Progressive: ______________________________.

   ______________________________.

   Passive: ______________________________

   ______________________________.

EXERCISE 5 *Check the following sentence groups for errors in present tense endings. Correct any errors that you find.*

1. Fred just got a new pair of glasses. He is supposed to wear them when he are reading. Although he paid a lot of money for the glasses, he still feels self-conscious, and he are not wearing them when he should be.

2. The bus company is on strike, so the men is standing in front of the entrance to the terminal. They are carrying signs and making it difficult for anyone to enter. The police is standing by to make sure there is no trouble.
3. Disco dancing are becoming very popular lately. One reason is because of several popular movies on this subject. Another is the fact that the driving age is only sixteen in many states. As a result, many more teenagers is going out to the discos.
4. The team has lost too many games lately. One of the reasons for this is that the members of the team is always fighting with the team owner. Apparently, the players are complaining about the mistakes the coaches and the manager is always making.
5. The girls in the crowd is strolling down the avenue, looking into the different shop windows. One of the girls are searching for a birthday present for her boyfriend. She is hoping she will be able to find something that is clever and unusual.

Compound Subjects and Verbs

Recall from Chapter 2 that a sentence may also have a **compound subject**. This means that a sentence may have more than one person, place, thing, idea, or action as its subject. Look at the following examples:

SINGULAR ADD -s

George works on weekends.

COMPOUND SUBJECT NO -s

George and Harvey work on weekends.

When a sentence has a compound subject, as in the second example above, the subject becomes plural, so the verb has no *-s* ending. If you made the mistake of looking only at the subject closest to the verb, you might think that "Harvey" was the only subject in the sentence. To avoid making this kind of mistake, always ask "who" or "what" of the verb. "Who or what work on weekends?" "George and Harvey" work on weekends.

Also, remember that a compound subject may consist of a combination of nouns or pronouns, or several pronouns without any nouns. For example:

COMPOUND SUBJECT
NOUN PRONOUN NO -s
George and I work on weekends.

COMPOUND SUBJECT
PRONOUN PRONOUN NO -s
She and I go everywhere together.

PRACTICE EXERCISE

*EXERCISE 6 *In the following sentence groups, circle the correct form of the verb. The subject in each sentence may be either a pronoun, a noun, or compound.*

1. Spring is my favorite season because the trees and flowers (bloom, blooms) and the long winter ends. It is interesting to watch the people come outdoors again when the warm weather (arrive, arrives).
2. There is no limit to the number of different mixed drinks it (is, are) possible to make. Every time my wife and I (think, thinks) we know all the names, somebody tells us about a new one.
3. More than anything else in the world, Shelly (want, wants) to make a million dollars. She is always coming up with some scheme she (claim, claims) will make her an instant millionaire.
4. The veteran policeman and his rookie partner (walk, walks) the beat slowly, looking into the shop windows and checking to make sure all the

doors are locked. Every half hour the rookie (call, calls) in to the desk sergeant from one of the call boxes.

5. The advertisement (state, states) that all the appliances are on sale this week. However, the televisions (is, are) still much too expensive for me.

Some sentences may have more than one verb *and* more than one subject. In sentences like this, you must find what subject each verb goes with, and then apply the rule. For example:

S V S V
Shirley goes out every night while the other girls stay home.

In this sentence there are two sets of subjects and verbs. The first subject is singular, so the verb that goes with it ends in *-s*. The second subject is plural, so the verb that goes with it does not end in *-s*.

Some sentences have one subject and several different verbs.

S V V V
The entertainer sings, dances, and tells corny jokes.

In this sentence, all three verbs end in *-s* because the subject of all three verbs is "entertainer," a singular noun.

In all of the exercises so far, the verbs have been identified for you. All you had to do was find the subject and then decide which form of the verb was correct. However, when you write your own sentences you will have to find the verbs yourself in order to check the endings. The only way to be absolutely sure your endings are correct in the present tense is to follow the three-step procedure:

1. Find the verb or verbs in the sentence.
2. Find the subject or subjects in the sentence.
3. Apply the rule.

PRACTICE EXERCISES

EXERCISE 7 *Return to any of the writing assignments for which you wrote a paragraph in the present tense. Check each sentence to be sure that the subjects and verbs agree.*

*EXERCISE 8 *Some of the following sentences contain more than one verb. Check the endings of all the verbs and correct any that are wrong.*

1. The basketball player leap for the rebound, grab the ball, and pass it off to another player. Then he runs back to the other end of the court to get into position.
2. Every day at rush hour all the main bridges into the city get clogged with traffic heading home for the day. The drivers are usually patient because they are used to a slow ride home. When the weather is bad it take even longer to get home.
3. Myron's hobby is buying and refinishing antique furniture. He goes to a sale every weekend and buy whatever antiques he can find. Someday he hope he can open an antique shop.
4. Lillian plays piano in a jazz group. They play at a small nightclub downtown called "The Lonesome Pit." They like to play old blues songs more than anything else, and Lillian sometimes sing.
5. I enjoy school most of the time, but the tests in school really bother me. I have difficulty sitting down and calmly taking a test. I always gets upset and forgets everything I know.

EXERCISE 9 *Now check the verbs in the following paragraph and correct any that are wrong.*

I believe it is a good idea for mothers to hold jobs. First, I think it is good for the mother and child to get away from each other once in a while. Next, I feel that if children goes out during the day to a day care center, they have a big advantage. Most day care centers has learning programs set up, while at home a young child has to sit and watch television. Finally, a working mother enjoy her child more when she get home. Since she is away for eight hours, she have more of a chance to miss her child. As a result, the mother is eager to get home and share the rest of the day with her child.

EXERCISE 10

Write!

Now write some sentences of your own. Write ten sentences, using the subject that is provided for each number and choosing one of the verbs from the list. Make sure each sentence is written in one of the correct present tense forms. Use each verb only once.

Verbs:

need	eat	burn	are	win
crawl	look	belch	feel	suspect

1. The detective ____
____

2. Warm spring breezes ____
____

3. The subway ____
____

4. Susan and Jeff ____
____

5. Our beloved mayor ____
____

6. The city street ____
____

7. My best friend Monty ____
____

8. The sun and the sand ____
____

9. My favorite plant ____
____

10. A colorful snake ______________________________

____

LOCATE THE SUBJECT-VERB PAIRS

Subject-Verb Pairs with Prepositional Phrases

You have probably noticed by now that the key to checking verb endings in the present tense is first to locate the subject that belongs to the verb. In most of the exercises so far, the subject has come next to the verb in the sentence. For example:

The boat glides through the water.

In this sentence, the subject is easy to find because it comes directly before the verb. In many sentences, however, the subject is separated from the verb by another element in the sentence. For example:

The warm breeze on summer evenings feels wonderful.

You find the subject in this kind of sentence the same way you first learned to find subjects: by finding the verb first and then asking "who" or "what."

Verb: "feels"
Question: "Who or what feels wonderful?
Answer: "breeze"; so "breeze" is the subject of the verb "feels."

As you find the subject in this example sentence, notice that "evenings" is not the subject that goes with "feels." However, if you did not find the subject by the questioning process, you could have mistaken "evenings" for the subject.

Finding the right subject, of course, makes a big difference when a sentence is in the present tense. As you know, the ending on present tense verbs depends upon whether the subject is singular or plural. Note in the sentence above that "evenings" is plural but "breeze" is singular. Since "breeze" is the subject, the verb "feels" ends in *-s*.

Always find the subject by identifying the verb first and then asking "who" or "what."

PRACTICE EXERCISES

*EXERCISE 11 *Circle the correct form of the verb in each of the following present tense sentences.*

1. The attorney for the defense (plead, pleads) with the jury.
2. The letters in the desk drawer (is, are) very important.
3. The players on the baseball field (wait, waits) for the pitcher to tie his shoelace.
4. My speech to the deans (has, have) to be forceful and dramatic.
5. Her problem with men (make, makes) her miserable.

*EXERCISE 12 *Now check the verbs in the following present tense sentences to see if the endings are correct. In this exercise, the verbs are not identified for you. Correct any errors that you find.*

1. The trees around my house is beautiful in the fall.
2. The packages by the door belongs in the living room.
3. Sharon's trip to the Caribbean islands begin next month.
4. The most common duck on city ponds are the mallard.
5. Her opinion of my family present problems.
6. The doors of the car have to be painted.
7. The spots on her dress does not come out.
8. The rule for present tense verbs are easy to learn.
9. A house in the suburbs cost too much money.
10. The beach in the summer is covered with sunbathers.

Now that you have completed these exercises, you should recognize that a *phrase* often separates the subject and the verb. These phrases usually have a noun in them that can be mistaken for the subject, but if you go through the questioning process for each sentence, you will always find the subject that belongs with the verb in the sentence.

PRACTICE EXERCISE

EXERCISE 13

Write!

Now write some present tense sentences of your own. In this exercise, you are given a phrase and you are to write a sentence using that phrase. Make sure that the sentence is in present tense and that the endings on your verbs are correct. Do not begin *your sentences with these phrases.*

Example:
in the newspaper
Sentence: The advertisements in the newspaper often contain valuable coupons.

1. *in the beginning*

   Sentence: ______________________________

   ____

2. *with the brown shoes*

   Sentence: ______________________________

   ____

3. *of my supervisors*

   Sentence: ______________________________

   ____

4. *in the exercise*

   Sentence: ______________________________

   ____

5. *to my girlfriend*

Sentence: ____

____

Subject-Verb Pairs with Relative Pronouns

Another sentence element that often separates subjects and verbs is the **relative pronoun**. In Chapter 2, you learned the three most common relative pronouns.

who	*relates* to people
that	*relates* to things
which	*relates* to things

Notice that each of these words *relates* to another word in the sentence. The word they relate to is the subject that goes with the verb in the sentence. Here is an example.

The driver who swerves in and out of traffic should get a ticket.

To check the agreement of verbs and subjects, you can find the subject in this kind of sentence the same way you do for any sentence.

Verb:	"swerves"
Question:	"Who or what swerves?"
Answer:	"driver"; so "driver" is the subject that must agree with the verb "swerves."

Remember that the relative pronouns always relate to another noun in the sentence, and it is this noun that determines the ending on the present tense verb. You cannot use the relative pronoun to determine the verb ending because the relative pronoun does not indicate whether the subject is singular or plural. For example:

SINGULAR / -S ENDING / -S ENDING

The *student* who talk*s* in class bother*s* everyone.

PLURAL / NO -S / NO -S

The *students* who tal*k* in class bothe*r* everyone.

Note that the relative pronoun ("who") is the same in both sentences, even though the subject of the first sentence is singular and the subject of the second is plural.

PRACTICE EXERCISES

EXERCISE 14 *Return to the paragraph you wrote for Writing Assignment 7. See if you used any relative pronouns in your sentences. If you did, circle the noun in the sentence that the relative pronoun refers to.*

EXERCISE 15 *Complete the following sentences, making sure that the endings on the verbs are correct.*

Write!

1. The thing that bothers me ______________________________

____

2. The people who I like the most ______________________________

____

3. The houses that I have lived in ______________________________

____

4. My car, which is my biggest problem, ______________________________

____

5. Money, which is always hard to find, ______________________________

____

Subject-Verb Pairs with Sentences Beginning with "There"

Another situation in which a subject may be separated from a verb occurs when the sentence begins with the word "**there**." The important point to remember is that *the word "there" can never be the subject*. For example:

There is a fly in my soup.

The ending on the verb in this sentence is determined the same way as in all other present tense sentences:

Verb: "is"
Question: "Who or what is in my soup?"
Answer: "fly"; so "fly" is the subject of the verb "is."

Since "fly" is singular, the verb ends in *-s*. Notice that the word "there" only starts the sentence; it is never the subject. Now find the subject in this sentence:

There are three beans in my bean soup.

If you questioned the sentence according to the regular method, you should have found that "beans" is the subject; "beans" is plural, so the verb is "are."

When a present tense sentence begins with the word "there," find the subject before you check the verb endings.

Caution: Remember that a sentence may have a compound subject:

There are a bicycle and a skateboard in the garage.

Verb: "are"
Question: Who or what are in the garage?
Answer: "a bicycle and a skateboard"; so "a bicycle and a skateboard" are the subjects of the verb "are."

Since the subject is plural, the verb is "are." This may not sound right to you, but sound is not always a reliable way to tell if something is correct. If you have written the sentence and it sounds wrong to you, turn the sentence around.

A bicycle and a skateboard are in the garage.

After you have turned the sentence around, you can decide which version you prefer; whether you start the sentence with "there" or with the subject, *both versions are correct.*

Subject-Verb Pairs in Questions

The final way that a subject is often separated from the verb is in a question. In this type of sentence structure, the subject comes after the verb. For example:

Where is my chemistry book?
Where are my chemistry books?

Note that the verb ending still depends on whether the subject is singular or plural. To find the subject in a question, turn the question into a statement.

Question:	Where is my chemistry book?
Statement:	My chemistry book is
Question:	Where are my chemistry books?
Statement:	My chemistry books are

After you have turned the question around, you can find the subject by asking "who" or "what" of the verb, exactly as you did in the other sentences.

PRACTICE EXERCISES

*EXERCISE 16 *In the following sentences, circle the correct form of the verb. Decide which verb to use by underlining the subject first.*

1. There (is, are) several reasons for my opinion about television.
2. There (is, are) a new neighbor in the apartment downstairs.
3. There (is, are) many advantages to eating health foods.
4. There (is, are) a cat and a dog fighting outside.
5. There (is, are) too many different choices on the menu.
6. When (do, does) we meet again?
7. Who (is, are) the people standing on the corner?
8. Why (do, does) Barbara comb her hair so much?
9. Where (is, are) all the friends who said they would help me paint the house?
10. What (is, am, are) I supposed to do now that I am out of school?

EXERCISE 17 *Now write some sentences of your own. Write five sentences starting with "There" and five sentences starting with a question.*

Write!

1. ____

____

2. ____

____

3. ____

____

4. ____

____

5. ____

____

6. ____

____

7. ____

____

8. ____

____

9. ____

____

10. ____

____

Special Subjects

So far you have learned to check the endings on present tense verbs according to a three-step process:

1. Find the verb or verbs.
2. Find the subject or subjects (by asking "who" or "what").
3. Apply the rule.

Some **special subjects** may appear to be plural but are always considered singular.

Collective nouns

The following words are considered to be singular subjects:

group	family
team	collection
club	gang
class	organization

These nouns are called **collective nouns**. They may *appear* to be plural (since there is more than one person in a group, team, club, class, and so on), but they are actually singular. One way to keep this in mind is to test the word to see if it can be made plural.

one group	two groups
one team	two teams
one club	two clubs
one class	two classes
one family	two families
one collection	two collections
one gang	two gangs
one organization	two organizations

This is not a complete list of collective nouns. There are many others, but you can always tell whether a noun is collective by trying to make the noun plural. Test the following nouns to see which ones are collective. If you cannot make the noun plural, it is not collective.

Noun	*Plural?*
men	
association	
women	
company	
children	
committee	
band	

When a collective noun is the subject in a present tense sentence, the verb must end in *-s*.

SINGULAR -S ENDING
/ /
The *group* meet*s* again next Tuesday.

PLURAL NO -S
/ /
The *groups* meet again next Tuesday.

Remember to test each sentence to find the subject before applying the rule. Look at the following sentence:

The players on the team are going to Texas.

Why is the verb in this sentence "are" instead of "is"? What is the subject? Even though "team," a collective noun, comes right beside the verb, the subject is "players" (who is going to Texas?), so the verb does not end in *-s*.

PRACTICE EXERCISE

*EXERCISE 18 *Check the verbs in the following sentence groups and correct any that do not agree with their subjects.*

1. The special committee meet every Tuesday for one hour. During that time, the members discusses important matters like the football game on the *Monday Night Game of the Week.*
2. Her family have always been close. Her brothers and sisters call each other frequently just to say hello. A family like that are hard to find nowadays.
3. The gang hang out in the old playground building. Most of the kids in the gang is only fourteen or fifteen years old, but the gang leader is twenty-one.
4. The paper company treat its employees fairly. All of the employees in the company receive a bonus check at the end of the year, and the company try to hire its executives from people who are already working for the company.

5. The singer in the band are conceited. He wants to get more money than anyone else, and he thinks the other members of the band is terrible musicians.

Indefinite pronouns

The following words, when used as subjects, are considered to be singular:

each   every   neither   either   one

For example:

Each of the cars *has* its own advantages.

The subject of this sentence (''who or what has?'') is ''each,'' not ''cars.'' Therefore, the verb ends in *-s*. This rule also applies to words beginning with ''every-,'' ''no-,'' ''some-,'' and ''any-.''

everybody	nobody	somebody	anybody
everything	nothing	something	anything
everyone	no one	someone	anyone

For example:

Everyone *brings* his own special dish to the party.

These words may not sound singular to you, especially when they are separated from the verbs in the sentences. The best way to learn them is simply to memorize these few words as singular subjects and practice recognizing them as singular in sentences.

PRACTICE EXERCISES

EXERCISE 19 *Now try selecting the correct verbs in a paragraph. Circle the correct verbs.*

One of the most interesting of my friends (are, is) Pete. The thing that (make, makes) Pete so unique is his obsession with keeping lists. Almost everything that (happen, happens) to Pete eventually (finds, find) its way onto one of his lists. When he drives to work, for example, he (list, lists) the location and number of traffic lights he stops at. When he walks to work, Pete counts each out-of-state license plate he (see, sees) and lists it on a card he carries with him. If he goes on a trip, he gets to the airport an hour early so he can keep a record of the time at which each plane (arrive, arrives). He also keeps track of every television or radio program that he (watch, watches) or (listen, listens) to. All of his lists are kept in a huge master file. And how does he find the lists when he wants them? He finds out exactly where each of the lists (is, are) filed by looking it up on his master list!

EXERCISE 20

Write!

Now write some sentences of your own. In the following exercise, a sentence has been started for you. Complete the sentence by adding to the subject. Make sure each sentence is in present tense.

1. Anyone who knows me ______________________________

____

2. Nobody in the army ______________________________

____

3. Either of the horses ______________________________

____

4. Each of the books ______________________________

____

5. In the spring, everybody ______________________________

____

WRITING ASSIGNMENT 9

Now write a paragraph, applying everything you have learned up to this point about sentences and subject-verb agreement. Remember the following points:

- Make sure you *understand the topic*.
- *List* all of the thoughts you have about the topic.
- *Select* the most convincing items from your list and arrange them into an order.
- *Expand the ideas* you will be using for support.
- *Write the rough draft*.

When you finish writing your paragraph, rewrite each sentence, one at a time, on a separate piece of paper according to the instructions on p. 76 of Chapter 3. Identify and correct any sentence fragments, run-on sentences, comma splices, or subject-verb agreement errors in your paragraph, and then write the sentences on a new piece of paper in regular paragraph form.

Topics

1. Name your favorite season and explain why you prefer it.
2. Describe a friend who has an unusual quality or habit. Be sure to provide specific examples to "show" the reader what your friend is like.
3. Present your opinion on whether mothers should or should not hold jobs. Give clear reasons to support your opinion.

CHAPTER REVIEW

In this chapter, you learned several important points about the present tense form of verbs.

First, you learned that present tense verbs must "agree" with their subjects. This means that they may or may not end in *-s*, depending on the subject that goes with them. If the subject is "he," "she," or "it," the present tense verb must end in *-s*.

You also learned that the verb "be" is the most irregular verb in present tense, and that the best way to deal with this verb is to memorize its different present tense forms.

Finally, you learned a three-step procedure for checking the endings on present tense verbs.

1. Find the verb or verbs.
2. Find the subject or subjects (by asking "who" or "what").
3. Apply the rule for present tense verbs: if the subject is "he," "she," "it," or any singular noun, the verb must end in *-s*.

Several types of sentences and special subjects can make it slightly more difficult to locate the subject, but if you always follow the same three-step procedure, you will have few problems checking the endings on your verbs.

SUPPLEMENTAL EXERCISES

Use the exercises below for additional practice in making sure that your subjects and verbs agree when you write in present tense.

EXERCISE 21 *The following sentences are written in the present tense and have one of the subject pronouns as a subject. Circle the correct form of the verb. Remember, if the subject is "he," "she," or "it," the verb must end in -s.*

1. He (stand, stands) up for what he believes in.
2. On weekends we eat out because she (cook, cooks) dinner all week.
3. When they (shop, shops) for new clothes, he spends more money than his wife.
4. I (do, does) not want to see that movie, so you go without me.
5. We watch the horse as it (feed, feeds) in the pasture.

6. I wonder if smoking really (do, does) cause cancer.
7. He (think, thinks) now is the time to look for a new house.
8. During the summer they (take, takes) long drives in the country.
9. The exam is on Friday, and it (include, includes) questions on three chapters.
10. She (drive, drives) too fast on her way to work.

*EXERCISE 22 *In the following exercise, the verb is not identified. Check the endings of the verbs and correct any that are wrong.*

1. With the rising costs of new houses, the average person do not make enough money to buy a house.
2. Within the next twenty years, the average cost of a new home are going to be 100 or 120 thousand dollars.
3. Economists gives several reasons for this.
4. For one thing, building materials costs more.
5. Lumber is getting harder and harder to find.
6. Building contractors charges more to build a new house.
7. This are because of higher wages for the working man.
8. The interest rates on mortgages also increases.
9. The banks has to charge higher rates to make a profit on their investment.
10. All of these things combine to paint a gloomy picture for the prospective house buyer.

*EXERCISE 23 *Now do the same for the following sentence groups:*

1. Most of the high school seniors wants to go to New York for the class trip. Freddy hope the principal will give his approval for the trip.

2. The government allows four and a half months for citizens to submit their tax returns. With all this time to figure their taxes, millions of Americans still turns in their forms late.
3. Zoos is depressing places. The animals are all in cages. They always looks miserable, lying around or pacing back and forth in their cages.
4. Every summer Jane go to Virginia for her vacation. She stays with her relatives. Most of the time she just relax on the beach, getting a tan and reading a novel.
5. Jerry always talks about sunken treasures. He are studying oceanography in college. He want to explore the floor of the Caribbean Sea.

*EXERCISE 24 *The following paragraph is written in the present tense, but some of the verb endings are incorrect. The subjects in each sentence may be attached to the verbs or they may be separated by a phrase or a relative pronoun. Check each verb and correct any that are wrong.*

Although all of my friends own new cars, I prefer to keep my old pickup truck. I drive that truck everywhere I go, and it never give me any trouble. My friends tell me how great their new cars are, but most of them spends more on gas and oil than I spend. They all own big new cars, which gets less than fifteen miles per gallon, while my beat-up old truck still gets a steady eighteen miles per gallon. The convenience of having a truck have come in handy many times. There are many times when I have to haul some furniture or something large, and this job is made simple with a pickup truck. My friends always jokes about my old truck, but all of them have borrowed it at one time or another.

*EXERCISE 25 *The following paragraph is written in the past tense. Rewrite the paragraph in the present tense by changing the verbs.*

The number of vehicles in the downtown areas grew each year. When something unexpected happened, like a transit strike, the congestion in the city became even worse. Many drivers who normally came into work on public transportation vehicles brought their own cars. This increased the number of dirty, noisy vehicles that ended up jammed together in the center of town. Some possible solutions to this problem were to encourage car-pooling by commuters and to restrict the flow of traffic in the downtown areas. Whatever the solution, something had to be done before the machines caused our cities to choke to death.

EXERCISE 26 *Circle the correct verbs in the following present tense paragraph.*

In spite of all the marvels of modern engineering, many of our cities (is, are) still vulnerable when a heavy rainstorm (strikes, strike). The two major highways in the city where I live have recently been redesigned and modernized. However, each of the roads (go, goes) through several low-lying areas, and it is in these areas that problems (arise, arises). On a sunny day, a car (travels, travel) either of these roads at a smooth fifty or sixty miles per hour. But if the sky suddenly (opens, open) and (dumps, dump) a substantial amount of rain, the highways (look, looks) more like rivers than roadways. In many places the water quickly (rise, rises) to a level approaching two feet. Drivers (proceed, proceeds) through the torrent with great misgivings, hoping that their electrical systems will not get drenched. If the rain (continues, continue), the water (rise, rises), and soon the highways (is, are) littered with stalled vehicles abandoned by their owners.

When they are criticized for this dismal state of affairs, road engineers (respond, responds) with a helpless shrug. They (insist, insists) that the problem (is, are) not engineering, but the simple fact that storm drains (is, are) unable to handle a flow of water as massive as that created by the more severe summer storms. One major problem, they point out, (are, is) that most of our cities have become "concrete jungles." Virtually every ground surface in a city (is, are) paved in some way; thus the natural absorbing effect of the earth cannot take place. This (is, are) just one of the many "advantages" of having an extensive superhighway system in our cities.

The following paragraphs (Exercises 27–28) are written in the present tense, but they contain some errors in subject-verb agreement. Check each paragraph by the three-step process and correct any errors that you find.

EXERCISE 27

In properly completing a double play in baseball, a team have to do quite a few different things. For example, if the ball is hit to the shortstop, he field the ground ball. After he catch the ball, he throw it to the second baseman. The second baseman catch the throw, then step quickly on the base and hurls the ball to the first baseman. The first baseman stretches to catch the throw so he will get the ball before the batter reach first base. If all of the fielders catches and throws without a mistake, the double play work.

EXERCISE 28

Spike is a good friend of mine, but I still think he is a little crazy. He want to be Mr. Universe, and everything he does is directed towards that goal. He belongs to a body-building group which meet each week to hear a lecture or see a film on muscle development. His eating habits are especially hard for an average person to understand. His lunch, for example, consist of forty-three different pills. There is vitamins, protein pills, and some kinds of pills that I have never even heard of. Along with all the pills, Spike drinks a pint of liquid protein. Spike says that eating these kinds of lunches make him feel fat and uncomfortable for the rest of the day, but it is the only way he can continue to develop his body. After work, Spike goes to a gym and works out for at least two hours. In addition to maintaining this difficult schedule, Spike does not drink any alcoholic beverages or eat any junk foods. Fruit is the only thing he will eat for a snack. I have never met a person so thoroughly dedicated to a single goal.

8 / Verbs: Learn the past tense

In Chapter 7 you learned to recognize the various tenses that use a present tense form of the verb, and you learned how to make subjects and verbs agree by adding endings to verbs. In this chapter, you will learn to recognize tenses that use a past tense form of the verb, and you will practice proofreading for endings that have been left off past tense verbs.

LEARN THE PAST TENSE ENDINGS

Checking the endings on past tense verbs is much easier than checking those on present tense verbs because, with one exception, past tense verbs do not have to agree with their subjects. Look at the following conjugation:

I looked	we looked
you looked	you looked
he, she, it looked	they looked

Notice that *the verb is spelled the same way with each of the different subjects*; this is because past tense verbs do not have to agree with their subjects.

Your only concern with past tense verbs should be how the past tense form is spelled. This depends upon the verb's principal parts. As you learned in Chapter 6, there are two different types of verbs—regular and irregular. Regular verbs form the past tense and the past participle by adding *-ed* to the present tense form.

Principal Parts of a Regular Verb

Present	*Past*	*Past Participle*
look	looked	looked

Irregular verbs, however, may form their past tense and past participle in any number of different ways. Look at the following examples:

Principal Parts of Irregular Verbs

Present	*Past*	*Past Participle*
see	saw	seen
bring	brought	brought
do	did	done
go	went	gone
cut	cut	cut

As you can see, no single rule describes all the possible forms an irregular verb may take. But, whenever you are in doubt as to the correct form of a verb, you can look it up in a dictionary.

PROOFREAD FOR PAST TENSE ENDINGS

The most common problem students have with past tense verbs is that they sometimes misspell the past tense form or leave off the *-ed* ending. Both errors can be corrected simply by careful proofreading.

PRACTICE EXERCISE

EXERCISE 1 *Proofread the following paragraph for any errors in the past tense. If you are uncertain about the spelling of a verb, look it up in a dictionary.*

Last week there was a tremendous traffic jam on the expressway. I was catched in the middle of it, and I sitted in my car for half an hour waiting for the traffic to start moving. What cause the mess was a dog that was trotting pleasantly down the center of the west-bound lanes. Some of the drivers behind the dog stop their cars and got out to try to catch the dog. They want to move him off the expressway so he wouldn't get killed. The dog thinked the people were playing with him, and while the traffic back up for several miles, he dodged the people who chase up and down the expressway after him. Finally the dog got tired enough to allow a man to catch him. The man put the dog in his car and taked him home to his family. A lot of people were upset at the delay, but at least the dog do not get hurt.

You probably found the following errors easiest to correct: "catched" should be "caught"; "sitted" should be "sat"; "thinked" should be "thought"; "taked" should be "took"; "do" should be "did." This kind of error in spelling the past tense verbs stands out most clearly because we are not accustomed to reading or hearing the word "catched" or "sitted." Similarly, you will probably not make too many errors of this type in your own writing.

But did you find the other errors? Here is the corrected paragraph with the corrections circled for you.

Last week there was a tremendous traffic jam on the expressway. I was caught in the middle of it, and I sat in my car for half an hour waiting for the traffic to start moving. What caused the mess was a dog that was trotting pleasantly down the center of the west-bound lanes. Some of the drivers behind the dog stopped their cars and got out to try to catch the dog. They wanted to move him off the expressway so he wouldn't get killed. The dog thought the people were playing with him, and while the traffic backed up for several miles, he dodged the people who chased up and down the expressway after him. Finally the dog got tired enough to allow a man to catch him. The man put the dog in his car and took him home to his family. A lot of people were upset at the delay, but at least the dog did not get hurt.

Notice that five of the verbs were wrong because the *-ed* ending had been left off. Did you find all these errors when you proofread the paragraph? If not, it is probably because the misspelled irregular verbs ("catched," "sitted," etc.) stand out more prominently in a sentence or paragraph than the regular verbs that are missing an *-ed* ending ("cause," "stop," etc.). Many students tend to skip over words when they proofread their own writing, and if you skip over entire words, imagine how easy it is to skip over something as small as a word ending!

The best way to make sure all your past tense verbs are correct is to improve your proofreading procedure. This means you must proofread *word by word* until you develop the skill to spot important details while reading at a normal speed. You will develop this skill in time, but, to begin with, follow these steps when checking your writing for errors in past tense:

1. Underline all verbs.
2. Determine the tense.
3. Check the endings.

Look at the following example:

> When we <u>reached</u> the top of the mountain, we <u>sat</u> on the ground and <u>rested</u> our weary legs. From where we <u>sat</u> we <u>looked</u> out upon a spectacular view of the entire valley below us. As we <u>sat</u> there, a golden eagle <u>soared</u> over our heads and <u>sailed</u> off into the distance. There <u>were</u> so many interesting sights that none of us <u>wanted</u> to leave, but the approaching darkness <u>forced</u> us back down the mountain.

Underline all verbs. Remember that verbs preceded by "to" or ending in *-ing* are not true verbs, so they are not underlined.

Determine the tense. There are two simple ways to do this: One, check for a time indicator early in the sentence or paragraph. This might be a word or phrase like "yesterday," "last weekend," "when I was a child," and so on. The second way is to see what tense you used in the first sentence of your paragraph. In the sample paragraph above, the verbs in the first sentence are in past tense ("reached," "sat," "rested"), so the paragraph should be written in past tense unless the time period changes.

Check the endings. Check each verb you underlined to make sure that it is spelled correctly. In past tense, as you know, the verb may end in *-ed* or it may be spelled another way (for example, "sat").

This is a very mechanical way of checking to see if you have left off any word endings. However, once you develop that habit of looking at the endings on the verbs in your sentences or paragraphs, you will be able to check the endings as you read.

PRACTICE EXERCISES

EXERCISE 2 *Return to any of the writing assignments you wrote in the past tense and proofread the paragraphs for any errors in the spelling of past tense verbs.*

*EXERCISE 3 *Proofread the following paragraph and correct any errors in the spelling of past tense verbs.*

I had my first car accident on January 23. We were having a bad winter, and the schools were close that day due to poor driving conditions. My mother warn me not to drive the car anywhere, but, as usual, I didn't listen. I had a date with my girlfriend at eight o'clock that night. Because of the snowy roads, I arrived at her house at eight-thirty, and she immediately start yelling at me for being so late. We got in the car, and she keeped this up for about fifteen minutes until I finally decided the only way to shut her up was to go faster. I push the accelerator to the floor, and the car started fishtailing. Then it happen: the back tire blew out. At this point the car was out of control and taking us anywhere it want to go. I tried hitting the brakes, but that made it even worse. Finally the time came for a decision: I had to decide whether to slide the car into a telephone pole or try to maneuver it onto someone's front lawn, where a giant snowman was watching the whole performance. I turn the steering wheel and hope for the best. When the car finally came to a stop, my girlfriend and I were unharmed and my car suffered only a few minor dents, but the snowman need major surgery.

EXERCISE 4

Write!

In the following exercise, you are given the beginning of a sentence. Complete each sentence any way you want, but use a past tense verb in each. After you complete each sentence, proofread it for errors.

1. When I was fourteen, ______________________________

____

2. Gary's best friend ______________________________

____

3. When the students graduated, ______________________________

____

4. Our trip to the beach ______________________________

____

5. Shopping in the city ______________________________

____

6. Although television was once considered a wonderful invention, ______

____

7. Sherry and I both enjoyed the movie; however, ______________

____

8. When the plane landed safely, ______________________________

____

9. Because she said she saw a UFO, ______________________________

____

10. Last year at this time ______________________________

____

THE PAST TENSE OF "BE"

As you have seen, writing the correct past tense form in most cases is simply a matter of remembering to put *-ed* on the end of the verb or knowing the past tense form of the irregular verbs. There is only one verb in past tense that is likely to give you problems, and that is the verb "be."

The verb "be" is the only verb in past tense that must agree with its subject in the same way that all present tense verbs must agree with their subjects. Note the difference between the conjugation of "be" and the conjugation of "look" in the past tense.

look		*be*	
I looked	we looked	I *was*	we were
you looked	you looked	you were	you were
he, she, it looked	they looked	he, she it was	they were

As you can see, the verb "be" changes forms in past tense, depending on the subject with which it is used. The best way to remember the different forms is to memorize the conjugation. To apply this knowledge to your own writing, remember that the rules for the verb "be" in past tense are the same as the subject-verb agreement rules for present tense.

PRACTICE EXERCISE

*EXERCISE 5 *Circle the correct form of the verb in each of the following sentences.*

1. When I (was, were) in high school, physics (was, were) my favorite class.
2. Physics (was, were) not an easy subject for me, but the class (was, were) always a lot of fun.
3. The students (was, were) always able to sidetrack the teacher into discussing other subjects.
4. The teacher, Mr. Palmer, (was, were) a supermarket manager in the evenings, and he (was, were) always telling stories about things that happened in his store.
5. By the end of the term, no one in the class (was, were) very good at physics, but we all knew exactly what (was, were) happening at the local supermarket.

After completing this exercise, you should recognize that the use of "was" or "were" in a sentence depends on the subject with which it must agree. When using the past form of "be,"

> If the subject is singular, use "was."
> If the subject is "you" or any plural noun or pronoun, use "were."

Remember: When trying to decide between "was" and "were," always find the subject first.

PRACTICE EXERCISE

EXERCISE 6

Write!

In the following exercise, you are given the beginning of a sentence. Complete each sentence by using either "was" or "were."

Example:
The men on the boat were ready for the race to begin.

1. Each of the girls ______________________________

____

2. Every one of the dishes ______________________________

____

3. The special committee ______________________________

____

4. The birds in the tree ______________________________

____

5. All of his money ______________________________

____

THE PAST TENSE OF HELPING VERBS

In past tense, just as in present tense, helping verbs are used to form the **past perfect tense**, the **past progressive** (*-ing* form) and the **passive**. Again, the helping verbs that form these constructions are "have" and "be." As you just learned, only the verb "be" must agree with its subject in past tense; the verb "have" remains the same with all subjects in past tense, as shown in the following conjugation.

I	had	we	had
you	had	you	had
he, she, it	had	they	had

Thus, the only time you need to check the ending of a helping verb in past tense is when a form of the verb "be" is used. This will be in the formation of the past progressive and the passive.

Past tense:	Barry paid the rent.
Past progressive tense:	Barry *was* paying the rent.
Passive:	The rent *was* paid by Barry.

PRACTICE EXERCISES

*EXERCISE 7 *The most important part of learning the past progressive tense is knowing when to use "was" and when to use "were." In the following paragraph, fill in the blank spaces with either "was" or "were."*

The other day my friend and I ______________ standing on a street corner downtown, watching the crowds of people. We ______________ playing a little game with the faces, trying to make up a story to go with each face. I think Frank ______________ being a little too creative; he ______________ always saying that this man was a detective or that woman was an actress. On the other hand, I liked to imagine the people I saw as just plain ordinary folks. I guessed that one woman in the crowd ______________ going to her hairdresser's, and a distinguished-looking man with a beard was actually a plumber. The game was a lot of fun, but we will never know which one of us was closer to the truth about the faces in the crowd.

EXERCISE 8

Rewrite each of the following past tense sentences, using the past progressive and the passive. Make sure you use the correct past tense form of the verb "be."

Example:
Past: A severe storm caused flooding in the streets.

Past Progressive: A severe storm was causing flooding in the streets.

Passive: Flooding in the streets was caused by a severe storm.

1. *Past:* They completed the project on time.

   Past Progressive: ______________________________

   ______________________________.

   Passive: ______________________________

   ______________________________.

2. *Past:* The child read the book on Saturday.

   Past Progressive: ______________________________

   ______________________________.

   Passive: ______________________________

   ______________________________.

3. *Past:* The maintenance workers paved the city streets.

   Past Progressive: ______________________________

   ______________________________.

   Passive: ______________________________

   ______________________________.

4. *Past:* The cats ripped the rug to shreds.

   Past Progressive: ______________________________

   ______________________________.

   Passive: ______________________________

   ______________________________.

5. *Past:* An old man in the audience challenged the new law.

   Past Progressive: ______________________________

   ______________________________.

   Passive: ______________________________

   ______________________________.

As was noted above, the past tense form of the helping verb "have" is always "had," no matter what the subject of the sentence may be. Thus, the helping verb should not be a problem in past perfect tense. More often, the difficulty with the past perfect tense concerns the use of the past participle form. To avoid this problem, remember these two points.

1. *The past participle form should not be used as a verb without a helping verb*. Take, for example, the verb "see."

Present	*Past*	*Past Participle*
see	saw	seen

Participle without helping verb: We *seen* the movie twice.

To correct this problem, the form of the verb must be changed, according to the meaning of the sentence, to either the simple past tense, present perfect tense, or past perfect tense. Note that in the perfect tenses a helping verb has been added to the participle.

Simple past: We *saw* the movie twice.
Present perfect: We *have seen* the movie twice.
Past perfect: We *had seen* the movie twice.

2. *Make sure you use the past participle when you form a perfect tense.* Do not use the simple past tense form in one of the perfect tenses. Take, for example, the verb "go."

Present	*Past*	*Past Participle*
go	went	gone

Perfect tense without participle: They *had went* to the beach for a swim.

To correct this problem, use the correct principal part: the past participle.

Past perfect: They *had gone* to the beach for a swim.

PRACTICE EXERCISE

EXERCISE 9 *Proofread the following sentence groups and correct any errors in the use of simple past tense or past perfect verbs.*

1. The telephone repairman had came to the house to fix the phones, but no one was at home. The family had already went on their vacation.
2. She should have began studying for the exam long before she actually did. Instead, she done something stupid; she went out to a party the night before the exam.
3. The outfielder had threw the ball back to the infield in plenty of time to catch the runner. However, the second baseman seen a pretty girl in the stands and the ball went right by him.
4. We had took the night flight to Chicago before, but it had never been so crowded. The whole trip was noisy and uncomfortable, and we soon begun to think we picked the wrong time to fly.
5. If you had took what I had gave you, you would not be in this trouble now!

WRITING ASSIGNMENT 10

Now write a paragraph, applying everything you have learned up to this point about sentences and verb tenses. Remember the following points:

- Make sure you *understand the topic*.
- *List* all of the thoughts you have about the topic.
- *Select* the most convincing items from your list and arrange them into an order.
- *Expand the ideas* you will be using for support.
- *Write the rough draft*.

When you finish writing your paragraph, rewrite each sentence, one at a time, on a separate piece of paper according to the instructions on p. 76 of Chapter 3. Identify and correct any sentence fragments, run-on sentences, comma splices, or verb tense or agreement errors in your paragraph, and then write the sentences on a new piece of paper in regular paragraph form.

Topics

1. Recall a *pleasant* childhood experience. Describe what happened, making sure that you provide enough specific details to *show* what made the experience pleasant.
2. Recall an *unpleasant* childhood experience. Describe what happened, making sure that you provide enough specific details to *show* what made the experience unpleasant.
3. Recall the first time you ever did a particular thing. It could be your first day on a new job, your first day at college, or even your wedding day. Describe the experience of that day in detail.

CHAPTER REVIEW

In this chapter, you learned to proofread your writing for past tense endings on verbs. The following are the most important points for you to remember.

The past tense of a verb is formed either by adding an *-ed* ending to a verb or by changing the spelling completely. The past tense form of a verb is the second principal part, and this form can easily be found in a dictionary.

With the exception of the verb "be," past tense verbs do not have to agree with their subjects.

The most frequent error in the use of the past tense occurs when the *-ed* ending is left off. Checking for this error requires careful proofreading. Until you are able to spot mistakes of this type while reading through your paragraph, you should follow this procedure after you have finished writing your rough draft:

1. Underline all verbs.
2. Determine the tense.
3. Check the endings.

The verb "be" is the only verb that in past tense must agree with its subject. When using either of the past tense forms ("was" or "were"), check to see whether the subject is singular or plural. If the subject is singular, use "was." If the subject is plural or "you" use "were."

Finally, you learned that the past progressive tense consists of a past tense helping verb (usually "was" or "were") plus a verb ending in *-ing*. This tense is used to show action in progress. It is especially important to check progressive verbs to make sure the helping verbs agree with their subjects.

Remember, the proofreading procedures described here are intended as a beginning point for you. You will not always have to go through a paragraph word by word to check all the word endings. Once you master the techniques described in this chapter, you will find it easier to spot word-ending errors simply by reading through your paragraphs.

SUPPLEMENTAL EXERCISES

Proofread the following paragraphs and correct any errors in the use of past tense.

*EXERCISE 10

When we got to the party we were late, but we had a good excuse. First of all, I could not find the map that came with the invitation. My wife said that she seen it somewhere in the dining room. When I finally did find it, my wife decide that she did not want to go because she did not want to leave the cats at home alone. I managed to drag her out of the house, but that were not the end of my troubles. On the way to the party, my wife got the hiccoughs. She told me that she would not walk into any party with the hiccoughs. I tryed to scare her a few times, but she keeped on hiccoughing. She insisted that the only thing that would cure her of the hiccoughs were a Slurpee. By now we were near the party, but I was not familiar with the neighborhood, so I could not find a 7-11 store. I continued to turn to my wife every few minutes and yell like a madman in an attempt to scare her. This failed to do anything for her, however, except to make her laugh at the ridiculous faces I were making. In the end I agreed to look for a 7-11 store for a Slurpee. It took half an hour to find one. I bought her a Slurpee, she slurp it, and her hiccoughs gone away. Then, when we finally arrived at the party, I start hiccoughing.

EXERCISE 11

When I was going to school I hated to get up in the morning, so I tryed a lot of different techniques. The first thing I tried was an alarm clock on the nightstand beside the bed. This didn't work, though, because I just turn it off and roll over in the morning. The next device were a radio alarm clock which play music at the time for which it was set. This waked me up, but I always manage to get back to sleep either by covering my head with a pillow or by turning the radio off and getting back in bed. It finally got to the point where I could ignore almost any type of alarm. In the end I solve my problem by placing the radio on the counter top in the bathroom. Before I went to bed I would set the alarm and turn the volume all the way up. When the alarm went off in the morning, it were so loud that I could not ignore it. By the time I manage to turn off the radio, I was out of bed, wide awake, and already in the bathroom, ready to prepare myself for another day of school.

EXERCISE 12

A moment in my life that I'll never forget was the time I was select from the fifth grade class to recite the American's Creed. Each student in the class stand up and recited a line, and then the teacher selected who she though was the best three speakers. Each of these three then recited a few more lines, and she made her final selection. I could not believe it when she select me for the part. I studied my lines very carefully and even practiced in front of the mirror.

The big day finally came, and soon it was my turn to go on stage. The auditorium was fill to capacity with the relatives of the students who were performing. As I walked out on stage, the auditorium became totally quiet and my knees begin to shake. When I reached the center of the stage, I turned toward the audience and pronounce the first few lines in a loud, clear voice. Then my mind went blank! For some reason, I could not remember the next line. I stood there in that terrible silence for what seem like hours, trying to remember that line. I thought of starting all over again, but I was not sure that would help. Then the last line of the creed flash in my mind. Very clearly, I recited the last line, turned, and walked offstage. The audience must have been as uncomfortable as I was, because they applauded as I left the stage.

9 / Use pronouns correctly

In this chapter you will learn how to use the various forms of subject pronouns and how to make sure that pronouns agree with their antecedents.

PRONOUN CASE

The **subject pronouns** are words that take the place of nouns. These words should look familiar to you by now.

Singular	*Plural*
I	we
you	you
he, she, it	they

Most pronouns *change in form* when they are used as something other than a subject. Look at the following example.

Pronoun as subject:	*I* am giving the book to Harry.
Pronoun as object:	Harry is giving the book to *me*.
Pronoun as possessive:	I am giving *my* book to Harry. The book I gave to Harry is *mine*.

The different forms that pronouns take are referred to as the **case** of pronouns. The chart below shows the different cases of these subject pronouns.

Subjective	*Objective*	*Possessive*
I	me	my, mine
you	you	your, yours
he, she, it	him, her, it	his, her, hers, its
we	us	our, ours
you	you	your, yours
they	them	their, theirs

To decide which form of a pronoun is correct, you must first decide how it functions in the sentence. Is it a subject, an object, or a possessive? Remember the following points.

- The subject is the *actor*. (*Who* gave the book?)
- The object is the *receiver of the action*. (The book was given to *whom*?)
- The possessive is the *owner*. (*Whose* book is this?)

PRACTICE EXERCISES

*EXERCISE 1 *In the following sentences, identify the underlined word as either* subjective case, objective case, *or* possessive case, *and then write the correct form of the pronoun in the space provided.*

Example.
The commuters take the train to work every morning.

Case: Subjective ________ Pronoun: They ________

1. The car with the whitewall tires belongs to *Harry*.

   Case: ________________ *Pronoun:* ________________

2. *Harry* owns the car with the whitewall tires.

   Case: ________________ *Pronoun:* ________________

3. The car with the whitewall tires is *Harry's*.

   Case: ________________ *Pronoun:* ________________

4. *Linda* completed the project in record time.

   Case: ____________________ *Pronoun:* ____________________

5. The project was completed by *Linda* in record time.

   Case: ____________________ *Pronoun:* ____________________

6. The project was *Linda's*.

   Case: ____________________ *Pronoun:* ____________________

7. *The truck* has a powerful engine.

   Case: ____________________ *Pronoun:* ____________________

8. The engine is *the truck's* best feature.

   Case: ____________________ *Pronoun:* ____________________

9. *Susan and Joyce* earned the top honors.

   Case: ____________________ *Pronoun:* ____________________

10. The visiting dignitary awarded the top honors to *Susan and Joyce*.

    Case: ____________________ *Pronoun:* ____________________

*EXERCISE 2 *In this exercise, fill in the blank with the correct form of the pronoun.*

Example.

I dreamed of the day when the boat would be __mine__________.

1. The boss warned José and me that if he caught ____________________ again, he would fire ____________________.
2. José and I complained that it was not ____________________ fault.
3. The boss insisted that the fault was entirely ____________________.
4. Skunks are timid animals, but they will use ____________________ natural defense if anything frightens ____________________.
5. The two supervisors congratulated themselves that the credit was all ____________________.

6. I didn't realize that the policeman wanted ______________ to pull ______________ car over to the side.
7. I told him that I didn't have the owner's card with ______________, but the car really was ______________.
8. He knew my mother and thought that the car was ______________.
9. If you're going there for a vacation, don't forget ______________ swimsuit.
10. "If you really want the painting," said the generous uncle, "it's ______________."

Compounds

Remember from Chapter 2 that subjects can be compound and can include nouns, pronouns, or a combination of both.

Helen and Frank both earned promotions.
Helen and I both earned promotions.
She and I both earned promotions.

The same is true of pronouns in the objective and possessive cases, as you can see in the following examples:

Objective:	The company gave promotions to *Helen and Frank.*
	The company gave promotions to *Helen* and *me.*
	The company gave promotions to *her* and *me.*
Possessive:	The car is *Helen's,* but the boat is *Frank's.*
	It is *her* car and *his* boat.
	The car is *hers,* but the boat is *his.*

PRACTICE EXERCISES

*EXERCISE 3 *In this exercise, rewrite each sentence according to the form provided in version B.*

Example:
A. You and I will win the prize.
B. The prize will be won by ___you and me___.

1. A. She and I wrote a letter to the mayor.

   B. The mayor received a letter from ____________________ .

2. A. You and I have responsibility for the project.

   B. The project is the responsibility of ____________________.

3. A. The cottage is shared by the Fredericks and us.

   B. ____________________ and the Fredericks share the cottage.

4. A. The credit belongs to me and you.

   B. The credit is ____________________.

5. A. You and I will share the secret.

   B. The secret is just between ____________________.

EXERCISE 4 *In the following sentences, correct any errors you find in pronoun case.*

1. The mechanic lost his wrench somewhere in my wife's car. Now, thanks to he, the car doesn't work right and he claims the fault is all her's.
2. His grandmother and him agreed that it would be best for the baby to stay with he.
3. I'm sure that the accident was not my fault, but the insurance company claims that my friend and me were driving recklessly.
4. All of our neighbors and us are planning a huge block party.

5. The owners said it was their land, they intended to keep it, and nothing could persuade them to sell it to us.

A Special Case: "Who," "Whom," and "Whose"

Another subject pronoun that you use frequently is "who." This pronoun changes to "whom" in the objective case and to "whose" in the possessive.

Subjective:	Kathy is a person *who* knows her job. *Who* knows what she likes?
Objective:	The person *whom* he most admired came to his aid. To *whom* did he give his aid?
Possessive:	She is the person *whose* job it is to schedule the appointments. *Whose* job is it to schedule appointments?

Students often find it difficult to determine when to use "who" and when to use "whom." There are two ways around this problem. The first is to recognize when "who" is being used as a subject; the second is to consider rewriting a sentence to avoid using "whom," since it is considered appropriate only in formal situations.

First, recognize when the pronoun "who" is being used as a subject. Consider this sentence from the examples above. "Kathy is a person who knows her job." If you were uncertain whether to use "who" or "whom," you could break the sentence down to determine the *function* of the pronoun in the sentence. You can see that this sentence consists of two clauses, one independent and one dependent.

Independent clause: Kathy is a person

Dependent clause: who knows her job.

After you break the sentence down into its component parts, it is easy to see that the pronoun "who" is functioning as the *subject* of the dependent clause. When the pronoun acts as the subject, the correct form is "who."

If the pronoun is *not* the subject, but is instead receiving the action of a verb, the correct form is "whom."

The person *whom* he most admired came to his aid.

In this sentence, "whom" is the *object* of "admired." "Whom" didn't do the admiring in this sentence; "he" did the admiring, and "whom" was the "object" of it. Another clue that the pronoun should be in the objective case is when it follows a preposition.

> To *whom* did he give his aid?
> For *whom* were all the people waiting?
> With *whom* are you going to dinner tonight?

Because the word "whom" is used only in formal writing, you can avoid the problem entirely by omitting it. Look at the example below.

> The person *whom* he most admired came to his aid.
> The person he most admired came to his aid.

In the revision, the word "whom" remains unstated, but the meaning of the sentence is still clear.

If you are confused about whether to use "who" or "whom" in a sentence, first check to see if the pronoun is being used as a subject. If it is, the correct form is "who." If it is being used as an object, you can either use the form "whom" or try rewriting the sentence and omitting "whom" entirely.

PRACTICE EXERCISES

*EXERCISE 5 *In the following exercise, fill in the correct form* ("who," "whom," *or* "whose").

1. The mail carrier couldn't determine to ____________________ the letter should be delivered.
2. The individual ____________________ can best handle that assignment happens to be on vacation.
3. He has absolutely no interest in ____________________ wins the World Series.
4. Everybody wanted to know ____________________ idea it was to start working every Saturday.

5. She is a responsible executive ______________________ you can trust completely.
6. ______________________ should handle the new account was the big question in the office today.
7. The boss said that the new account should be handled by the person ______________________ experience included some work with feathers.
8. People ______________________ are afraid of flying should take trains.
9. The person ______________________ we hired has proved invaluable.
10. ______________________ we hired for the new position must remain a secret for another two weeks.

EXERCISE 6 *Proofread the following paragraph and correct any errors you find in pronoun case.*

Chuck and me went jogging the other night around the lake and we found ourselves surrounded by a bewildering variety of joggers. I couldn't figure out whom was a jogger and who was just dressed up in jogging clothes, but Chuck had it all figured out. The first type he pointed out to me were the joggers whom wore tennis shoes. These people, Chuck explained, ran only when the mood struck them. That didn't seem to slow any of them down, though, for some of them ran right by him and I. Another type Chuck pointed out was represented by a girl who wore the latest running shoes. Her outfit consisted of an old sweatshirt and a faded pair of bluejeans. Her's was a very distinctive style. The final type was the jogging-suit runner, whom both Chuck and me thought was pretty funny. This person never allows himself to be seen jogging in anything but his nylon pin-striped jogging suit, his color-coordinated sweatband, and his Marathon Man running shoes.

PRONOUN AGREEMENT

Just as verbs must agree in number with their subjects, pronouns must agree in number with their antecedents. The **antecedent** is the word or words a pronoun refers to. In the following sentence, for example, "people" is the antecedent of the pronoun "their."

The people piled into their cars.

Three problems arise with making pronouns agree with their antecedents: The first is the use of the wrong *relative pronoun*; the second is the use of a pronoun that is different in *number* from its antecedent; the third occurs when a pronoun *shifts* to a form different from its antecedent.

Relative Pronouns

The relative pronouns "who," "which," and "that" were presented in earlier chapters. As a "relative" pronoun, each of these words *relates* back to a particular kind of antecedent:

who relates to people;
which relates to things or ideas;
that relates to things, ideas, or animals; it is also used sometimes to relate to people.

Notice in the following sentences the nature of the antecedent these pronouns refer to.

CORRECT
Gregory is a man who has made many enemies.
Antecedent: man *Pronoun:* who
Judy's report, which had been lost for weeks, was found in the bus station.
Antecedent: report *Pronoun:* which
I can still remember the song that was playing.
Antecedent: song *Pronoun:* that

Most problems with the use of these pronouns occur when the pronouns "which" and "that" are used to refer to people, as illustrated below.

INCORRECT
Gregory is a man which has made many enemies.
Gregory is a man that has made many enemies.

Remember, when the antecedent is a person or people, "who" is the appropriate relative pronoun. The relative pronouns "which" and "that" are appropriate for referring to things, ideas, animals, and so on.

PRACTICE EXERCISE

EXERCISE 7 *In the following sentences, underline the antecedent and write the correct form of the pronoun in the space provided.*

1. Anyone ______________ witnessed the accident should contact the police.
2. When you are finished pruning the bushes, please return the tools ______________ you borrowed.
3. For their wedding, Kim and James chose a song ______________ was special to them.
4. The babysitter ______________ took care of the children last week charged more than the one ______________ came this week.
5. Students should complain about grading policies ______________ ______________ are unfair.
6. Clothing ______________ is collected by charities is donated to the poor.
7. Joan slammed the ball back over to Phyllis, ______________ ______________ was winning the tennis match.

8. Food ______________________ contains starches, sugar, and fat is the most fattening.
9. The woman ______________________ introduced us made jokes about it afterwards.
10. The problem is one ______________________ will require study.

Agreement in Number

The second major difficulty in pronoun agreement occurs when pronouns are different in *number* from their antecedents. As you know, nouns and pronouns have both singular and plural forms. When an antecedent is singular, the pronoun that refers to it must also be singular.

antecedent **pronoun**
When the mouse got angry, it roared.

In this example, the antecedent "mouse" is singular, so a singular pronoun, "it," is used to refer back to it. This is usually not a problem when the number and identity of the antecedent are clear, as in the following examples:

The *man* wanted more of a challenge, so *he* quit his job.
Theresa was happy because *she* was moving to Chicago.
My friends and I decided that *we* needed a long vacation.
Roxanne and Ronald announced that *they* were getting married.

The problem of agreement in number arises when the identity of the **antecedent** is **indefinite** or **unclear**, as in the following examples:

INCORRECT
Each of the men in the group decided that *they* wanted to join.
One of the companies gave *their* employees a raise.
Neither of the bands knew that *they* were scheduled to perform.
A *person* must choose *their* profession carefully.

You might recognize the antecedents in the sentences above as one of the *special subjects* you reviewed in Chapter 7. These special subjects were considered to be singular for purposes of subject-verb agreement. They are also considered to be singular for purposes of pronoun-antecedent agreement. Thus, since these antecedents are singular, the pronouns that refer to them must also be singular.

CORRECT
Each of the men in the group decided that *he* wanted to join.
One of the companies gave *its* employees a raise.
Neither of the bands knew that *it* was scheduled to perform.

Opinion is divided on which pronoun is appropriate when the antecedent is of **indefinite gender**, as in the following examples:

A person must choose ______________ profession carefully.
A good *student* is able to organize ______________ schedule effectively.
A truly great *athlete* knows ______________ limitations.

When the antecedent is indefinite, "his" and "his or her" are both considered acceptable, though not all readers will agree on which is the best pronoun to use.

A person must choose *his* profession carefully.
A good *student* is able to organize *his or her* schedule effectively.

A more effective—and more widely accepted—method of referring to indefinite antecedents is to use an article instead of a pronoun, or to make the antecedent plural.

Use an article instead of a pronoun:
A person must choose *a* profession carefully.
A good *student* is able to organize *a* schedule effectively.

Make the antecedent plural:
People must choose *their* professions carefully.
Good *students* are able to organize *their* schedules effectively.
Truly great *athletes* know *their* limitations.

Either of these two methods, especially making the antecedent plural, is more effective than trying to use singular pronouns with indefinite antecedents because it makes sentences, and especially paragraphs, read more smoothly.

PRACTICE EXERCISES

*EXERCISE 8 *Fill in the spaces in the sentences below with the pronoun that agrees with its antecedent. You may want to change the antecedent from singular to plural in some sentences. You may also use an article instead of a pronoun if it does not change the meaning of the sentence.*

1. All of the drivers lost ____________________ patience.
2. Each of the husbands had ____________________ day to drive the children to school.
3. Neither of the cats would sit still for ____________________ ____________________ distemper shots.
4. One of the women sales representatives won ____________________ ____________________ second award for highest sales of the month.
5. Every person who wants a driver's license must demonstrate ____________________ ability to drive safely.

EXERCISE 9 *In this exercise, make the following paragraph read more smoothly by changing the antecedents and pronouns from singular to plural. The first sentence has already been changed to provide an example. Note that some verb endings must also be changed to make the verbs agree with their subjects.*

~~A person~~ People who want~~s~~ to study law can begin to prepare ~~himself~~ themselves well in advance. The best way for a student to prepare is by doing a lot of reading and writing. This kind of practice will help the student when he or she gets into his or her first law school course. A good undergraduate major for a student who wants to attend law school is English. The study of English requires a student to read critically and express himself or herself clearly. The same skills are required of a student in law school, where he or she must study important cases and write a brief on the major issues involved in the case. A student who can read critically, use the library, and write effectively will find himself or herself on familiar ground in law school.

Pronoun Shift

The final problem in the use of pronouns occurs when a writer *shifts* from one pronoun to another without reason.

> *I* have found taking good pictures easy if *you* just keep a few things in mind.
> *One* must keep a positive attitude if *you* want to succeed.

Remember to remain *consistent* in your use of pronouns. That is, continue to use the pronoun you begin with in a sentence or paragraph unless the antecedent of the pronoun changes.

PRACTICE EXERCISE

*EXERCISE 10 *In the following sentences, correct any errors in pronoun shift. You may eliminate the shifts by changing either antecedents or pronouns.*

1. A competitive person has the desire to do well and to win. They can be counted on to give it their best effort.
2. One must be polite and attentive at all times during a job interview. Otherwise, you have little chance of getting the job.
3. I never have had any difficulty understanding mechanical things. You just take things apart carefully and pay attention to what you're doing.
4. Most people never know how good one has it until you feel the pinch of truly hard times.
5. Sometimes one has to appreciate the little things in life, like your friends, your family, even your old dog.

CHAPTER REVIEW

In this chapter you learned that the form a pronoun takes depends upon its function in a sentence. If the pronoun is a subject (actor), it is in the subjective case; if the pronoun is an object (receiver or recipient of an action), it is in the objective case; if the pronoun owns something, it is in the possessive case. You also learned that antecedents are the words pronouns refer to. Pronouns must agree with their antecedents in number, and pronouns should be used consistently, without shifting from one type to another.

SUPPLEMENTAL EXERCISES

In exercises 11–13, correct any errors in pronoun case and antecedent agreement.

*EXERCISE 11 A high school athlete should not be required to take regular physical education classes. They get all the exercise they need during their practice sessions and games. A young man or woman on the track team, for example, practices every day after school for about two hours. This is far more physical activity than that required of those students who are in a physical education class. Also, if a student is excused from physical education classes, they could replace the class with a study period. A student athlete often doesn't get as much time as he or she needs to do their best on a test. If their physical education period were replaced with a study period, you could gain valuable time to catch up with your studies.

EXERCISE 12 My friend Sheila and me recently wandered around an old junkyard just to see what kinds of interesting things we could find. We saw hundreds of old cars in all kinds of shapes, sizes, and stages of decay.

Some of them were so torn apart you couldn't tell what it was originally. The best part of the junkyard for me was the mountain of bicycle parts up against the corner of a fence. They were so tangled up that you couldn't tell where one began and where they ended. Sheila, meanwhile, was off in another part of the yard. For she, the best part was an old cement statue of a nameless person whom must have been famous at least once. Now it was just an old cement relic, gathering dirt in a junkyard; he was so isolated not even the pigeons bothered him.

EXERCISE 13

When I was a high school student I worked in a chicken restaurant. I liked the job pretty well, except for an occasional troublesome customer. Everybody has seen the kind of a customer who has to have their way and is very pushy. They get on your mind, and they got on mine, too. One evening, a man came into the store and wanted the barbecued chicken that was the hardest one to reach in the oven. He barged right ahead of other customers who were waiting for their orders. I was feeling harried at the time, so I told him he couldn't have the chicken. He was very offended and demanded an explanation of me. I asked him whom he thought he was speaking to. He called me a chicken man and pointed again to the chicken whom he wanted me to get for him. I felt that he had insulted me. A customer is always right, as the saying goes, but they shouldn't call you a chicken man! I told him to get out of the store—without his chicken—and he said, just between he and I, he'd go somewhere else for his chicken. After everything settled down, each of the other customers told me they thought my actions were correct. And the chicken in the oven was burnt to a crisp.

WRITING ASSIGNMENT 11

Now write a paragraph, applying everything you have learned up to this point about sentence skills and usage. Remember the following points:

- Make sure you *understand the topic*.
- *List* all of the thoughts you have about the topic.
- *Select* the most convincing items from your list and arrange them into an order.
- *Expand the ideas* you will be using for support.
- *Write the rough draft*.

When you finish writing your paragraph, rewrite each sentence, one at a time, on a separate fold of paper according to the instructions on p. 76 of Chapter 3. Identify any sentence skills or usage errors in your paragraph, and then write the corrected sentences on a new piece of paper in regular paragraph form.

Topics

1. Describe a vacation or a trip you have taken. Provide enough specific details to *show* the reader the experience.
2. Describe another person in the class. Do not give the person's name in your paragraph. You may describe the person in any way you want, concentrating on appearance, habits, friendliness, personality, and so on.

PART TWO REVIEW

By now you have learned how to proofread your writing to check your use of verbs and pronouns. A great many rules govern the use of both verbs and pronouns, but you should try to keep in mind at least these three major guidelines:

1. *Be consistent.* Do not change tenses in a sentence or paragraph unless the time period changes. Likewise, do not shift without reason from one pronoun to another in a sentence or a paragraph.

2. *In the present tense, verbs must agree with their subjects.* This means that the endings on present tense verbs depend upon whether their subjects are singular or plural. Pronouns must agree with their antecedents, depending upon whether the antecedents are singular or plural.

3. *Be sure that your past tense verbs are spelled correctly, especially those that require an -ed ending.* If you do not know the correct spelling of a verb or its three principal parts, look it up in a dictionary. Also, make sure that you are using the correct *case* of a pronoun in your writing. Determine which is the correct case by deciding upon the function of the pronoun in the sentence.

The following review exercises will test your understanding of verbs and pronouns. If you have difficulty with any of these exercises, return to the material in Chapters 6–9 and review it.

Also included in this review are several paragraphs that contain errors in the use of verbs, pronouns, and sentence skills. By now, you have learned what common errors to look for and how to correct them. Apply this knowledge by proofreading for the different kinds of errors.

REVIEW EXERCISES

*EXERCISE 1 *In the following paragraph, correct any verbs that are* inconsistent.

The first time I ever went deep sea fishing was an experience I will never forget. I was very young at the time, and I had no interest in going fishing. However, my father was a dedicated fisherman and he was determined to make a fisherman out of me. I had a hard time getting excited about the trip until we arrived at the marina. When I saw all the beautiful boats there, I was filled with enthusiasm. The boat we went on was around 45 feet long, and I was amazed at all the different instruments and gadgets it had on it. For most of the day, I wander around the boat imagining that I am the captain and I am sailing to some uninhabited tropical island. But then some people started catching fish so I decided to try fishing for a while. The first time a fish bit my hook I get so excited that I start jumping up and down and I let go of the fishing rod. It went right over the side and sank. I was so disappointed that I didn't fish for the rest of the day. That was the end of my career as a fisherman.

EXERCISE 2 *The following paragraph is written in the present tense, but there are some errors in* subject-verb agreement. *Proofread the paragraph and correct any errors that you find.*

There are always one sure way to start your day off wrong, and that is by taking public transportation. It does not matter where you are going; if you are going by public transportation, you are almost always in for problems. First of all you have to get up earlier, because it take a half hour longer to get anywhere by public transportation than by any other means. If you leave your house right on schedule, you will probably get to the bus stop just in time to see your bus go speeding by. If and when you catch the bus to the train station, you will hear the train doors close just as you are buying your ticket. This gives you a chance to read the morning paper, because the next train never arrives in less than twenty minutes. When the train finally does arrive, so many people is packed into it that you have to stand, wedged between two passengers who insists on trying to read their newspapers while they are on the train. If you are lucky, you will manage to fight your way out of the train by the time it reaches your station. Then, as you run to your job or class to get there on time, you can think about going through the same ordeal again when you want to go home.

EXERCISE 3 **Write!**

In this exercise, a present tense sentence has been started for you. Complete the sentence by adding to the subject, and make sure each sentence is written in present tense.

1. The curtains that are hanging in the window ______________________

____

2. Each of the flowers ______________________________

____

3. The company that she works for __________________________

____

4. One of these streets ______________________________

____

5. Everyone at the party ______________________________

____

*EXERCISE 4

Proofread the following paragraph for both sentence skills *and* usage (verb tense and pronoun) *errors. Correct any errors that you find.*

I have noticed that there is three clearly different types of writing teachers. They can be classified according to the way they teach the subject. First there is what I call the literature type. This kind of teacher tells the class that they are going to teach writing, he or she spends all of his or her time talking about different kinds of literature that no one in the class has ever read. They is so concerned with explaining famous works of literature that he rarely gives writing assignments. Another kind of instructor is the grammar teacher. This kind of teacher is the one who believe that a student must know the parts of speech before they can write well. The class time is spent in long and tiring drills, and students memorizes dozens of sentence patterns and parts of speech. This instructor may give a writing assignment, but only after all the parts of speech is correctly memorized. Finally there is the last kind of teacher this is the one who teaches grammar and writing at the same time. He does not emphasize grammar, but they teach all the grammar the student needs to know in order to write well. Much of the class time is spent in doing writing assignments, since this kind of teacher uses the students' papers when he is teaching the grammar rules. Although each of these three have their own special talent. I prefer the third type. After all, if I have to be in a writing class, I would rather be writing than doing anything else.

EXERCISE 5 *Proofread the following paragraph for both* sentence skills *and* usage *errors. Correct any errors that you find.*

Many of the more popular games in American society imitates American life. The one parlor game that is especially famous is Monopoly. The winner in a game of Monopoly is the person whom is able to acquire the most money and property, they must do this through a combination of luck and cleverness. The game's resemblance to American life is the idea that all Americans is trying to accumulate fortunes in property and money. Another popular game is "Let's Make a Deal." On this show, contestants are eager to do anything at all, no matter how ridiculous, in order to gain a chance to bargain for money. The costumes and actions of the audience demonstrates that there are no limits to what he or she will do for money. Perhaps the most popular American game is football. It is a rough and sometimes vicious game the winner is the team who capture the opposing team's property. This appeals to many Americans. Since they too are involved in a fierce struggle to gain more property and possessions. The more property a person own, the more you can claim to be "winning" in the game of life.

10 / Learn paragraph organization

In Chapter 1 you learned how to get started on a writing assignment and how to transform your ideas from a general listing to a first draft of a paragraph. In Writing Assignments 2–11, you practiced this method of writing on a variety of topics. You also learned to proofread your first draft for additional kinds of errors so that your final draft could be written as effectively as possible.

REVIEW THE WRITING PROCESS*

In this chapter, we will review and expand upon the writing process you learned in Chapter 1. During the review, we will focus on evaluating the effectiveness of your paragraphs by deciding how well you convince your reader of your main point. Then we will suggest some specific methods for making your writing more convincing, both by strengthening the support you use and by organizing the support effectively. Finally, you will learn how the essay form allows you to express ideas that may be too detailed or extensive for a single paragraph.

Listing Ideas

As you will recall from Chapter 1, after you have determined exactly what a particular topic is asking you to do, a good way to get started is to list

*See Chapter 1 for more information on understanding a topic, creating a list, selecting ideas from a list, and deciding upon a main idea.

all of the ideas that come to mind about that topic. At this stage of the process, don't try to limit or restrict your ideas—simply write down every possible thought you have about the topic. Remember that the longer you make your list, the more ideas you will have to choose from when you begin writing your draft.

PRACTICE EXERCISE

EXERCISE 1

Write!

For the two topics presented below, determine exactly what you are being asked to write. On a separate sheet of paper, list all of the ideas you have about the topic.

A. Name your favorite sport and explain why it is your favorite. If you do not have a favorite sport, explain why not.

B. What are the advantages or disadvantages of owning a pet? You may write about just the advantages, just the disadvantages, or both.

The Main Idea

After you have listed your ideas for a topic, you should be able to decide what kind of response you are going to make to the topic. Making this decision is a matter of "adding up" the different entries on your list to see what kind of general idea they make. This "total," or more general, idea is the **main idea** you can work with. Look at the following list to see how this process works.

Topic: Some people claim that competition is what makes America work. What do you think? Is competition a good thing or a bad thing?

List:

1. helps achieve perfection
2. motivates
3. puts people under pressure
4. Super Bowl
5. sales
6. realize full potential
7. life is full of competition
8. children in little leagues
9. makes economy work

Evaluating the List

Since this topic, like many you will be asked to write on, asks you to make a value judgment about the subject (''Is competition good or bad?''), a good way to evaluate the items in the list is to separate them into categories of ''good (positive),'' ''bad (negative),'' or ''in between (neutral).'' You will find that you can categorize items into three groups like this for most topics that ask you to answer a question or take a position on an issue. Here is an example of how you might evaluate the items in the list above:

Positive	*Negative*	*Neutral*
helps achieve perfection	puts people under pressure	Super Bowl
motivates		sales
realize full potential		life is full of competition
makes economy work		children in little leagues

Notice in this list that there are as many items in the ''neutral'' category as there are in the ''positive'' category. This will often be the case because many of the ideas you will get about a topic could be either positive or negative, depending on how you choose to view them. For example, the item ''children in little leagues'' could be used as an example to show how much fun competition is for children, a good thing. Or it could be used to show how competition can turn an innocent children's game into an event in which winning means everything. The items ''Super Bowl'' and ''sales'' seem to be useful as examples of competition in our lives; and both of these, like the ''little leagues'' item, could be used to support either a positive or a negative position on the topic. The other item in the neutral category, ''life is full of competition'' is truly in between. It is more of a general statement and would probably be most useful as part of an introduction or conclusion rather than as a supporting statement.

As you know, the main idea of a paragraph is a general statement that is supported by most of the details in the paragraph. After you have evaluated the items in a list, you will be able to see what kind of a main idea statement would be general enough to be supported by most of the items in the list. Write a sentence stating a possible main idea for the items in the list above.

Main idea about competition: ______________________________

____

____.

The most general idea that arises from this list would probably be that competition is a good thing. Check to see if your statement expresses that idea. That statement would be the main idea a writer could work with because the list includes more items under "positive" than under "negative," and several of those under "neutral" could be used as positive examples.

The example above is one kind of list, a type that you might create when you have no clear and immediate answer to the question asked in a topic. Thus, you can use a list to help you discover what position you want to take on an issue.

Sometimes you will have an immediate answer to the question asked by a topic. For example, in responding to the above topic, you may have thought immediately "Competition is wonderful!" In this case, you have already formed your main idea, so instead of listing *all* of the ideas that come to mind, you might try listing only the ideas that support your view. However, if you find that you cannot think of many ideas that support your view, you should go back to the method of listing everything you can think of about the topic. After you do create your list, you may discover that you are supporting a main idea completely different from the one you first thought of! Listing allows you to explore and discover your ideas *before* you begin writing your actual paragraph.

PRACTICE EXERCISE

EXERCISE 2

Write!

In this exercise, a topic is presented, followed by several lists that can make up the support in the paragraph. For each list, write a sentence expressing a main idea that could be supported by most *of the items in the list. If the items in the list are divided equally between positive and negative, write a main idea that presents both sides of the issue.*

Topic: Is television a good or a bad influence on children? State your opinion and support your view with specific reasons, details, and examples.

List 1: violent police shows

cartoon shows with violence

soap operas and series with "adult" situations

TV time takes away from reading time

children committing "copy cat" crimes

Main Idea: ______________________________

____

____

____

List 2: children learning alphabet by watching TV

TV can be used as reward for doing homework

Sesame Street

nature and educational shows

news shows increase awareness

Main Idea: ____________________

____

____

____

List 3: Violence on prime time shows

Sesame Street

sex and sensationalism in most shows

nature and educational shows

national news shows increase awareness

TV watching keeps kids from doing homework

Main Idea: ____________________

____

____

____

Sometimes a topic does not ask the writer to make a value judgment or answer yes or no, as does the topic above. Instead, it asks for a description or an explanation. For example, look at the following topics:

> *Topic:* Name your favorite restaurant and explain what makes it your favorite.
>
> *Topic:* What is your worst habit? Identify what it is and explain what makes it such a bad habit and why you have not been able to get rid of it.

As you can see, if you were to create lists of ideas to help you respond to these topics, the items in your lists probably wouldn't fit into categories of "positive," ''negative,'' and ''neutral.'' Instead, the lists would include reasons, details, and examples to *show the reader* what you mean. Look at the following example:

Topic: What are the qualities of a ''good'' neighborhood?
List: friendly and helpful neighbors
good schools
well-maintained houses
stores within the area
police and fire protection
recreational facilities nearby
low property taxes

If you were to sort through the list above and evaluate the items, you would quickly see that they are all ''positive'' features, as they should be, because the topic asks for *only* the positive features of a neighborhood. To sort through the items in this kind of a list, you would simply select those you felt were the *most important* characteristics of a good neighborhood.

General Statements

Writing a sentence that expresses the main idea for this kind of a topic is a little different because the main idea does not have to indicate what kind of a position you are taking on an issue. Instead, your main idea should be a *general statement* that is broad enough to include the items from the list that you intend to use. To continue with our example, suppose you had decided to use only the following items from the list:

friendly and helpful neighbors
good schools
well-maintained houses
stores within the area

If you were planning to use these items in a paragraph, which of the following sentences would best convey the main idea?

A. A good neighborhood is a place where there are friendly and helpful neighbors.

B. A good neighborhood is a place where the houses are always well-maintained.

C. A good neighborhood has features too numerous to mention.

D. A variety of important features make up a good neighborhood.

E. To be considered a ''good place to live,'' a neighborhood should have friendly neighbors, good schools, well-maintained houses, and stores nearby.

What is wrong with Sentences A and B? Since each identifies only one characteristic in the list, neither of them is *general* enough to state the main idea. How about Sentence C? If you used this sentence as your main idea, what could you write in the rest of your paragraph? If your main idea is that the features are too numerous to mention, then you certainly cannot go ahead and try to describe them in your paragraph.

Sentence D is a good main idea; it is general enough to serve as a main idea that would include all of the items in the list. It simply states that there are a number of features and suggests that these features will be specified in the paragraph. Sentence E is an even better statement of the main idea. It is not only general enough to include all of the items in the list, it names the items so that the reader knows immediately what to expect in the rest of the paragraph.

Remember: When writing a sentence to express the main idea of your paragraph,

- the sentence must be *general* enough to include the items on your list that you intend to use;
- the sentence must *answer the question* or *take a position on the issue* presented in the question.

PRACTICE EXERCISE

EXERCISE 3

Write!

For each of the topics presented below, list *all of the ideas that come to mind,* select *the best items from your list, and then* write *a sentence that expresses the main idea for the items you selected from your list.*

Topic A: Name your favorite restaurant and explain what makes it your favorite.

List: ____________________

____

____

____

____

Main Idea: ____________________

____

____

Topic B: What is your worst habit? Identify what it is and explain what makes it such a bad habit and why you have not been able to get rid of it.

List: ______________________________

____

____

____

____

Main Idea: ______________________________

____

____

Attracting Interest

The main idea does not always have to be presented as the first sentence of a paragraph. It is often presented as the final sentence. Also, a writer may decide to use the first sentence or two of a paragraph to attract the reader's interest before presenting the topic sentence. One way of creating interest is by using the first sentence to make a statement *opposite* to the main idea of the paragraph. This technique is especially effective if the main idea of the paragraph is opposite to a commonly held belief. Look at the following examples.

Topic: Air travel
Main Idea: *Air travel* is safer than any other form of travel.
Beginning of paragraph:

STATEMENT TO ATTRACT INTEREST.	People are always telling stories about frightening experiences on airplanes and describing how close they came to being killed in a crash. But the fact is that air travel is safer than any other form of travel.	MAIN IDEA

Topic: Description of a good friend
Main Idea: My *friend* Sharon is a warm, considerate person.
Beginning of paragraph:

STATEMENT TO ATTRACT INTEREST.	Most people who meet my friend Sharon think she is extremely self-centered. However, Sharon is really a warm and considerate person.	MAIN IDEA

PRACTICE EXERCISE

*EXERCISE 4 *Read the following paragraph and determine the main idea.*

I have always been told that it is best to buy American-made products, especially cars. However, I have come to the conclusion that foreign cars are a better investment than American cars. For one thing, the foreign cars get better gas mileage. The price of gas and oil is getting higher and higher, so any car owner must be concerned about how far his car will take him on a gallon of gas. In this category the foreign cars leave the American cars far behind. Another important advantage of the foreign cars is their dependability. While parts and labor for foreign car repairs are expensive, the facts show that foreign cars do not require repair nearly as often as American cars.

Main Idea (What is the most important point the writer is making about the topic?): ______________________________

____

Limiting the Topic

While the sentence that states the main idea must be general enough to include all of the items in your list, it must also *limit* the topic enough so that it is manageable. "Limiting" a topic simply means restricting it further—placing some controls upon it. This becomes necessary when the topic deals with an issue or idea that is too broad or too general to be treated effectively within a single paragraph. One response to this situation is to expand the paragraph into an essay; this process is explained in detail in Chapter 11. However, if you want to restrict your response to a single paragraph, you will need to place some limitations on the topic. Let's look at an example of topics that are too broad and consider how they might be limited by the main idea to become more manageable.

Topic: capital punishment

This is an example of a topic that is too broad to be covered fully in a single paragraph, or even in an essay. To limit this or any topic, try thinking of a particular *aspect*, or part, of the topic. For example, instead of trying to write on capital punishment in general, consider one of these ideas *about* capital punishment:

—the history of capital punishment in America
—capital punishment and minorities
—what's wrong with capital punishment
—what's right with capital punishment

As you can see, even some of these limited topics are still too broad to be treated fully in a single paragraph. "The history of capital punishment in America," for example, could easily take up one or more volumes.

To test whether or not you've limited your topic effectively, simply ask yourself whether you could *convince* your reader of the point you want to make in a single paragraph. For example, the main idea for the topic "the history of capital punishment" might look something like this:

> The history of capital punishment in America demonstrates this country's struggle with the need for justice while maintaining the ideals of compassion and fairness.

To convince a reader of this assertion, a writer must provide "proof"—a series of examples throughout American history illustrating the central aspects of the main idea—and such an extensive amount of proof would certainly require more than a single paragraph.

Now look at this main idea on another of the sample topics.

> Capital punishment has never been effective for two main reasons: it discriminates against the poor, and it does not deter hardened criminals.

Convincing a reader of the points in this main idea would seem a bit more manageable because they have been limited to a much greater extent.

Here are some examples of other broad topics and how they might be limited in the statement of a main idea.

Broad Topic:	soap operas
Main Idea Too Broad:	Soap operas offer a good example of everything that is wrong in American life.
Activity:	List the elements your paragraph would have to include to *convince* your reader of the broad main idea above.
Limited Main Idea:	Soap operas offer a harmless means of escape for millions of television viewers.
Activity:	List the elements your paragraph would have to include to *convince* your reader of the limited main idea above.

Broad Topic: nuclear power

Main Idea Too Broad: Nuclear power represents the largest single threat to the continued existence of mankind.

Activity: List the elements your paragraph would have to include to *convince* your reader of the broad main idea above.

Limited Main Idea: The risks of using nuclear power outweigh the potential benefits.

Activity: List the elements your paragraph would have to include to *convince* your reader of the limited main idea above.

PRACTICE EXERCISE

EXERCISE 5

Write!

For each of the broad *topics presented below, write a main idea that limits it, and then list the elements a paragraph would have to include to convince a reader of your main idea.*

Topic 1: boxing

Limited Main Idea: ______________________

____

List of Elements: ______________________

____

Topic 2: drunk drivers

Limited Main Idea: ______________________

____

List of Elements: ______________________

____

Topic 3: child abuse

Limited Main Idea: ______________________

____

List of Elements: ______________________

____

Topic 4: buying a house

Limited Main Idea: ______________________________

____

List of Elements: ______________________________

____

Topic 5: athletic scholarships

Limited Main Idea: ______________________________

____

List of Elements: ______________________________

____

SUPPORT: STRENGTHENING THE ARGUMENT

Get Specific

The **support** in your paragraph is the way you convince your reader of your main idea. In general, the more convincing your writing is, the better it is. But what makes your writing convincing? To answer this question, let's look at the following examples:

Sentence 1: The television shows that children watch are too violent.

Sentence 2: In a typical half hour of watching television, a child may witness a murder, an attempted rape, half a dozen cases of assault, and the kind of driving that is real only in a demolition derby.

Both sentences support the main idea that watching television can be harmful to children. Obviously, the second sentence is more effective in making this point. It is not only a more interesting sentence to read, it is *more specific* than Sentence 1. Notice that Sentence 1 *says* the word "violent," but Sentence 2 never uses the word at all; instead it *shows* the violence that a child is seeing.

The best way to be specific is to try to *show* the reader what it is you mean. To do this, think of your support as having different **levels of specificity**.

To see how this works, let's go back to a topic and list we used earlier in this chapter.

Topic: What are the qualities of a "good" neighborhood?
List: friendly and helpful neighbors
good schools
well-maintained houses
stores within the area
police and fire protection
recreational facilities nearby
low property taxes

Recall that we selected the following items from this list:

friendly and helpful neighbors
good schools
well-maintained houses
stores within the area

These items look as if they could be useful in explaining what it is that makes a good neighborhood. Let's look at a paragraph that uses these items as support.

> A variety of important features make up a good neighborhood. The neighbors must be friendly and helpful. It must have good schools. The houses in the neighborhood should be well maintained. There should be enough stores located within a reasonable distance from the neighborhood.

This paragraph states a main idea and supports it, but the way the paragraph is written, it is little better than the list. Remember that the *purpose* for writing is to convince a reader of the truth of your main idea. To do this, you must *expand and develop* the support to make it specific and convincing. Look at the way the paragraph begins now:

> A variety of important features make up a good neighborhood. First, the neighbors must be friendly and helpful. Even the most beautiful and convenient community can be little more than a prison if the people who live there are unfriendly. A "place to live" becomes a "neighborhood" when the neighbors offer to help with a weekend project, keep an eye on each other's children, and collect the mail and newspapers for a family that is away.

By making the supporting statement *more specific*, the writer *shows* the reader what the terms "friendly" and "helpful" mean. Always try to expand the items in your list by making them as specific as possible.

PRACTICE EXERCISE

EXERCISE 6

Write!

Expand each of the following supporting statements by making it more specific. Use the example above for your model.

1. good schools

____

____

____

____.

2. well-maintained houses

____

____

____

____.

3. stores within the area

____

____

____

____.

4. police and fire protection

____

____

____

____.

5. recreational facilities nearby

____

____

____

____.

Use Examples

Another way to make the support more specific is by using examples. An **example** illustrates, or shows, the point the writer is making. The important point to remember about using examples is that they should *show, not tell.* When used in this way, examples add a great deal to a paragraph, especially to paragraphs that explain or describe. Look at the following pairs of sentences and decide which ones are more effective at showing what the writer means.

Sentence A: The mayor is corrupt.

Sentence B: The mayor has fixed local elections, bribed judges, and received kickbacks on city contracts.

Sentence A: Driving conditions were bad.

Sentence B: The road was slick with rain, and the fog was so thick that I could not see more than twenty feet in front of me.

Notice that in each of the pairs of sentences, Sentence B *defines* or *describes* what is simply *stated* in Sentence A. People have different ideas of what words mean; for example, "corrupt" and "bad" will certainly convey different meanings to different people. Therefore, in order to convey your own particular meaning of the term, you should *show* what it means to you by using an example. Of course, an obvious advantage to using examples is that they make sentences and paragraphs much more interesting to read. How often, in conversation, after you say to someone: "I had a great time last night!" has he or she asked you for the details? The statement that you had a great time is, by itself, only mildly interesting. But if you describe what specifically made it great, and let your listener or reader "see" each event, you create much more interest and make your point more convincing.

PRACTICE EXERCISES

EXERCISE 7

Write!

In the following exercise, write a sentence that gives one or more examples of the descriptive phrase provided.

1. A generous person ______________________________

____

2. An honest person ______________________________

____

3. A rude salesperson ______________________________

____

4. An athletic person ______________________________

____

5. An attractive house ______________________________

____

6. A good teacher ______________________________

____

7. A busybody ______________________________

____

8. A stingy person ______________________________

____

9. A pleasant day ______________________________

____

10. An aggressive football player ______________________________

____

EXERCISE 8

Write!

In this exercise a paragraph is provided, including a topic sentence and three reasons, but the details and examples have been left out. Fill in each of the spaces with a detail or example that develops or illustrates the reason that is given.

TOPIC SENTENCE: *A number of different factors led to my car accident.* I got up late and had to drive faster than normal on my way to school.

Detail: ______________________________

____

____

____

____

I had neglected to have the proper maintenance done on the car.

Detail: ______________________________

____

____

____

____

The weather that day was terrible.

Detail: ______________________________

____

____

____

____

Eliminate Irrelevant Details

When you are developing a paragraph by adding explanation or description, it is often easy to add a detail that does not really belong in the paragraph. This is called an **irrelevant detail**. An irrelevant detail is one that does not support the main idea. Remember that a paragraph must contain support for the main idea, and all of that support must relate to (by explaining, describing, or defending) the main idea. Look at the following paragraph.

> I prefer swimming over all other forms of exercise. For one thing, it is recognized as one of the best forms of physical exercise available. Many different muscles are used in the act of swimming, and all of these are strengthened and conditioned when swimming is done regularly. Another reason I like swimming is that it is one of the few ways I can cool off and exercise at the same time. A quick swim in the pool after school or work is always refreshing. Unfortunately, I have to drive across town because the pool in my community always has too much chlorine in it. The final reason I prefer swimming is that it is something I can do all year. Other kinds of exercise, like tennis and softball, are seasonal, but I can go swimming at any time of the year.

Can you identify the irrelevant detail? To check for an irrelevant detail, first recall your main idea. The main idea of this paragraph is "I prefer swimming over all other forms of exercise." Once you have found the main idea, check the other sentences in the paragraph to make sure that they relate to it. If a sentence does not relate to the main idea by explaining or describing something about it, it is an irrelevant detail.

The irrelevant detail in the above paragraph is "Unfortunately, I have to drive across town because the pool in my community always has too much chlorine in it." This sentence is irrelevant because *where* the writer goes swimming (or why he has to go there) does not explain, describe, or defend his main idea—that he prefers swimming over other forms of exercise. Always check your paragraph for irrelevant details after you finish the first draft. *Note:* A statement presented to attract the reader's interest is *not* an irrelevant detail. Such a statement is usually used in a paragraph to *introduce* the topic sentence; it is *not* used as part of the support in the paragraph.

PRACTICE EXERCISES

*EXERCISE 9 *The following paragraph contains one or more irrelevant details. Underline the sentence or sentences that are irrelevant, and be prepared to explain* why *they are irrelevant.*

During the evening hours, it is very hard to get any studying done in my house. First of all, there is nowhere in the house to be alone. We have a seven-room house with ten people occupying it. It is an old row house that was built sometime after the Second World War. In addition, there are entirely too many interruptions. As soon as I begin to concentrate on my studies, the telephone starts ringing. Then the children become very inquisitive and start asking me all kinds of questions. Finally, the noise is unbelievable. Someone is watching television in the living room with the volume turned all the way up, and my brother has his stereo blasting away upstairs. The result is that it is so loud I can hardly hear myself think.

*EXERCISE 10 *Underline any sentences that are irrelevant and be prepared to explain why they are irrelevant.*

I like watching *Monday Night Football* for many reasons. To begin with, most of the time the two teams that are playing are contenders and are evenly matched. This means that the games are usually pretty exciting. Also, I am one of the few people around who likes the announcer and enjoys listening to him. He makes some ridiculous comments once in a while, but most of the time he is fun to listen to. In addition to those features, I also enjoy the halftime program, which shows all the highlights of the Sunday games. Most of all I love to play football as much as I love to watch it, but I can never find a group of guys who can organize a good game.

Use Transitions

You may have noticed, in the paragraphs used in the last few exercises, that some key words or phrases were included: "first of all," "in addition," "finally." These phrases actually take the place of numbers in the paragraphs since they indicate the order of the reasons. The phrases also separate the three reasons from each other. These words and phrases are called **transition words** or **signal words**. A transition is a change; when used in paragraphs, these words indicate the "change" from one idea to another.

In addition to, explaining or defending the main idea, the support in a paragraph must also be logically developed. The transition words help to establish a logical relationship between the different parts of the support, and they help the reader see the relationship more clearly.

The following list gives many of the different transition words and phrases that can be used for this purpose.

To indicate a first reason:

first of all,	first,
to begin with,	on the other hand,
in the first place,	

To indicate a second or third reason:

second,	in other words,
also,	consequently,
furthermore,	therefore,
in addition,	however,
next,	on the other hand,

To indicate a final or most important reason:

finally,	in summary,
in the last place,	in conclusion,
most important,	as a result,

ORGANIZE THE PARAGRAPH

After you have decided on a topic, a main idea, and sufficient support, it is time to think about putting the ideas into a logical order. The arrangement you use for your paragraph will depend on the purpose of your paragraph. For an example, look at the following paragraph in which the writer explains how to change a tire.

> Anyone can change a flat tire by following a few simple steps. First, jack the car up until the tire is no longer touching the ground. Be sure to stop the car on a level surface. Use a lug wrench to remove the lug nuts on the tire. Take the flat tire off and get the spare tire out of the trunk. Put the lug nuts back on the wheel and tighten them in equal amounts a little at a time. Take the spare tire out of the trunk and put the flat tire in. Place the spare tire on the wheel. Place the hubcap back on the wheel after tightening the lug nuts. Do not forget to get the flat tire fixed. Put the jack back in the car.

Can you tell what is wrong with this paragraph? It has a main idea and plenty of details, all of which relate to the topic, but there is still something wrong. The problem in this paragraph is that there is no order to the sentences. The writer's purpose in this paragraph is to explain a process: how to change a tire. But if you had no idea how to change a tire, would this paragraph help you? Probably not, since the writer tells you to tighten the lug nuts *before* putting the spare tire on the car. In short, the instructions are out of sequence, so they do not accomplish the writer's purpose.

Now that you have seen why a paragraph needs to be organized according to a certain plan, you are ready to learn about the different kinds of writing purposes and the different types of plans each of them requires.

Among the methods often used to organize paragraphs are:

1. Explaining a process.
2. Presenting an opinion.
3. Defining.
4. Explaining a cause-effect or effect-cause relationship.
5. Comparing and/or contrasting.

Explaining a Process

This is one of the simplest ways to organize a paragraph. It is used to **describe** or **explain how to do something**; it is often called a "how-to" paragraph.

Before giving the steps involved in a process, you should indicate just what process you are going to describe. One good way to do this is to encourage the reader to follow the steps by telling how important or how simple the procedure is. Notice, in the sample paragraph about changing a tire, that the first sentence does this: it gives the main idea of the paragraph, and it encourages the reader to follow the steps. If you start a process paragraph right off with the steps, the reader will not know what process is being described.

The **steps** in the process are the most important part of this type of paragraph. Remember that your purpose in writing anything is to communicate an idea to a reader. As you saw with the example paragraph, if the steps are presented out of sequence, or if one or more steps are missing, you will not communicate your idea. Remember to give all of the important steps in the process, and to give the steps in the proper sequence.

A final point about explaining a process is the need to define special terms. When you are explaining a process, be sure to consider whether your reader is likely to know the meanings of the terms you use. In the sample paragraph, there is no need for any definitions, since most people are familiar with terms such as "jack" and "lug nuts." However, if you explain a more technical or unusual process, you may have to use a word that needs to be defined. For example, if you were explaining how to pot a plant, you might want to use the word "vermiculite," which you should define, in your own words, for the reader.

Outline for a Process Paragraph

Topic sentence:	Statement that names the process to be explained and encourages the reader to follow the steps.
Support:	Steps involved in the process. Include all important steps and make sure they are in the correct sequence.

Sample Process Paragraph

If you are interested in getting the best deal when you buy a car, you should follow these few simple steps. First, decide exactly how much money you can spend on the car, and determine whether you want a full-sized car, a compact, or a subcompact. Next, read some consumer and automotive magazines to get the facts about the different cars that are available within your price range. Now you are ready to go do battle with the car salesman. If you have done the proper amount of research on the car that you are interested in, the salesman will not be able to tell you anything about the car that you do not already know. This means that he will be forced to talk about the price of the car right away. This is the most important stage of car-buying for most people. Do not assume that the price the salesman gives you is the final figure. The first price he offers is usually a few hundred dollars higher than the lowest price he is able to accept. After he gives you a price, offer to buy the car on the spot for a price a few hundred below what you intend to pay for the car. This usually forces the salesman to drastically reduce his price. If he does not reduce it enough to satisfy you, visit another dealer and follow the same procedure. Also, be sure to tell the second dealer about the price offered by the first dealer. This will force him to offer a lower price. If you follow these steps, and go to enough car dealers, you will be sure to get the best possible deal.

PRACTICE EXERCISES

EXERCISE 11

Write!

Rewrite the paragraph on how to change a tire. Make sure to describe the steps of the process in order. Also, an important step in the process has been left out. Write a sentence describing this step and include it in the paragraph.

EXERCISE 12

Read and evaluate the following paragraph according to what you know about explaining a process. Make any corrections that you feel are necessary.

To begin with, understand your camera thoroughly. Know how to focus the lens and how to set the exposure properly. Next, hold the camera steady. Do this by placing your left hand under the lens and your right hand on the side of the camera. Also, hold your elbows close to your sides. This will minimize camera movement, which can lead to a blurred picture. Now set the exposure properly, and carefully focus the camera on the image. Finally, push the shutter release button very slowly, making sure the camera does not move.

EXERCISE 13

Write!

Select any two of the topics from the following list. For each topic, write a topic sentence, and then construct an outline by adding the steps involved in the process. Do this on a separate sheet of paper.

1. How to register for classes
2. How to wash a car
3. How to baby-sit
4. How to drive on snow or ice
5. How to select the best stereo equipment
6. How to study for an exam
7. How to grow a plant or vegetable
8. How to ask someone for a date
9. How to do a popular dance
10. How to act at a party

WRITING ASSIGNMENT 12

Write a paragraph, using one of the two outlines you prepared in Exercise 13. After you finish writing your paragraph, proofread it for any errors in sentence structure, verb tense or agreement, or paragraph organization. Correct any errors that you find.

Presenting an Opinion

The **opinion-reason** paragraph is a useful method of organizing sentences that present and defend opinions. In this type of paragraph the opinion is the main idea, and it is often presented as the first sentence. The support for the main idea is in the form of reasons that explain or defend the opinion. In addition, descriptive details or examples are usually provided to develop each reason.

The reasons in an opinion-reason paragraph should be presented in a logical order, just as the steps of a process paragraph are presented in a sequence. In a process paragraph, the order of the steps depends upon how the process is completed. In an opinion-reason paragraph, the order of the reasons depends upon the amount of emphasis the writer wants to give to each reason. The most important reason is usually given last in the paragraph since the reader tends to retain the last idea he or she sees. The writer may also decide to organize the reasons according to a time or space arrangement, when that is possible.

Outline for an Opinion Paragraph

Main Idea: The writer's opinion
Support: Reason 1
Detail explaining or giving an example of the reason
Reason 2
Detail
Reason 3
Detail

Sample Opinion Paragraph

I hate television commercials for a number of reasons. First of all, they insult my intelligence. The people who make those commercials really expect me to believe that all women just *love* to clean and do laundry! They also want me to believe that if I use a particular brand of after-shave lotion, I will capture the heart of every girl in sight. Another thing wrong with the commercials is that they are often dishonest. Many companies make claims and promises they simply cannot keep, while others announce "test results" that leave out important facts or details. Finally, I do not like the kinds of ideas that commercials put into children's heads. The commercials encourage children to eat sugar-coated cereals and drink outrageous quantities of soda. They also mislead the children into believing that a McDonald's or a Burger King is a kind of playground.

As you can see from the example, many of the paragraphs you have written so far in this book have been opinion paragraphs. What makes an effective opinion paragraph, like any other paragraph, is the support. In an opinion paragraph, it is especially important for the support to be *convincing* because the *purpose* of the paragraph in this case is to convince the reader of an opinion or point of view. Some of the ways you can make an opinion paragraph convincing are to present opposing arguments, use evidence, and predict consequences. We will look at each of these methods below.

Presenting opposing arguments

One very effective method of defending an opinion is to show what's wrong with the **opposite point of view**. Look at the following example:

> There are several good reasons why deer hunting should be permitted. Many people claim that shooting a poor, defenseless animal with a high-powered rifle is the height of cruelty. But is that as cruel as starving to death? Without hunters, the deer herds would grow so large that thousands of the animals would starve to death during the winter months when food becomes scarce.

In this example, the second sentence *does not* support the main idea expressed in the first sentence. Instead, it offers a reason often given to support the opposite point of view. That point of view is then challenged by the third and fourth sentences, which attempt to show what is wrong with it. This is an effective method of supporting an opinion, especially when your main idea expresses an opinion opposite to the one normally held by most people.

Using evidence

Another effective method of support is to use **evidence** to support your opinion. There are many kinds of evidence, but the two types most often used to support arguments are facts and expert testimony. **Facts** are simply a form of detail that you can use to support your position. As you know, the more specific you make your support, the more effective it is in defending your position. Facts are one of the most specific of all types of support. Which of the following sentences is more convincing?

Sentence 1: For example, last winter after hunting season was over, a lot of deer starved to death in the snow.

Sentence 2: For example, last winter after hunting season was over, more than a thousand deer starved to death in the snow.

The second sentence, of course, is more convincing because instead of the phrase "a lot of deer," it gives a specific fact: "more than a thousand deer."

Expert testimony is another form of evidence. By using the opinion of an expert to support your view, you strengthen your argument. Here are two more supporting sentences to consider:

Sentence 1: I also think that the deer in our forests are getting bigger and stronger because hunting "thins out" the weaker members of the herd.

Sentence 2: According to a game biologist for the state department of natural resources, the deer in our forests are getting bigger and stronger because hunting "thins out" the weaker members of the herd.

A reader is much more likely to be convinced of the truth of a supporting statement if that statement comes from a person who is considered an "authority" on the subject. For you as a writer to state that you "think" something is so is considerably less persuasive than to report that an authority in that field believes this.

Predicting consequences

Yet another effective means of support for an argument is to **predict the results** if the course of action you recommend is followed or is *not* followed. Look at these examples:

Sentence 1: By permitting deer hunting, we strengthen our deer herds and raise significant revenues through the sale of hunting licenses.

Sentence 2: If deer hunting were not permitted, we would soon find our farmlands overrun with destructive deer in the summer, only to see thousands of them die a horrible death by starvation in the winter.

Sentence 1 illustrates the kind of supporting sentence that predicts a consequence if a recommendation *is* followed. Note that this kind of sentence can also serve as an effective conclusion in a paragraph. Sentence 2 shows an example of a consequence of *not* following a recommendation. Note that this kind of sentence is similar to the supporting statement that presents the opposing argument.

PRACTICE EXERCISES

EXERCISE 14 **Write!** *Using the* Outline for an Opinion Paragraph *as a model, construct an outline for the paragraph on television commercials presented in this section.*

EXERCISE 15 **Write!** *The following list names some broad issues about which many people have strong opinions. Select any* two *of the phrases, list some ideas, and then write a sentence expressing the main idea in the form of an opinion.*

Remember to limit *the topic when you write your main idea, as discussed earlier in this chapter (see Exercise 5). Then, construct an outline of the reasons and details you will use to support your opinion. Try to use one or more of the techniques presented in this section to construct your supporting statements.*

1. The 55-mile-per-hour speed limit
2. Capital punishment
3. Legalizing marijuana
4. The legal drinking age in your state
5. Adult book stores
6. Mandatory attendance at school or college
7. Nuclear power
8. Violence on television

WRITING ASSIGNMENT 13

Write a paragraph, using one of the two outlines you prepared in Exercise 14. Be sure to use effective arguments in your paragraph. After you finish writing the paragraph, proofread it for any errors in sentence structure, verb tense or agreement, or paragraph organization. Correct any errors that you find.

Defining

As discussed earlier in this chapter, effective writing usually requires the limiting of a subject. In many kinds of explanatory writing, the primary task of the writer is to **define** an important term or concept. The two uses you will most likely make of the definition method of organization are: to define a term in the course of an explanation, and to present an opinion by using definition as support.

Defining a term

We typically think of a definition as "what a word means," and this is the first use of the definition scheme of organization that we will explore. Look at the following example:

> Word processing is a type of computer program used to create and manipulate text.

What are the elements of this definition? First, of course, is the word or phrase being defined—in this case, "word processing." The next element of the definition is the **category** or group to which the word to be defined belongs. Here, the category to which "word processing" belongs is "computer program." Identifying the category to which a word or phrase belongs is a critical element of the definition method because it is the first step in *limiting* the possible meanings the word or phrase might have. For example, if the above definition read: "Word processing is something used to create and manipulate text," many things besides computer programs would come within the definition of word processing, including typewriters, pencils, pens, tape recorders, and so on. Thus, the first important step in definition is limiting the term to be defined by identifying precisely the category to which it belongs.

Notice, however, that the definition does not end with the naming of its category. Look at what would happen if it did:

> Word processing is a type of computer program.

This sentence is accurate so far, but it is not an adequate definition because it does not enable the reader to say whether word-processing computer programs are different from other kinds of computer programs. The identification of **specific features** is the second important function of a definition. After identifying the category to which a term belongs, an effective definition then *separates the term from other elements in that category.* The table below illustrates this idea.

Term	***Category***	***Specific Features***
word processing	computer program	creates and manipulates text

Without the specific features, word processing could be confused with any other member of the category that includes computer programs. Computer programs include disk operating systems, spreadsheets, games, inventory controls, and many, many others, but these are not used "to create and manipulate text." It is that phrase that separates word processing from other types of computer programs.

This type of writing is useful when you are explaining something and your reader is unlikely to know or be familiar with a term that you are using. For example, a writer presenting a series of investment options may want to define terms such as "annuity," "capital gains," "depreciation," and others. In the same way, a writer explaining how to wire an electrical outlet may want to define terms such as "circuit," "ground," and "short." The definition pattern can also be used to explain a **particular sense** of a term that is already familiar to most people. The following paragraph illustrates this use of the pattern:

> To be an effective teacher, a person must have some particular knowledge or experience and must know how to create the opportunity for others to learn it. A good teacher knows something, and knows it thoroughly. This means that the teacher not only has a background of knowledge in the subject, but a background of experience as well. A good art teacher, for example, should be something of a photographer, too. But there is something beyond mere knowledge and experience in a truly effective teacher. Someone could be the world's foremost authority on a particular subject and still not be a particularly good teacher. To be effective at teaching requires a blend of the knowledge with the ability to create the right atmosphere for learning. This involves making the subject matter interesting and important to students. Also, the right learning environment exists when students feel free to offer their ideas without fear of ridicule, when they can learn from their mistakes as well as their successes, and when the students are the people in the classroom who are doing most of the work. This balance of a thorough background with an ability to stimulate and foster interest in the subject is a rare combination and is the mark of a truly effective teacher.

Explaining or presenting an opinion

The definition organizational pattern can be used in a broader way in order to explain something or present an opinion. For example, look at the following paragraph:

> "Fast food" is a frequently inedible substance distinguished by its texture, the way it's served, and its aftereffects. Fast food is easy to tell from real food, first of all, because it usually has the texture of a piece of wet cardboard. If the piece of meat you're eating tastes like it's held together with epoxy, you can bet you're eating fast food. But if that method of identification fails you, there are others you can try. Historically, the care and method of serving prepared foods

have been as important as the ingredients themselves. That's how parsley got invented. But when it comes to fast food, the emphasis is on *fast*. You know you're in a fast-food restaurant when the manager, instead of studying the appearance of a dinner or trying to taste here and there, is using a stopwatch to time the speed with which your order is shoved into your hands. However, the ultimate mark of fast food comes later, during the agony of digestion. When the battle is raging down there, and you wonder who deposited that sack of flour in your belly, you know you've sampled some fast-food fare. This is the most important sign of fast food because it is sending a critical message to whoever's in charge of your body's digestion. In all likelihood, however, the message will be forgotten in the very next yearning for that fast, tasty, cardboard stuff we have taken to calling food.

The writer's purpose in the above paragraph clearly goes beyond defining fast food. Rather, the writer uses the definition method of organizing to present a particular opinion about fast food.

PRACTICE EXERCISES

EXERCISE 16 *For both of the sample definition paragraphs presented in this section, list the term that is defined, the category it belongs to, and the specific features used to distinguish the term from others in the same category.*

EXERCISE 17 **Write!** *Select any three terms or phrases from the following list. Write a sentence providing a definition, including the category and the specific features, for each of the topics.*

1. Happiness
2. Wealth
3. A good job
4. A college course (in general, or a specific course)
5. A true friend
6. A parent
7. The ______________________ curriculum
8. An adult
9. Television
10. Football (the game or the object)

WRITING ASSIGNMENT 14

Write a definition paragraph using one of the definitions you prepared in Exercise 16. Before you begin writing, decide on the purpose of your paragraph. You may want to provide an interpretation of a familiar term, or you may want to present an explanation or opinion by using a definition. After you finish writing the paragraph, proofread it for any errors in sentence structure, verb tense or agreement, or paragraph organization. Correct any errors that you find.

Explaining Cause-Effect and Effect-Cause

Both cause-effect and effect-cause paragraphs are organized like the opinion paragraph. In a **cause-effect paragraph**, the main idea is a statement of the cause of something, and the support is a listing of the effects of that cause. An **effect-cause paragraph** is organized the opposite way: the main idea is a statement of an effect, and the support is a listing of the causes that produced the effect.

To fully understand these methods of organization, you must first understand the difference between a cause and an effect. A cause is a *reason* why something happened. An effect is the *result* or *consequence* of one or more causes. Look at the following cause-effect paragraph and note the relationship between the cause and the effects:

> Since I have changed my curriculum to law enforcement, there have been amazing consequences. First of all, I am now interested in my courses. I am so interested, in fact, that I have done a lot of extra reading for the course. Also, my parents are much more involved with what I am doing in school since my father is a policeman. Finally, my grades have shown a remarkable improvement. I expected better grades to result from the switch, but I never thought I would get all the A's I have been getting. I am beginning to wish I had never heard of the data processing curriculum.

Now look at an effect-cause paragraph:

> Several factors led to the Bears' defeat in the playoff game. First, they lost because they did not have enough starting pitchers. Two of the starters they used had started in only one or two games all year. Second, three of the best hitters on the team were in a slump. Without the hitting ability of those three players, the team simply did not have any offensive power. Also, the team's general attitude seemed to be poor. There were several players who were in the middle of contract disputes this year, and this could have been one major cause of the numerous disputes between players and the management. But, most important, the team they played was ready to play baseball. The Bobcats played aggressively and skillfully, and they deserved to win, no matter who they played against.

As you can see, the method used to organize these paragraphs is quite similar to that used with the opinion paragraph. This is a useful method for organizing sentences when the writer wants to explain what happened (cause-effect) or why something happened (effect-cause).

Outline for a Cause-Effect Paragraph

Main Idea:	Cause:	The *reason* that something happened.
Support:	Effects:	The *results* or *consequences* of the cause described in the statement of the main idea.
	Details:	As in the opinion paragraph, each effect may be followed by a detail that describes or gives an example of the effect.

Outline for an Effect-Cause Paragraph

Main Idea:	Effect:	The result, *what happened.*
Support:	Causes:	The *reasons* that explain or describe why the effect occurred.
	Details:	As in the opinion paragraph, each cause may be followed by a detail that describes or gives an example of the cause.

Sample Cause-Effect Paragraph

Several serious consequences result when an oil spill occurs. The most immediate effect is the death of large numbers of fish and waterfowl from the oil in the water. Many birds that are not killed consume quantities of oil which cause disease or death later. When a spill occurs close to shore, another result is the destruction of beaches. Enormous amounts of work and money are required to clean the oil from beaches. The most serious consequence of a spill may be the damage done to microorganisms on the ocean floor. More research is required to determine the precise extent of the damage, but scientists do know that a large spill can destroy all forms of life on the ocean floor.

Sample Effect-Cause Paragraph

Several factors led to Fred and Linda's divorce. One important cause was money problems. With two cars and a house to make payments on, there was rarely ever any money for extras like entertainment or vacations. In addition, both Fred and Linda worked and attended school, so they were always busy. Whenever one of them was at home, the other was either at work or at school. It was a rare moment when they were together. The final contributing factor was their disagreement on the subject of children. Fred wanted Linda to quit working so that they could start a family, but Linda was not ready to give up her career. This proved to be an insurmountable obstacle to the success of their marriage.

PRACTICE EXERCISES

EXERCISE 18 *Construct an outline for the two sample paragraphs on the change in curriculum and the baseball team's defeat.*

EXERCISE 19 **Write!** *Select any two topics from the following list. Write a main idea for both topics, and construct an outline for the support. Use a cause-effect method of organization for one statement and an effect-cause method for the second. Be sure you understand whether the statement you use is a cause or an effect before you begin an outline of the support. Write your outlines on a separate sheet of paper.*

1. My biggest problem at home
2. Coping with a car that is a lemon
3. Causes for my poor attendance
4. Causes for my lateness in school
5. Why I chose the curriculum I am in
6. Results of being in the ______________________ curriculum
7. Results of being in the ______________________ class

8. Results of a fear of heights
9. Results of a fear of women (or men)
10. Causes of marital difficulties

WRITING ASSIGNMENT 15

Write a paragraph, using one of the two outlines you prepared in Exercise 19. You may want to use transition words in your paragraph. After you finish writing the paragraph, proofread it for any errors in sentence structure, verb tense or agreement, or paragraph organization. Correct any errors that you find.

Comparing or Contrasting

The comparison or contrast method of organizing is used when a writer wants to describe the relationship between two or more subjects. The subjects may be almost anything: objects, animals, emotions, people, or ideas. When the *similarities* of the subjects are being presented, the method of organization is called **comparison**. When the *differences* between the subjects are being presented, the method of organization is called **contrast**.

Writers normally organize comparison or contrast paragraphs in one of two ways. The first method is to write the main idea (which will usually just state that there are similarities or differences between the subjects being discussed), and then present the support by completely describing one subject. This is followed by a complete description of the next subject. The following paragraph illustrates this method of organization:

> I was very anxious to leave my old job, but I discovered a big difference between my old job and my new one. First of all, my new job was very dull. I sat for seven hours and did nothing but type. My co-workers were not the friendliest

people I have ever met. Our coffee breaks reminded me of a funeral; no one said a word the whole twenty minutes. I also took a cut in salary. I made $50 less than before. The company did not have as many benefits either. I got ten sick days and two personal holidays. My supervisor was not an easy person to get along with. Everything had to be her way or no way at all. In contrast, the job I left was very interesting. I had a variety of duties to perform. The people I worked with were very friendly; someone always had a nice thing to say. Every now and then someone had a good joke to share with the rest of us. My salary was also higher. I even had more benefits. I received fourteen sick days and four personal holidays. The supervisor was easy to get along with and very understanding; he would help me in any way he could. I am now considering returning to my old job if they will take me back.

The second way to organize a comparison or contrast paragraph is to present the support by describing one aspect or feature of the first subject, and then describing the *same* aspect of the next subject. The following sentence then describes another aspect of the first subject, and then the same aspect of the second subject, and so on. The following paragraph illustrates this method of organization:

There are several major differences between fast food restaurants and old-fashioned diners. First of all, the service in a fast-food restaurant is, as you would expect, fast. In a diner, the customer may have to wait a few minutes before his order is taken. But there is no atmosphere or comfort in a fast-food restaurant; the customer steps up to the counter, gives the order, and is handed a bag containing the food. A customer has more opportunity to relax in a diner, where he or she can give the order to a waiter or waitress and then sit back and be comfortable until the food arrives. The quality of the food at a fast-food restaurant is subject to considerable doubt. Since the food must be ready fast, it has to be prepared in advance, and thus many of the items, like hamburgers and french fries, can be cold and dry by the time a customer gets them. The food in a diner is prepared as it is ordered, so it is generally fresh and hot when the customer is served. Finally, the price of food at the fast-food places is unbeatable; their low prices are their entire reason for success. The diner prices are, of course, considerably higher, since the customer must absorb the expense of service, atmosphere, and better food.

Note that in both methods, the aspects that are described are the same for both subjects, and they are presented in the same order for both subjects.

Outline for Comparison or Contrast Paragraph

Main Idea: Statement that identifies the two subjects being described and indicates whether they are being compared ("There are several similarities . . . ") or contrasted ("There are several differences . . . ")

Support: Method 1

Description of first subject

Aspect 1

Aspect 2

Aspect 3

Description of second subject

Aspect 1

Aspect 2

Aspect 3

Support: Method 2

Description of first subject

Aspect 1

Description of second subject

Aspect 1

Description of first subject

Aspect 2

Description of second subject

Aspect 2

Description of first subject

Aspect 3

Description of second subject

Aspect 3

Sample Comparison Paragraph

It should come as no surprise that the two most popular police shows on television have similar formats. In *Chicago Beat*, for example, the hero is a veteran cop who has worked his way up from being a street cop to being a chief of detectives. In a typical show, this hero will be challenged by a crime that is seemingly unsolvable. But, somehow, the cop will unravel the series of mysterious clues and arrive at a solution. In the process he will meet up with a stunning female, often a suspect in the case. Finally, the weekly show must include at least one car chase, either at the beginning or at the end of the show. Although *Scarpata* is a show about a private investigator, it is not all that different from *Chicago Beat*. In *Scarpata* too, the hero is an older man who was once a policeman but who now works on his own. Scarpata's weekly case may not involve a crime, but the facts of whatever case it is are sure to be as hopelessly tangled as in *Chicago Beat*. The television viewer will not miss seeing one or more gorgeous women by watching *Scarpata*, either. In addition, the hero of *Scarpata* is a former race-car driver, so there are always plenty of chase scenes in this show, too.

Sample Contrast Paragraph

Where I work there are two supervisors, one for the day shift and one for the night shift. Since I have worked on both shifts, I have had a chance to compare both of them. Although they are both the same age and have exactly the same responsibilities, they are quite different in several ways. The first of these ways is their appearance. The day supervisor always dresses very formally. He usually wears a tie and a sports jacket, and he always wears a pair of neatly pressed dress slacks. The night supervisor, on the other hand, typically wears a pair of old blue jeans and a sweater. The way they dress does not indicate anything about their personalities, though. The day supervisor is very liberal with the employees, and never gets excited or irritated when something goes wrong. The night supervisor always looks relaxed in his casual clothes, but he is quick to yell and shout at the employees for the slightest mistake, and he constantly watches over everyone. I think these differences just prove that the way a person dresses does not necessarily indicate anything about his personality.

PRACTICE EXERCISES

EXERCISE 20 *Read the following paragraphs. On a separate sheet of paper, outline each paragraph, making sure to indicate (1) whether the paragraph is comparison or contrast, and (2) which method is used to organize the support.*

Although the two candidates for the governor's job represent different political parties, their views on important issues are very much alike. The Democrat has promised that he will not increase the state income tax, but he may raise business taxes. He says unemployment is the most important problem in the state and he hopes to relieve the problem by obtaining more support from the federal government. The Republican has also insisted that he will not increase the state income tax, although he said nothing about business taxes. Unemployment is the state's major problem from the Republican point of view too, and the candidate, like his Democrat opponent, has talked about requesting additional federal funds to help solve the problem.

Main Idea: ______________________________

Support: ______________________________

____

EXERCISE 21 *Now outline the following paragraph in the same way:*

Anyone who has had both a fireplace and a wood-burning stove knows that there are several important differences between the two. The first is the matter of safety. Sparks often fly out of a fireplace and can possibly damage or ignite wooden floors. In a stove, the fire is completely enclosed and there is no danger of flying sparks. In terms of heating power, the fireplace is at a disadvantage since most of the heat from the fire escapes up the chimney. On the other hand, a wood-burning stove generates heat throughout an entire house, losing almost no heat to the chimney. Finally, the fireplace requires a constant supply of logs, and it consumes them as fast as they are piled on. The wood-burning stove is much more efficient: it generates ample heat from only two or three large logs per day.

Main Idea: ______________________________

Support: ______________________________

____

EXERCISE 22

Write!

Select any two of the topics from the following list. For the first topic, construct an outline for a comparison *paragraph. For the second topic, construct an outline for a* contrast *paragraph. Write the outlines on a separate sheet of paper.*

1. Compare or contrast two jobs you have had.
2. Compare or contrast the personalities of two people you know.
3. Compare or contrast two cars you have owned.
4. Compare or contrast two houses you have lived in.
5. Compare or contrast two teachers you now have.
6. Compare or contrast two of your favorite musicians or singers.
7. Compare or contrast your two best friends.
8. Compare or contrast two of your favorite restaurants.
9. Compare or contrast your present attitude toward school and your previous attitude.
10. Compare or contrast your neighborhood with another neighborhood.

WRITING ASSIGNMENT 16

Write a paragraph, using one of the two outlines you prepared in Exercise 22. After you finish writing the paragraph, proofread it for any errors in sentence structure, verb tense or agreement, or paragraph organization. Correct any errors that you find.

Combining Several Methods of Organization

As you have probably noticed by now, some subjects lend themselves to more than one method of organization. The best way to explain how to drive a car with a manual transmission, for example, might be to contrast the way a manual transmission works with the way an automatic transmission works. Also, when the overall purpose of your paragraph is to present and support an opinion, you can use any number of methods to organize your supporting arguments. As you have seen, a position can be defended by defining, by analyzing causes and effects, or by comparing or contrasting. All of these methods of organizing ideas are *tools* to help you achieve your purpose in a particular writing situation. Now that you have practiced these methods, you should use them whenever they are appropriate for the subject you are writing about. The following examples illustrate some ways in which more than one method of organization can be used in a single paragraph.

Example 1

Almost everyone dreams of someday buying an old, run-down house and fixing it up on weekends until it becomes a showplace. Having been through the experience and lived to tell about it, I can offer some advice to anyone who still has this foolish dream. People who want to do some major house renovations must first become acquainted with some basic terminology. A "carpenter" is a craftsman who builds and repairs things. Anyone thinking of renovations as a form of recreation isn't a carpenter; carpenters know better. The rest of us who aren't carpenters are usually referred to as "do-it-yourselfers." The name itself suggests the term's true meaning: a "do-it-yourselfer" is a person who thinks he doesn't need the services of a craftsman and who proceeds to try to build and repair things without very much prior experience. The main difference between a carpenter and a do-it-yourselfer, of course, is that when a carpenter leaves a job, it is likely to appear improved for the effort. When a do-it-yourselfer leaves a job, it is usually time to call in a carpenter to repair the damage.

Example 2

One of the major stumbling blocks to the success of the ecology movement in the United States is the inability of environmentalists and hunters to see themselves as allies. For their part, many environmentalists have a one-dimensional view of hunters. They see them as drunken, brawling bullies whose only reason for going into the forest is to maim and kill as many creatures as possible and to deposit empty beer cans in otherwise scenic locations. To environmentalists, hunters are invaders in a world of peace and beauty. On the other hand, quite a few hunters don't have an accurate view of environmentalists, either. When they think "environmentalist," they see a little old lady fussing over her bird bath in a quaint English garden. To many hunters, environmentalists are the folks who are intent on *closing* the environment to any productive use, not saving it. Clearly, both groups have a good many misconceptions about each other. Environmentalists and hunters have much in common, even if they don't always recognize it. If the people in both camps could cast out the old stereotypes and join forces, collectively they would represent a powerful force for both the preservation and the judicious use of natural resources in this country.

PRACTICE EXERCISES

EXERCISE 23 *Prepare an outline for the two paragraphs in this section. In each outline, indicate the paragraph's main idea and what methods of organization were used.*

EXERCISE 24 *Select any three topics from the following list. For each topic, write a sentence expressing a main idea that would require the use of more than one method of organization.*

Write!

1. Marijuana and alcohol: what's the difference?
2. Why "work" is no fun
3. Why cable television is more popular than network television
4. A college course: What it is and how to succeed in it
5. Why typewriters are becoming obsolete
6. Antiques: What they are and how to find them

WRITING ASSIGNMENT 17

Write a paragraph on one of the topics listed in the previous exercise. Try to use more than one method of development to write the paragraph. After you finish writing the paragraph, proofread it for any errors in sentence structure, verb tense or agreement, or paragraph organization. Correct any errors that you find.

CHAPTER REVIEW

In this chapter you reviewed some of the points you learned about the writing process: understanding the topic, listing your ideas, selecting the most convincing ideas from the list, and writing a statement of the main idea that is general enough to cover all of the supporting ideas.

You also learned that the more specific the ideas you use for support, the more convincing your writing will be. The best way to make your ideas specific is to try to *show* the reader what you mean. Often, using examples is the best way to do this.

In the last section of this chapter you learned some of the most common methods for organizing ideas in paragraphs. As a writer, you will decide which of these methods is appropriate by determining the purpose of your paragraph. If the purpose of the paragraph is to give instructions, the best type of organization is the process method. The opinion paragraph is used to present and support a point of view, or an opinion. The definition pattern can be useful when you want to present a particular interpretation of a word or phrase, or when you want to present an explanation or opinion by means of an extended definition. The cause-effect and effect-cause methods of organization are useful for explaining the results of or reasons for something. If the purpose of the paragraph is to describe the relationship between two or more subjects, the best method of organizing is comparison or contrast. Finally, in some types of writing you will find it useful or necessary to use more than one organizational pattern.

SUPPLEMENTAL EXERCISES

Use the exercises below for additional practice in paragraph organization.

*EXERCISE 25 *Each of the sentences below expresses the main idea for a paragraph. For each sentence, indicate which* method of organization *would be the best way to write a paragraph using this main idea.*

Example:
Washing a car is no problem if you have the proper materials and follow a few simple steps.

Method of Organization: Process

1. State lotteries do nothing but encourage citizens to waste their money on pipe dreams.

   Method of Organization: ______________________

2. The problem of teenage gangs is the result of serious inequities in our economic system.

   Method of Organization: ______________________________

3. Parallel parking scares the wits out of most new drivers, but it's really not that hard to learn.

   Method of Organization: ______________________________

4. There are several reasons why I decided to go to college.

   Method of Organization: ______________________________

5. Several things happened to me after I was late for my mathematics class for the tenth time.

   Method of Organization: ______________________________

6. Elma and Irma are so different you'd never guess that they are sisters.

   Method of Organization: ______________________________

7. A fly rod and a shotgun look different to most people, but fishing and hunting are really quite similar.

   Method of Organization: ______________________________

8. Golf is the only professional sport left that is truly a game for gentlemen and ladies.

   Method of Organization: ______________________________

Read and evaluate the paragraphs in Exercises 26–28 according to what you know about paragraph organization. Remember that a paragraph must contain a main idea and the main idea must be supported by relevant details.

*EXERCISE 26

I think mothers should hold jobs for several reasons. First, it is good for the mother and child to get away from each other. This makes the time they share together that much more valuable. I remember once, when I was a child, my mother went to Texas to visit her sister. She was gone for over two weeks. I missed her, but she had a wonderful time with her sister. Next, a child who goes out to a day-care center while the mother goes to work has an advantage over the child who stays at home, because the child at the day-care center has the benefit of a special learning program. Last, a mother should not feel compelled to stay home just because she has a child. If she has the desire and the opportunity to work, she should be able to take a job.

Identify exactly what is wrong with the paragraph:

____

____

Now make the necessary corrections to the paragraph.

*EXERCISE 27

There are several reasons why I walk in my sleep. First I fell down a full flight of steps at three-thirty in the morning. The next time I was found wandering around in the back yard in the middle of the winter night, sound asleep. A week after that I was discovered happily eating a bowl of Cheerios—with bananas—in my bedroom. My parents have found me sleeping in the bathtub, springing up and down upon the bed, creaking back and forth in the old rocker on the porch, and they have even retrieved me from jogging around the neighborhood with nothing on but a happy smile.

Identify exactly what is wrong with the paragraph:

____

____

Now make the necessary corrections to the paragraph.

EXERCISE 28

There are several reasons why *Cosmopolitan* is my favorite magazine. First, it is published primarily for women, and its editorials deal with issues of interest to just about all women. The last issue, for example, gave a detailed history of the struggle to get the Equal Rights

Amendment passed through the state legislatures. Next, the magazine keeps its readers abreast of what is current in books, movies, plays, and music. Each issue offers a number of well-written reviews in each field. The drama reviews are my favorite since I was in the drama club in high school. My advisor thought I should major in drama in college, but my parents persuaded me to pursue a more practical field. Another reason *Cosmopolitan* is entertaining is because it has great short stories and fun quizzes to read and complete. Last, when I want to get ideas for decorating, fashions, hairstyles, or menus, I only have to pick up the latest issue of *Cosmopolitan*.

Identify exactly what is wrong with the paragraph:

____

____

Now make the necessary corrections to the paragraph.

The paragraphs in Exercises 29 and 30 contain a main idea and relevant details, but there is a problem with the way each one is organized. Read the paragraph and answer the questions that follow.

EXERCISE 29

There are a few important differences between communicating by phone and communicating by letter. A telephone call, of course, is more convenient. It not only takes less time, but it allows me to talk to someone immediately. Also, I feel closer to a person when I can talk to him and hear his voice. Another reason is that I am sure to get an answer if I talk to someone on the phone. If I send someone a letter, I may never get an answer.

Identify exactly what is wrong with the paragraph:

____

____

Now make the necessary corrections to the paragraph.

EXERCISE 30

Washing windows can be easy if you just follow a few simple steps. The first step is to squirt the window with the window cleaner and wipe the window with a paper towel, making sure to get all the corners. Next, wipe the window dry with another towel or cloth. Use a commercial window cleaner like "Windex" or prepare your own solution with ammonia and water. You should use cotton towels or paper towels because these will not smear the window or leave lint on it. After you finish the bottom window, follow the same procedure on the top window. Do the outside of the windows first.

Identify exactly what is wrong with the paragraph:

____

____

Now make the necessary corrections to the paragraph.

For each of the paragraphs in Exercises 31–34, construct a detailed outline on a separate sheet of paper.

*EXERCISE 31

There are several reasons why the death penalty should be abolished. To begin with, it is inhumane. The U.S. Constitution forbids "cruel and unusual punishment," and the electric chair and gas chamber are certainly cruel and unusual punishments. Also, there is no guarantee that the sentence will be given without regard to sex or race. In the past, a poor man or woman was much more likely to receive the death sentence than a rich man or woman, even if they were both guilty of the same crime. Last, there is absolutely no evidence to indicate that the death penalty would significantly reduce the amount of crime in our society. Every major study that has been done so far has concluded that individuals convicted of violent crimes do not usually think about the crime before they commit it, so the thought of the death penalty would not even occur to them.

*EXERCISE 32

Making an attractive flower bed is a lot of fun, and it does not take very long to do if these simple steps are followed. The first thing to do is to find a well-lighted location where the soil is loose and relatively free of stones. Next, gather together your tools (especially something to dig with), fertilizer, seeds, plants, and water. Now the real action begins. Start by clearing an area the size you want your flower bed to be, and then turn over the soil in that area. Remove as many weeds as possible from the area, and mix the fertilizer in with the soil according to the directions on the package. Rake the soil smooth. Now read the directions on the seed package to learn how deep and how far apart to plant the seeds. After planting the seeds, cover them with soil and water them thoroughly. Be sure to water your flower bed every day until the plants are showing. If you devote time and care to your flower bed, the result will be rewarding.

EXERCISE 33

I personally enjoy the summer months rather than the bitter cold winter. Summer is the fun time of the year, a time for vacations and weekend trips. I love to visit the various beaches and amusement parks. In the summer outdoor adventures are everywhere. There are carnivals, festivals, water skiing, surfing, camping, and fishing, just to name a few. Needless to say, the air is always filled with the sweet fragrance of flowers. Unfortunately, though, summer does not last forever. Soon winter comes along, signaling a time to stay indoors and read a book or watch television. The only outdoor adventures in the winter are the bitter cold weather, the blizzards, harsh and howling winds, sleet, hail, and icicles. To venture out in the winter is to risk frostbite or a broken limb from a slip on a patch of ice. Instead of the aroma of flowers, the winter air is filled only with a dry coldness that makes your head ache when you breathe. You can have the winter wonderland; give me the sunshine and warmth anytime.

EXERCISE 34

Although my new job pays less than my old job, there are several good reasons for taking a cut in pay. My new job is closer to home, for one thing. Now I can walk to work in the morning. This means that I can sleep later in the morning, get home earlier in the evening, and spend less on transportation during the work week. The new job also has great benefits. After my first year on the job, I get four weeks of vacation time, three weeks of sick leave if I need it, and five personal days. In addition, the company pays for my hospitalization insurance. Another reason for taking the job is that there are more opportunities for advancement. I may be starting at a lower rate, but I expect to be advancing very quickly. The company has a record of hiring all of its top-level executives from within the company. My final reason for accepting the job is security. I would rather work for an old, established firm, even at a lower rate, than with a new firm that may have to lay off all of its employees as soon as it runs into difficulties.

11 / The essay

WHAT IS AN ESSAY?

In some of your writing assignments, you have probably felt that you could have written more than just a single paragraph. This is particularly true when you have a very strong opinion on an issue or when the list of ideas you begin with is extremely long. The **essay** is a form of writing that allows a writer to develop ideas in greater detail. Whether a writer conveys an idea in a single paragraph or in an essay depends entirely upon the writer's purpose. If the purpose can be achieved within a single paragraph, then that one paragraph is enough. If the purpose demands a more extensive treatment than is possible in a single paragraph, then an essay might be a more appropriate form. The difference between a paragraph and an essay is the *extent of development*. The best way to see this is to look at both a paragraph and an essay written on the same topic.

Topic: If you had a choice, would you prefer to live in the city or in the country? Indicate which you would choose and explain why you would prefer it.

Paragraph

There are several reasons why I would prefer living in the country to living in the city. First of all is the matter of healthful living. In the city I am constantly breathing in noxious fumes from the millions of cars and the dozens of factories. In the country, the air is fresh and pure, and there are rarely enough cars or factories to pollute it. Secondly, I am tired of living a life of constant fear. Every day the newspapers and the evening news reports are full of stories about robberies, gang wars, and murders throughout the city. There is crime in the country too, of course, but there is a lot less of it. In most country towns, it's an event when the local police officer stops a car to issue a traffic ticket. But the most important reason for picking a place to live has to be the people. The people in my apartment house live only a few feet away from each other, yet most of them live solitary lives, and they barricade themselves in every night to protect themselves from their neighbors. Country people, on the other hand, need each other. Life in the country can be difficult without friends to help, so neighbors stay close and are always available to lend a hand. In the country there's a real feeling that the people care about each other. Because I value my health, don't like being afraid all the time, and do like people, country living is for me.

This is an effective paragraph. It has a clear main idea that is supported by effective reasons and details, and it ends with a good concluding sentence. But it could be made more effective still by the addition of specific examples. Look at what happens when this paragraph is expanded into an essay:

Model 1

The Country Life

Life in the country is by no means perfect. People who live in the country usually have to travel great distances to do things that city inhabitants take for granted—like shopping. Unemployment, too, is a bigger problem in the country, where there is not nearly as much industry as there is in the city. In spite of these hardships, however, I'd much rather live in the country than in the city. Country living is sometimes more difficult, but it is definitely healthier, safer, and friendlier than life in the city.

First of all is the matter of healthful living. The air pollution in cities is often frightful. Not only are there millions of cars coming into the city during the day and speeding back out to the suburbs in the evening, but there are also factories everywhere, belching black smoke into the air that people need to breathe. Country people don't suffer from these problems. "Rush hour" in the country is when you see more than two cars on a road at any one time. And although the lack of factories may make jobs hard to find, it also makes the air considerably cleaner to breathe.

Secondly, I am tired of living a life of constant fear. Every day the newspapers and the evening news reports are full of stories about robberies, gang wars, and murders throughout the city. I've spent $150.00 on deadbolt locks, and I still don't feel secure in my own house. There's no such thing as an evening walk for a city-dweller; you either drive or run as fast as you can. There is crime in the country towns too, but a lot less of it. The only "gang" you'll find in most country towns is the group of men who exchange gossip at the fire hall. A "crime wave" in the country is when the local sheriff catches some teenagers drinking beer out at the railroad tracks.

But the most important reason for picking a place to live has to be the people. The people in my apartment house live only a few feet away from each other, yet most of them live solitary lives, and they barricade themselves in every night to protect themselves from their neighbors. All of those deadbolt locks I've invested in not only protect me from the criminals, they also hide me from my neighbors. And the stories of some unfortunate person's calls for help being ignored by people who don't want to get involved are all too common by now. Country people, on the other hand, do get involved. Life in the country can be difficult without friends to help, so neighbors stay close and are always available to lend a hand. When a roof needs mending or firewood has to be cut for someone who is ill, there's never a shortage of volunteers to do the job. In the country, the word "community" really means something: the people care about each other.

There's no such thing as a perfect place to live. No matter whether the location is the city, the suburbs, or the country, there will be no shortage of problems. But for me, living in the country has much more in the way of advantages than does living in the city. Because I value my health, don't like being afraid all of the time, and do like people, country living is for me.

The Structure of an Essay

Because the essay form allows a writer to develop ideas in greater detail and provide more examples, the essay is more *convincing* than the paragraph; therefore, it is more effective in accomplishing the writer's purpose. As we'll see now by comparing the paragraph with the essay, the essay is just an *expanded paragraph* with an *introduction*, a *body*, and a *conclusion*. The following table illustrates how a paragraph can be expanded into an essay.

Paragraph	***Essay***
Main Idea	Introduction Paragraph Introduction Thesis statement
Support 1 Detail	Body Paragraph 1 Main idea Support
Support 2 Detail	Body Paragraph 2 Main idea Support
Support 3 Detail	Body Paragraph 3 Main idea Support
	Conclusion Paragraph Summary Conclusion

An **introduction paragraph** in an essay introduces the topic, captures the reader's attention, and presents the main idea for the essay, usually called the **thesis**. Notice in the introduction paragraph of the sample essay that the writer begins by making some statements that are the *opposite* of the point the essay will make. This is one effective technique of introduction that can be used to interest the reader. Usually, the introduction paragraph in an essay concludes with a **thesis statement**, which often mentions how the thesis will be supported. The final sentence of the introduction paragraph does just this: it states the writer's opinion and indicates why the writer believes this to be true. Also notice that the thesis statement of the essay states the same main idea as that used in the sample paragraph.

In the sample paragraph, the main idea is followed by the first supporting reason. In the essay, the first supporting reason makes up the first paragraph of the part of the essay called the **body**. Notice that the three sentences that make up the support in the sample paragraph are used to express the main ideas for the three paragraphs that make up the body of the essay. These main ideas are then expanded and supported with more specific details in each of the paragraphs in the essay. The body of "The Country Life" essay contains three supporting paragraphs. There is no absolute number of supporting paragraphs that the body of a paragraph must have. The rule for support in an essay is the same as the rule for support in a paragraph: the amount of support needed is the amount it takes to convince the reader of your thesis, or main idea.

The body of the essay is followed by a paragraph of **conclusion**. Usually, the conclusion paragraph *summarizes* or briefly *restates* the points made in the body of the essay. Notice in the sample essay that the concluding paragraph contains a brief summary of the reasons for the writer's opinion, along with a final restatement of the thesis.

Of course, not all essays are the same, either in content or in structure. The five-paragraph structure of "The Country Life" is the format usually suggested to beginning writers because it is simple, effective, and three supporting paragraphs are usually enough to adequately illustrate or defend a main idea. But sometimes you will want to vary this structure to suit your purpose. Remember, the key to deciding what structure to use is to decide which structure will make your writing more *convincing*. The following student essay, "The Athletes Come First," shows a variation of the structure used in "The Country Life."

Model 2

The Athletes Come First

Carol is a high school senior who plays piano. Throughout her four years of senior high school, she has earned nothing but A's and B's in her courses, and she has been a key member of the high school band. In addition, Carol has entered some local music competitions and has won first prize several times. All of Carol's teachers agree that she is a bright, promising student, but her music teachers, especially, think her potential as a musician or composer is boundless. Robert, a classmate of Carol's, couldn't be more different. Having always regarded school work as a form of agony, Robert avoided it throughout high school and passed his courses only with the greatest difficulty. Like Carol, Robert has a special interest at which he excels and for which he is widely acclaimed, but it is not music. It is football. Both Carol and Robert come from families that cannot afford the expense of a higher education. That is where all similarities end. While Carol has not been able to find a way to continue her education in music, Robert has been swamped with scholarship offers. Because he can play football, Robert—not Carol—will be going to college this fall.

The story of Carol and Robert is all too true today in American colleges. While the injustices of the system to the nonathletes—the Carols—are obvious, the system is also damaging to the athletes. The message that colleges are sending to high school athletes is that academic work is not very important and that the ability to play games will get you anything you want.

In the attention they devote to their athletic programs, colleges are sending a loud and clear message to high school students throughout the country. The message is simple: games are more important than academic achievement. At most major universities in the United States, the athletic programs not only get the bulk of the publicity, they also get a major share of the institution's budget. While the music department is told that there is no money for the piano it needs, the athletic department is installing the newest type of Astroturf in the football field. The most noticeable of these inequities is in the area of scholarships. The purely academic scholarship has become a thing of the past at many institutions, while you can rest assured that every player on the football and basketball teams at the university is there on a total scholarship. Advocates of college football and basketball defend the imbalance by pointing to the amount of revenue that these two sports bring into the university. But that is precisely where the problem lies. The universities have adopted the profit motive and are more concerned about making money than they are about the students they serve.

Contrary to popular belief, the student athletes are usually not the winners in this game. They, too, become victims of the universities' disproportionate attention to sports. The high school stars who get the football scholarships go to college with one goal in mind: to play professional football. As a result, football is what they concentrate on in college, not academics. It's not hard to see where they got this idea: this pattern of behavior in high school earned them a scholarship, so how important can school work really be? The bubble bursts after the player has played in his final college game, for it is then that he learns that he is not good enough to be a professional player. In fact, only about one of every hundred college players ever makes a career of professional football, and the ratio is similar for other sports. All of the players think of themselves as an O.J. Simpson or Doug Flutie, but only one such player—out of the legions who play college football—is likely to emerge in a given year.

The facts of the matter suggest that Robert will not be a professional athlete. About half of the time, he will drop out of college because he is totally unprepared for it academically. If he "graduates," he'll have no real skills or abilities, other than a knack for catching or throwing a football. Who is responsible? Robert—the athlete—himself, of course. But the colleges and universities that promote the value of athletics over that of academics, and then feed the athletes' illusions with more pipe dreams, must also share a large part of the blame.

Can you explain how these two essays differ? First, the introduction of "Country Life" begins with a statement that is the opposite of the thesis, and then the paragraph provides a thesis sentence and a plan of development. "Athletes," on the other hand, begins with an **anecdote**—a story to attract the reader's interest. This is another effective method of introduction because it draws the reader into the essay. Notice that the writer of "Athletes" devoted much more development to the introduction than did the writer of "Country Life." There is another important difference as well. What is the thesis sentence of "Athletes?" Where does it appear in the essay?

You are correct if you identified the final sentence of the second paragraph as the thesis sentence. In this essay, the introductory paragraph is quite extensive and tells a little "story" all by itself. Rather than disrupt the natural flow of that "story," the writer decided to let it stand on its own, as an example that illustrates the thesis. Then, in the second paragraph, the writer presented the thesis in a more straightforward way.

Now take a look at the rest of the essay. How did the writer of "Athletes" support the thesis? How many major supporting elements are there? Instead of the three supporting paragraphs used in "Country Life," there are just two in "Athletes." Is this acceptable? Again, the issue is not the *quantity* of support but rather the *quality* of it. If the writer supports the thesis convincingly, the support is adequate. In the case of "Athletes," the two supporting paragraphs are effective at explaining two major aspects of the athletic scholarship issue. Also, because the extensive introduction serves to illustrate the nature of the problem, it, too, strengthens the support for the thesis.

Finally, "Athletes," like "Country Life," ends with a conclusion paragraph that brings the reader back to the original anecdote and serves to "wrap up" the arguments the writer has presented. The final sentence of the concluding paragraph is a forceful restatement of the essay's thesis sentence.

Thus, both "Country Life" and "Athletes" are five-paragraph essays, but they differ significantly in structure. The form of "Athletes" could be represented by the following outline:

The Athletes Come First

Paragraph 1:	Introduction Anecdote
Paragraph 2:	Presentation of thesis
Paragraph 3:	First major support
Paragraph 4:	Second major support
Paragraph 5:	Conclusion

As you begin to write essays, you should follow the five-paragraph model presented in "Country Life." But, after you've had some practice and have written a few different essays, you needn't feel that every essay you write *must* fit that particular mold. Let your purpose for writing and the content of what you are writing dictate the form you should use to convey the message effectively. Your final criterion for evaluating your essay should not necessarily be "Does it have five paragraphs?" but rather "Does the essay convince the reader of my thesis?"

WRITING AN INTRODUCTION PARAGRAPH

As was discussed earlier, the introduction paragraph is very important to the success of your essay. It is in the introduction paragraph that you must capture the reader's interest and present the thesis that will control the development of your essay. This section illustrates several methods that can be used to write an effective introduction paragraph.

Method 1: General to Specific

Americans tend to be a society that values credentials. We believe that a doctor with a degree from Harvard is better than a doctor who graduated from anywhere else, and that a "certified" plumber is better able to fix a leaky faucet than a plumber without a certificate. Most of the credentials are earned, directly or indirectly, by taking tests. And most of the tests are standardized to ensure that they are as "fair" as possible. It may be that our use of credentials is a necessary and important feature of American life. But the route to those credentials—whether it is a high school diploma or a graduate school degree—needs to be called in question. Standardized testing is a dehumanizing and frequently inaccurate method of measuring student achievement.

The movement from **general to specific** is the method most often used to introduce a thesis. This introduction paragraph moves from the very broad—Americans and the value they place on credentials—to the specific thesis—what is wrong with standardized testing. By beginning with the broader aspect of credentials, the writer has made the link between testing, which will be the subject of the essay, and its applications in American society. Thus, in addition to providing an effective introduction, this paragraph sets up a context within which the discussion of testing is important. In short, the paragraph effectively demonstrates the subject's importance so that the reader will become interested in it.

Method 2: Opposites

Americans have great faith in technology. We put a man on the Moon, we can walk in space, and we believe we can solve all problems. This faith in technology and science pervades the realm of education, too, where it takes the form of standardized tests. As children we are given achievement tests in school year after year and informed, as if by magic, that we can read, or can't read, or can read but not as well as 47.5% of our classmates. In high school the testing barrage becomes greater—and more important. Now our test scores not only indicate what skills we do or do not have, they serve as licenses—to go to college, to graduate school, to the professions. And we all march dutifully to the tune of the scores spit out by the computer, impressed by the efficiency of it all and doubting, when we doubt at all, only our own inability to perform to the demands of the test. But it is the tests—and not ourselves—that we should be doubting. Standardized testing is a dehumanizing and frequently inaccurate method of measuring student achievement.

The **opposites** is another often-used and effective method of introduction. As you can see from the example, paragraphs using this method begin by making a point opposite to the point made in the thesis sentence. This is an effective technique especially when the thesis challenges a commonly held belief. By first subscribing to the belief, the writer secures the reader's agreement, and thus the reader's attention. Then, while the reader is feeling agreement with the points made, the thesis forces the reader to question some of those commonly held beliefs.

Method 3: Anecdote

It is 7:45 on a Saturday morning, and you are standing in line in a hallway at a school you've never been to before. The line crawls forward as each young person pauses before a grouchy, intimidating old man who seems to hate young people and clearly does not want to be there. You timidly present to him the papers that prove you are who you claim to be. The man gruffly dictates your seat number and permits you to enter the room, but you can sense that he does not believe you are really the person whose name is on your papers. You sit uncomfortably in a straight-backed wooden desk chair and stare straight ahead, knowing that if you speak to anyone you'll be branded as a cheater. For the next several hours you will be asked to answer questions—many of which will seem to have no reasonable answer—and the results will be used to decide the course of the rest of your life. A nightmare? No, this scenario is a reality for almost all high school seniors who aspire to a college career. It is the ultimate experience in standardized testing, a dehumanizing and frequently inaccurate method of measuring student achievement.

The **anecdote** method is often the most effective way to capture the reader's attention because it engages the reader in a story. As a writer, you can rely on the fact that everybody loves a good story, and you can use that fact to bring your reader step-by-step through an illustration that leads directly to your thesis sentence. The first paragraph of "The Athletes Come First" is another example of an introduction paragraph that uses the anecdote method.

Method 4: Quote from One or More Authorities

John Fredericks, a prominent educational psychologist, has this to say about standardized tests: "The whole concept of standardized testing came about because it is more economical to test large groups of people than it is to test them individually. Also, testing groups according to rigid procedures allows for comparisons of the groups. Those are good reasons. But standardized tests have become something of a good idea gone wild. They are overused, and people place entirely too much faith in their results." Fredericks's view is typical of a growing number of professionals in the field of educational measurement today. Increasing numbers of experts have begun to view standardized testing as a dehumanizing and frequently inaccurate method of measuring student achievement.

A little research will often produce a **statement by an expert** that supports your thesis or explains the nature of the issue you are treating. Because readers respect expertise, an expert's opinion can be effective at drawing a reader into an essay. Of course, the more familiar the name and reputation of the expert, the more likely they are to attract and hold your reader's attention. It is better to quote a household name, even if the opinion opposes your thesis. For example: "Freud was a big believer in the value of standardized testing, but in this respect, at least, the great expert was mistaken." Readers will continue to read an essay that begins this way, if only because you have challenged the opinion of a noted authority.

In addition to the methods of introduction illustrated above, there are several other possibilities. Sometimes it is useful to open a paragraph with a **rhetorical question**, such as "Just how fair are standardized tests?" A word of caution, however: be careful not to overuse this technique. Still another option is to list a **series of headlines** about the issue to illustrate its importance and topicality. Finally, it is possible in some cases to combine two or more of the introductory methods described here.

One *ineffective* method students frequently use to introduce a thesis is to announce their intentions. For example: "In this essay I will show that standardized testing is a dehumanizing and frequently inaccurate method of measuring student achievement." *This is one method to avoid.* It is ineffective as an introduction because it fails to involve the reader in the issue you are addressing, and it does not make a very convincing assertion. The more direct statement that "standardized testing is a dehumanizing and frequently inaccurate method of measuring student achievement" tells the reader in much more forceful terms what you think of the issue and how you plan to support your position. In short, don't *tell* the reader how you are organized; let your thesis *show* it.

WRITING ASSIGNMENT 18

Write an essay on any one of the following topics. After you finish writing the essay, check to make sure you have an effective introduction paragraph, enough support in the body paragraphs, and an effective concluding paragraph. Proofread your essay and correct any errors that you find.

Topics

1. Write an essay in which you argue that city living is better than country living.
2. Write an essay telling about the best house you ever lived in and explaining why it was the best.
3. Write an essay naming the person now living who has had the greatest influence on your life. Explain how that person has influenced you.
4. Write an essay presenting the benefits of college athletic programs.

PRACTICE EXERCISES

EXERCISE 1

Write!

Select any two of the following thesis statements and write an introduction paragraph *for each one. Make sure that the introduction paragraph includes the thesis sentence and an indication of how you will support the thesis.*

1. State lotteries do nothing but encourage citizens to waste their money on pipe dreams.
2. The problem of teenage gangs is the result of serious inequities in our economic system.

3. Parallel parking scares the wits out of most new drivers, but it's really not that hard to learn.
4. There are several reasons why I decided to go to college.
5. Several things happened to me after I was late for my mathematics class for the tenth time.
6. Elma and Irma are so different you'd never guess that they are sisters.
7. A fly rod and a shotgun look quite different to most people, but fishing and hunting are really pretty similar.
8. Golf is the only professional sport left that is truly a game for gentlemen and ladies.

EXERCISE 2 *Not all of the thesis sentences in Exercise 1 necessarily require three supporting paragraphs. Indicate which sentences could be developed with a structure* other than *that used for "The Country Life." Be prepared to defend your answers.*

EXERCISE 3

Write!

Return to any one of the paragraphs or outlines you wrote in Chapter 10. Prepare an outline that you could use to expand the paragraph into an essay, including an introduction and a conclusion.

12 / Learn the apostrophe

In the first three parts of this book you learned and practiced using the basic elements of writing: words, sentences, and paragraphs. Here you will learn about some of the smaller elements of writing, including punctuation, capitalization, and some words that are frequently misspelled. As you work through this part of the book, keep in mind that, even though you may now be able to write complete sentences and well-organized paragraphs, what you write cannot be understood by your reader if it is not properly punctuated. Similarly, if your writing contains numerous "minor" errors, your writing will not be as convincing as it could be.

In this chapter you will learn the two main uses of the apostrophe: (1) to form contractions; (2) to show possession.

CONTRACTIONS

One use of the apostrophe is to form contractions. A **contraction** is a word or phrase that has been shortened by leaving out one or more letters. The following list includes many of the most common contractions:

Phrase	*Contraction*
I am	I'm
you are	you're
he is	he's

it is	it's
she is	she's
we are	we're
they are	they're
I have	I've
you have	you've
it has	it's
he has	he's
she has	she's
they have	they've
I had	I'd
you had	you'd
he had	he'd
they had	they'd
I will	I'll
I would	I'd
you will	you'll
you would	you'd
he will	he'll
she would	she'd
they will	they'll
they would	they'd
is not	isn't
does not	doesn't
do not	don't
did not	didn't
has not	hasn't
was not	wasn't
should not	shouldn't
could not	couldn't

Notice that the function of the apostrophe in these contractions is to take the place of the missing letter or letters. The apostrophe is a signal to the reader that a letter or several letters have been left out.

You may have noticed that certain contractions can be used in place of different phrases.

he is = he's	they had = they'd
he has = he's	they would = they'd

The meaning of the sentence in which one of these contractions is used will indicate which phrase is being shortened.

HE IS
I heard that *he's going* on vacation.

HE HAS
I heard that *he's gone* on vacation.

THEY HAD
We all hoped *they'd recovered* from their illness.

THEY WOULD
We all hoped *they'd recover* from their illness.

For a further description of the differences between helping verbs (including "is," "has," "had," "would"), see Chapters 7 and 8.

PRACTICE EXERCISES

*EXERCISE 1 *In the following exercise, form a contraction for the phrase that is provided. Do this by leaving out the letters that are in parentheses and using an apostrophe to signal that the letter or letters have been left out.*

	Phrase	***Contraction***
1.	can(no)t	______________
2.	we (ha)d	______________
3.	I (ha)ve	______________
4.	would n(o)t	______________
5.	she (ha)d	______________
6.	she (ha)s	______________
7.	does n(o)t	______________
8.	were n(o)t	______________
9.	are n(o)t	______________
10.	did n(o)t	______________

*EXERCISE 2 *In this exercise, the letters that are to be omitted in the contraction have not been indicated for you. Form a contraction for each phrase and be sure to place the apostrophe correctly.*

	Phrase	***Contraction***
1.	has not	________________
2.	you will	________________
3.	he will	________________
4.	he is	________________
5.	it is	________________
6.	they are	________________
7.	should not	________________
8.	you are	________________
9.	I will	________________
10.	was not	________________

The contracted form of ''will not'' is a special case: in addition to substituting an apostrophe for one or more letters, in ''will not'' the ''-ill'' is replaced by an ''o'':

will not = won't (NOT willn't)

The purpose of a contraction is to shorten phrases so that they are easier to say. Writing that imitates speech or uses a conversational tone is called **informal writing**. Since informal writing often ''sounds'' like conversation, contractions may be appropriate. However, contractions should not be used in formal writing. Be sure to ask your instructor to explain his or her policy regarding the use of contractions in your paragraphs.

There are a number of other good reasons why you will want to avoid using contractions. As you go through the section on possessives, you will notice that many of the possessive pronouns look and sound like some of the contractions. This can sometimes become pretty confusing; if you do not use contractions, you will eliminate the confusion. Also, the use of contractions often presents special problems in subject-verb agreement. For example, if you use contractions in the present tense, you must remember that "don't" can be used only with plural subjects and "doesn't" should be used with singular ones. If you avoid the contractions, the decision is easier because "does not" has an *-s* ending.

In short, contractions are convenient to use in conversation and in informal writing. However, in formal writing contractions are usually considered inappropriate, and they frequently present more problems than they are worth.

POSSESSIVES

Singular Nouns

The second use of the apostrophe is to show possession. Look at the following examples:

the car belonging to the boy	= the *boy's* car
the average of the player	= the *player's* average
the radio belonging to the girl	= the *girl's* radio

As you can see, a possessive is formed by adding an apostrophe and an "s" to the noun that possesses something.

Some singular nouns already end in *-s*.

bus   Mr. Jones   hostess

Most writers form a possessive with these nouns in the same way as with other singular nouns: by adding an apostrophe and *-s*.

the bus's windshield
Mr. Jones's house
the hostess's uniform

PRACTICE EXERCISE

*EXERCISE 3 *Form a possessive from the following phrases by adding an apostrophe and an -s to the appropriate noun.*

Phrase	*Possessive*
1. The skateboard belonging to the boy	________________
2. The leaves of the tree	________________
3. The car of Bess	________________
4. The star of the team	________________
5. The policy of the school	________________
6. The hubcaps of the car	________________
7. The commission of the salesman	________________
8. The apron of the waitress	________________
9. The performance of the singer	________________
10. The rating of the movie	________________
11. The hair of Susan	________________
12. The favorite show of Clark	________________
13. The job of Mrs. Andrews	________________
14. The ingenuity of Cheryl	________________
15. The clear voice of the actor	________________
16. The tone of the radio	________________
17. The complaint of the mistress	________________
18. The appearance of the husband	________________

19. The reputation of the museum ______________________

20. The greatest concern of Carol ______________________

Plural Nouns

The apostrophe is also used to show possession with plural nouns. The rule for forming a possessive with a singular noun is to add an apostrophe and an *-s*. Since most plural nouns already end in *-s*, the possessive is formed by simply adding an apostrophe *after* the *-s*. Look at the following examples.

the car belonging to the *boys*	= the *boys'* car
the average of the *players*	= the *players'* average
the radio belonging to the *girls*	= the *girls'* radio

Remember that some nouns form their plurals without adding *-s*. The possessive case for these nouns is formed the same way as it is for singular nouns. For example:

Singular	***Plural***
the man's boat	the men's boat
the child's toy	the children's toy
the woman's house	the women's house

PRACTICE EXERCISES

EXERCISE 4 *Form a possessive out of the following phrases:*

Phrase	***Possessive***
1. The exhaust of the jets	______________________
2. The leaves of the trees	______________________
3. The cushions of the chairs	______________________
4. The attitude of the boys	______________________
5. The softball game of the men	______________________
6. The food of the kittens	______________________

7. The roost of the chickens ____________________
8. The playground of the children ____________________
9. The voices of the singers ____________________
10. The clothes of the women ____________________
11. The nest of the birds ____________________
12. The fur of the animals ____________________
13. The test scores of the students ____________________
14. The concern of the parents ____________________
15. The reaction of the teachers ____________________
16. The ambitions of the children ____________________
17. The achievement of the women ____________________
18. The restlessness of the men ____________________
19. The jokes of the comedians ____________________
20. The remarks of the contestants ____________________

EXERCISE 5 *Form a possessive out of the following phrases. The nouns may be either singular or plural.*

Phrase	***Possessive***
1. The eyes of the rat	____________________
2. The apron of the cook	____________________
3. The book of the children	____________________
4. The crime of the teenager	____________________
5. The grades of the students	____________________
6. The dream of an old man	____________________
7. The wealth of the Senator	____________________

8. The idea of the scientists ______________________

9. The role of the actress ______________________

10. The salaries of the athletes ______________________

Possessive Pronouns

Recall from Chapter 2 that a pronoun is often used to replace a noun. To form the possessive of a noun, you must add an apostrophe and an *-s*, but this is not the case with pronouns. Each subject pronoun has its own special form to indicate possession. Look at the following list:

Subject Pronoun	*Possessive Pronoun*
I	my
you	your
he	his
she	her
it	its
we	our
they	their

None of the possessive pronouns has an apostrophe. As was noted earlier, some possessive pronouns are often confused with some contractions. The easiest way to keep them clear in your mind is to remember that no possessive pronoun has an apostrophe. The three possessive pronouns that prove most troublesome for students are "your," "its," and "their."

Contraction		*Possessive Pronoun*	
you're	=you are	your	=possessive form of *you*
it's	=it is	its	=possessive form of *it*
they're	=they are	their	=possessive form of *they*

If you have used one of these words in a sentence and you are not sure whether to use the contraction or the possessive pronoun, try spelling out the contraction in the sentence. Look at the following example:

Sentence: She thinks *you're* house is beautiful.

To check the contraction, spell it out:

Test: She thinks *you are* house is beautiful.

Obviously, this does not make sense, so the possessive form should be used:

Corrected sentence: She thinks *your* house is beautiful.

You can perform the same test with any of the contractions to make sure you are using them correctly.

Sentence: The old dog has lost *it's* teeth.
Test: The old dog has lost *it is* teeth.
Correction: The old dog has lost *its* teeth.

Sentence: The newlyweds are on *they're* honeymoon.
Test: The newlyweds are on *they are* honeymoon.
Correction: The newlyweds are on *their* honeymoon.

Remember these two important points about the possessive pronouns:

1. None of the possessive pronouns has an apostrophe.
2. You can avoid all confusion between possessive pronouns and contractions if you simply avoid using any contractions.

PRACTICE EXERCISES

EXERCISE 6 *In the following sentences, correct any errors in the use or spelling of the possessive pronouns.*

1. Diane and Fred said they have lost they're ticket.
2. After the game, his pants were ripped and his' arm hurt.
3. The tree has caterpillar nests in all it's branches.
4. Our favorite television show is on tonight.
5. He thought he would be able to fix you're car.
6. They're house has a built-in swimming pool in the yard.
7. The duck is calling for it's mate.
8. When will he get a chance to meet you're cousin?

9. They have made they're decision, and now they're going to live with it.
10. The problem with my car is that its body is all rusted out.

*EXERCISE 7 *In the following sentences, circle the correct form of the words in parentheses.*

1. (They're, Their) going to have (they're, their) party whether it rains or not.
2. I understand that (your, you're) going to visit (your, you're) relatives in England this year.
3. (They're, Their) looking everywhere for (they're, their) lost dog.
4. (Its, It's) a shame that the old horse has lost (its, it's) teeth.
5. Happiness is knowing that (your, you're) going to pass all (you're, your) courses.

EXERCISE 8 *Write five sentences of your own, using each of the following possessive pronouns at least once.*

Write!

its your their

1. ______________________________
____
2. ______________________________
____
3. ______________________________
____
4. ______________________________
____
5. ______________________________
____

EXERCISE 9 *Proofread the following sentence groups and correct any errors in the use or spelling of the possessive pronouns.*

1. They spent weeks looking at different kinds of campers and trailers before they decided which one they wanted. Now they are planning a cross-country vacation so they can try out they're new camper.
2. When I first learned how to drive, my father was very nervous when he sat in the car with me. Any time I started to go over thirty miles per hour he would start giving advice: "If you don't slow down you'll get a ticket and lose you're license."
3. We always liked the big house on the corner. It had about twenty different rooms, three floors, and a magnificent garden. It's enclosed porch was what we liked more than anything else.
4. He tried to describe the exotic bird to the expert, but all he could remember was that it's wings were bright blue and it's call was a loud and ringing Bleep! Bleep!
5. They intended to paint the house on Saturday, so Norm prepared a lot of sandwiches and snacks. Unfortunately, only one person arrived to help out, so they're consumption of sandwiches and snacks surpassed the amount of painting they got done.

CHAPTER REVIEW

In this chapter you learned to use the apostrophe in two ways: (1) to form contractions, and (2) to show possession. You also learned two other important points:

1. Contractions are acceptable in speech and informal writing, but are generally considered unacceptable in formal writing. In addition, the use of contractions often creates confusion when the possessive pronouns are used. So, you should probably not use contractions in your college papers.

2. When showing possession with a pronoun instead of a noun, the apostrophe is not used; instead, a special set of possessive pronouns is used. There is a possessive pronoun for each of the subject pronouns.

SUPPLEMENTAL EXERCISES

Now apply your knowledge by proofreading for errors in the use of the apostrophe. Each of the following paragraphs (Exercises 10 and 11) contains some errors in the use of the apostrophe; the errors may be in the formation of contractions, the formation of possessive nouns, or the use or spelling of the possessive pronouns. Correct any errors that you find. You may want to eliminate any contractions you find by spelling out the phrase completely.

*EXERCISE 10

Its always more fun to plan something than it is actually to do it. This became quite clear to me a few years ago when my friend John and I were planning a trip to Italy. For weeks before we left, we spent every free moment discussing everything wed' do when we got there. Johns' greatest desire was to spend several day's touring the museums in Florence. Hed' read that they're displays were among the best in all of Europe. My ambitions were simpler. I only wanted to roam the streets of Venice, for Id' heard so much about it's charming alleys and canals. When we finally arrived at our destination, both John and I had imagined our adventures in such great detail that the actual experience was naturally less exciting than the imagined one. John saw Florences' art treasures, and I strolled through Venice, but both of us could'nt help feeling a bit sad that the great adventure was actually under way.

EXERCISE 11

Most people agree that the Sixties were exciting years, and the most eventful year of them all was 1968. It was in 1968 that students and young people throughout the world decided that their lives were being controlled by those in power. In Paris, students' nearly succeeded in overthrowing the French government. In the United States, the young people made they're biggest move at the Democratic National Convention and at Columbia University. The year was also marked by a great deal of violence. The Vietnam War was at its height, Russia's tanks invaded Czechoslovakia, and two of America's leaders—Martin Luther King and Robert Kennedy—were assassinated. The year was not without it's achievements in science, either. It was in 1968 that an American spacecraft successfully orbited the Moon and sent home dramatic closeup pictures of the Moon's surface. Its simply amazing that so many important events could've occurred in twelve short months.

13 / Learn to use the comma

The comma is one of the most frequently misused marks of punctuation in writing. It is an important part of writing because it signals the reader to pause for a particular reason. The key to using the comma correctly is knowing why you are using it. There are many different rules governing the use of the comma, but if you just learn the few that are presented in this chapter, and then use the comma only when you know why you are using it, your punctuation will be correct most of the time.

COMPLEX AND COMPOUND SENTENCES

Recall from Chapter 4 that a comma is often required in complex and compound sentences. A comma separates the dependent and independent clauses in a *complex sentence* when the sentence begins with the dependent clause. (The dependent clause often begins with one of the conditional words.)

CONDITIONAL WORD — DEPENDENT CLAUSE — COMMA — INDEPENDENT CLAUSE

When she unlocked the door to her apartment, she smelled the smoke.

If the independent clause comes first, no comma is required.

INDEPENDENT CLAUSE — NO COMMA — CONDITIONAL WORD — DEPENDENT CLAUSE

She smelled the smoke when she unlocked the door to her apartment.

A comma separates the two independent clauses in a *compound sentence* when one of the connecting words is used ("and," "but," "for," "or," "so").

INDEPENDENT CLAUSE   COMMA + CONNECTING WORD   INDEPENDENT CLAUSE

Matt has already graduated, but he wants to keep going to school.

PRACTICE EXERCISE

*EXERCISE 1 *Punctuate the following complex and compound sentences according to the rules in this section and in Chapter 4.*

1. When Frank reads spy thrillers and mystery stories he really gets involved in the book.
2. Linda went to England for the summer and John went to summer school.
3. Although the police responded quickly they were too late to catch the jewel thief.
4. If the subways were cleaner and safer more people would use the public transportation.
5. There were plenty of people to help with the job but the paint ran out before the house was finished.
6. People think she is strange because she always wears one gold earring.
7. Since anything artificial is dangerous I eat only natural foods.
8. You must follow the directions carefully or you will get lost and spend the night in the wilds of the city.
9. Whenever I feel like smoking I get up and take the dog for a walk.
10. The most important thing in life is peace of mind and it is usually the hardest thing to find.

ITEMS IN A LIST

Use a comma to separate items when there are three or more items in a list. For example:

> We bought eggs, bacon, and butter at the store.

Note that in the example there are three items and two commas, one after the first item and one after the second. Use a comma after the next-to-last item in the series, even if it is followed by "and" (as in the example).

The items in a list may be of any type. The list could include names, numbers, actions, and so on.

> 1 2 3
> Everyone was there except Bruce, Susan, and Jeff.
>
> 1 2 3
> My three grades in algebra were a 95, an 84, and a 76.
>
> 1 2
> Last weekend *I washed and waxed the car*, *took the children to the baseball*
> 3
> *game*, and *took my wife out to dinner*.
>
> 1 2 3
> *They cause inflation*, *they damage the environment*, and *they pay no taxes*.

Of course, a list may include more than three items.

> 1 2
> The wrestler's lunch consisted of a *two-pound steak*, *a half-gallon of milk*, *a*
> 3 4
> *large bowl of fresh salad*, *a double serving of mashed potatoes*, and a *king-*
> 5
> *sized pumpkin pie*.

PRACTICE EXERCISE

*EXERCISE 2 *Punctuate the following sentences wherever necessary. Not all the sentences require commas.*

1. When you buy a car you should consider the gas mileage the frequency of repair and the cost of parts.

2. Before we leave the house we must close all the windows turn off all the lights and make sure the stove is turned off.
3. Everyone was content except Greg, Mike, and Larry.
4. He won the batting championship he hit the most home runs and he stole the most bases that year.
5. Washing dishes doing laundry and writing letters are the three things I hate the most.
6. The leaders of the camping trip were the scoutmaster the pastor of the church and three volunteer parents.
7. What is wrong with city life is that there are too much litter inadequate public transportation and inefficient public schools.
8. The mayor of any large city should have a college education at least ten years' experience at a high level of city government the ability to get along with many different types of people and the ability to speak in public without making a complete fool of himself or herself.
9. Success in college requires some brains, a fair amount of time, and an overwhelming desire to learn.
10. The sun was bright there was not a cloud in the sky a gentle breeze was blowing and the air had the fragrance of lilacs.

INTRODUCTORY WORDS AND PHRASES

Use a comma to separate an introductory word or phrase from the rest of the sentence. Remember that a phrase is a group of words that does not have both a verb and a subject. (For a full description of phrases, review Chapter 4.) There are many different types of introductory phrases.

To begin with, I want to know why I was asked to be here.
On Tuesday, they were supposed to go to the new flea market.
On the other hand, he is the most conceited person I know.
In the end, everyone thought the show was a big success.

The following list includes some other introductory words and phrases.* Each of these should be followed by a comma when it is used to introduce a sentence.

In the first place, . . .	Consequently, . . .
In the second place, . . .	Therefore, . . .
First of all, . . .	However, . . .
In my opinion, . . .	Nevertheless, . . .
As a matter of fact, . . .	In addition, . . .
To conclude, . . .	Also, . . .
Finally, . . .	Furthermore, . . .
In conclusion, . . .	Thus, . . .

PRACTICE EXERCISE

*EXERCISE 3 *Punctuate the following sentences wherever necessary. Not all of the sentences require commas.*

1. First of all there was a certain amount of work to do.
2. By the way the plant on the patio needs watering.
3. In February the roads are usually covered with snow.
4. In addition, they were not sure they were going in the right direction.
5. For one thing he has done an outstanding job.
6. For another thing he happens to be my son-in-law.
7. In some ways a newspaper reporter and a policeman are very much alike.
8. Consequently the Senator missed his morning appointment with his staff.

*For other introductory words, see Chapter 4

9. Therefore the Board of Education asked for an increased budget.

10. At last all of the work was finished.

INTERRUPTIONS

An interruption is a word or phrase that comes in the middle of a sentence and breaks up the natural flow of the sentence. Interruptions are always set off from the rest of the sentence by commas.

INTERRUPTION
Tom spent a weekend in Maine, for example, at his parents' expense.

INTERRUPTION
The end of pollution, therefore, is what Americans must fight for.

INTERRUPTION
The restaurant on the corner, by the way, serves fine pastries.

INTERRUPTION
My favorite subject, however, is American history.

Many of the words and phrases used in interruptions are the same as those used in introductions. The only difference is that interruptions come in the middle of the sentence and must be completely set off from the rest of the sentence by commas.

PRACTICE EXERCISES

---

*EXERCISE 4 *Punctuate the following sentences wherever necessary. Not all of the sentences require commas*

1. The solution to the problem however is not an easy one.

2. The cost of living for example increases every year.

3. Some of the victims by some kind of miracle were able to survive.

4. The grass is always greener for some reason on the other side of the fence.

5. The policeman, to my amazement, decided to let me go with just a warning.

6. The best example of her ability in my opinion is the way she reduced taxes.
7. The alternative it seems to me is perfectly obvious: he will be forced to resign.
8. My appetite by the way has improved enormously.
9. Their marriage, in the beginning, was like a domestic cold war.
10. I would like to point out in conclusion that this has been an educational experience.

EXERCISE 5

Write!

Now rewrite the sentences in Exercise 4, using the interrupting word or phrase as an introductory element. Be sure to punctuate each sentence correctly.

1. ______________________________

____

2. ______________________________

____

3. ______________________________

____

4. ______________________________

____

5. ______________________________

____

6. ______________________________

____

7. ______________________________

____

8. ______________________________

____

9. ____

____

10. ____

____

ADDRESSES AND DATES

The comma is used to separate the different elements in addresses and dates.

Addresses Use a comma to separate street name, city, and state.

STREET NAME CITY STATE
4360 Dixon Avenue, Fort Worth, Texas
14 Hoover Place, Denver, Colorado

If an additional element is used in the address, such as an apartment number, that too must be separated by a comma.

STREET NAME APARTMENT NUMBER CITY STATE
4360 Dixon Avenue, Apartment 114, Fort Worth, Texas

OFFICE INSTITUTION
Learning Resources Center, Pennsylvania State University

CITY STATE
College Park, Pennsylvania

In short, each separate element in an address must be separated from the other elements in the address.

If the address is written on several lines rather than on one line, as it would be on an envelope, the street element is separated from the city and state elements by being placed on a different line, so no comma is required.

4360 Dixon Avenue
Fort Worth, Texas

Dates Use commas to separate the name of the day, the date, and the year.

DAY DATE YEAR
Thursday, June 14, 1979

If the name of the day is not used, only one comma is required.

DATE YEAR
June 14, 1979

PRACTICE EXERCISE

*EXERCISE 6 *Punctuate the following sentences wherever necessary. Not all of the sentences require a comma.*

1. We once lived at 3240 Bay Drive Monterey California.
2. Her favorite city in the world is Cortina Italy.
3. On February 18 1972, a major snowstorm struck the city of Buffalo New York.
4. We moved to Apartment 112 1348 West Monroe Boulevard Cleveland Ohio, on March 22 1968.
5. Send your opinion to Congressman John Murphy Congressional Office Building Washington D.C.
6. The jet's arrival time was 1:20 P.M., August 4, 1977.
7. The project started in Fairbanks Alaska, on May 1 1969.
8. The judges on the panel are from Memphis Seattle Detroit and Miami.
9. The date of my anniversary, November 12 1951, is engraved on my ring.
10. The paper reported that the car had been stolen April 1, 1978, from Okaloosa County Florida.

CHAPTER REVIEW

The most important point to remember when using the comma is to know *why* you are using it. In this chapter you learned the most common uses of the comma. A comma is used:

1. a. To separate dependent and independent clauses in a complex sentence when the dependent clause comes first.
   b. To separate independent clauses in a compound sentence when a connecting word is used.
2. To separate items in a list including three or more items, names, actions, and so on.
3. To separate introductory words or phrases from the rest of the sentence.
4. To separate interrupting words or phrases from the rest of the sentence.
5. To separate the different elements in addresses and dates.

More errors in the use of the comma are due to *overuse* of it than to anything else. *If you do not know why you are using a comma, you probably do not need one.*

SUPPLEMENTAL EXERCISES

Exercises 7–9 contain errors in the use of the comma. The errors may involve any of the different uses of the comma that you have learned. In addition, some commas may not be necessary. Proofread the sentences and paragraphs, and correct any errors in the use of the comma.

EXERCISE 7

1. After I had traveled for many years, I decided that my favorite places were San Francisco Rome and a little place called Friendly Idaho.
2. The attorney's argument was very convincing, and he appeared certain to win his case. The defense attorney however had a surprise witness in reserve.

3. He finally decided to buy the imported car, since it got better gas mileage. In the end it was a good decision because the car was comfortable it cost less to drive and it was reliable.
4. Although, the train arrived at the station on time it was packed to the doors with passengers. We decided however that it would be better to squeeze into this train than wait for another hour.
5. Professional golfers make a lot of money; in addition they get to travel all over the country and stay at some very fancy country clubs.

EXERCISE 8

The other night I stayed up late, to finish reading a novel about political terrorists. When I finally went to bed I fell asleep right away. However it was not long before I was awakened by a strange scratching sound coming from the living room. My mind was still full of the political terrorists and their ghastly crimes so I got a baseball bat out of the closet and made my way as quietly as possible toward the scratching noise. I checked every window in the apartment, and did not find any terrorists. I decided therefore that they were attempting to get in through the patio door. I made my way in perfect silence to the door as the scratching sound grew louder, and louder. I pictured the terrorists on my patio, using a glass cutter to gain entry into my apartment for some deadly reason. At last, I was in position. I lunged toward the door, ripping away the curtains and preparing to attack the nearest terrorist. However instead of a terrorist what I discovered was my cat trying to get at a moth that had landed on the outside of the patio door. The cat looked up at me with a quizzical expression I considered using the baseball bat on the cat and then I put my weapon back in the closet and returned to bed.

14 / Learn capitalization

There are as many rules for capitalization as there are governing the use of the comma. Included in this chapter are those capitalization rules that you will need most often. The basic rule of capitalization is this: *capitalize only when something is specifically named.* Keep this rule in mind as you study the following examples.

1. Capitalize the first word in a sentence.

The train is expected to arrive on time.

2. Capitalize the pronoun "I," regardless of its position in the sentence.

I intend to report this to the manager.
The manager and *I* will discuss this.

3. Capitalize names, including:
   a. Names of people:

The idea was to surprise *F*rank.

   b. Names of languages and nationalities:

He speaks fluent *S*panish and *F*rench.
His mother is *G*reek, and his father is *I*talian.

c. Names of specific courses of study:

This semester I am taking *B*asic *P*sychology.

Note: Do not capitalize the name of a discipline if a specific course is not named.

This semester I am taking a psychology course.

d. Names of holidays, companies, specific products, and so on.

We are planning a picnic for *L*abor *D*ay.
He is a top executive with *B*ell *T*elephone.
I always buy *S*hine car wax.

Note: Do not capitalize the name of a company or a product if it is not specifically named.

He is a top executive with the telephone company.
I always buy the same kind of car wax.

4. Capitalize the names of directions only when they are used as the names of specific geographic regions.

He has always lived in the *W*est.
The storm is centered over the *E*ast *C*oast.
I think the campground is *s*outh of here.

5. Capitalize the names of days and months, but *not* the names of the seasons.

I only hope I can survive until *F*riday.
Her favorite month is *M*ay.
The *w*inter is a good time to complete projects started in the *f*all.

6. Capitalize titles of books, magazines, movies, and so on. (When you title the paragraphs you write, follow this rule.)

a. Always capitalize the first word in a title.

*S*ailfish from the Beach
*A*n End to Inconsistency

b. Capitalize all the words in a title of three words or less.

*I*n *T*he *B*eginning
*O*f *H*uman *E*motions

c. In titles consisting of more than three words, capitalize the first word and all major words. Do not capitalize conjunctions, prepositions, or articles.

> *A*n *E*nd *to Madness.*
> *C*onsiderations *f*or *t*he *S*election *of* *R*eading *T*exts

7. Capitalize official titles when the titles are followed by names and capitalize the words "President" and "Presidency" when referring to the President of the United States.

> I came to see *D*octor *C*handler.
> I came to see the *d*octor.
> The newspaper reported that *S*enator *G*oode was involved in the accident.
> The newspaper reported that a *s*enator was involved in the accident.
> The *P*resident is working late tonight.
> The *p*resident of the university is working late tonight.

8. Capitalize family titles when they are followed by a name or when they are used to replace a name.

> She will borrow the money from *U*ncle *S*tan.
> His favorite relative is *A*unt *M*argaret.
> I have to tell *M*other about the invitation.
> She will borrow the money from her *u*ncle.
> His favorite relative is his *a*unt.
> I have to tell my *m*other about the invitation.

Notice that in every case, only what is *specifically named* gets capitalized (one person, one region, one brand, one company, and so on).

PRACTICE EXERCISES

*EXERCISE 1 *Proofread the following sentences and correct any errors in capitalization.*

1. On our vacation we are going west to see the grand canyon.
2. Last year on memorial day my uncle jimmy jumped into the pool with all of his clothes on.
3. The best book i ever read was called *the fury of angels*.

4. The sunshine brand unsweetened grapefruit juice is the best bargain around.
5. Next semester I am taking an english course, two history courses, a biology course, and a spanish course.
6. To get to their house, you drive South on the dirt road until you cross the chester river, and then turn left onto cheswick street.
7. I went to see father last Summer, but he was away on a business trip.
8. When you find yourself in trouble, the person to see for help is dean ray.
9. She planned on visiting the south over the easter vacation.
10. A favorite Uncle of mine once gave me some advice about college: "Whatever you do, don't major in english."
11. My report is on a magazine article in the *saturday evening post* entitled "the saga of american streets."
12. She was advised by her Counselor to get some tutoring so she could pass introduction to sociology.
13. The best time of the year to have a Family Picnic is the fourth of july.
14. I wrote a letter to congressman Phillips, but he never responded.
15. We told mother that the entire family would be there on mother's day.
16. The Autumn would be my favorite season except it means the beginning of College Classes again.
17. Her Grandfather's cottage on lake pleasant once belonged to senator Kane.
18. When officer Geralds received the emergency call, he was heading East on forty-second street.
19. The puritane chemical company has recently marketed a new weed-killing product called weedgone.

20. He is taking a course in italian, even though his Father is french and his Mother is irish.

EXERCISE 2 *Proofread the following paragraph and correct any errors in capitalization.*

Most automobiles in america today can be classified into three types according to their size. First of all is the compact car, like the volkswagen, which can seat from two to four passengers. The car usually costs between three and four thousand dollars and gets twenty-five to thirty miles per gallon. another type is the medium-sized car, such as the ford fairmont. This one will hold up to six passengers, costs around five thousand dollars, and gets about fifteen to twenty miles per gallon. A third type is the family-sized car. This is usually a Station Wagon, and it can sometimes seat seven or more passengers. It usually costs six or seven Thousand dollars and gets only ten to fifteen miles per gallon. Of the three types, i prefer the compact car since I need room for only my Wife and me.

15 / Recognize words that look or sound alike

The words listed in this chapter usually present students with some difficulty. Some of them look alike, others sound alike, but each word has its own particular meaning and uses, and these will be explained for you. The words are listed in alphabetical order.

This chapter is intended both as a lesson in the uses of these words and as a reference guide for you to use when proofreading your writing. You should remember, though, that each of these words is defined in any dictionary, and a dictionary is almost always available when you are writing. However, no reference can help you to use these words correctly if you do not refer to it regularly to check your use of these words.

There is one other point worth mentioning: when some of these words are used incorrectly, they create an unfavorable impression in the minds of some readers. If you are the writer and the reader happens to be an instructor or a potential employer, you will have failed to impress him or her with your point because of something as simple as a misspelled or misused word. Many people react to the misuse of these words more strongly than they react to a sentence fragment or a run-on sentence. Rather than letting that happen to something you write, whether it is a paragraph for a writing class or a letter of application for a job, check your use of these words as part of your regular proofreading procedure.

a/an/and
a = an article used before a word beginning with a consonant.

*A p*each fell from the tree.

an = an article used before a word beginning with a vowel.

*An a*pple fell from the tree.

and = a connecting word (conjunction) used to indicate addition.

A peach *and* an apple fell from the trees.

its/it's (see Chapter 12)
its = the possessive form of the pronoun "it."

The sheepdog is shedding *its* hair all over the house.

it's = contraction of "it is."

I think it's going to be a beautiful day.

knew/new
knew = the past tense of "know," "to be aware of."

She always *knew* that I liked her sister.

new = "first," "original," "unused."

I have decided to buy a *new* car.

know/no
know = "to be aware of," "to have knowledge of."

The swimming instructor said that I should *know* how to float.

no = "not at all," "not any," or a negative assertion.

There is *no* way that I can learn how to swim.

than/then
than = a word used only in a comparison (it often follows a word ending in *-er*).

My new car runs much better *than* my old one.

then = "at a particular time," or "next in order."

First we will talk, and *then* we will argue.

there/their/they're (see Chapter 12)
there = "at or toward a particular place or point in time or action."

He wanted to go *there* to see the plants.
He read up to page 292 and stopped *there*.

"There" may also be used as the first word in a sentence in which the subject follows the verb.

There is a cat in the tree.

their = possessive form of the pronoun "they."

Their tulips are healthy.

they're = a contraction of "they are."

We are staying home, but *they're* going to a movie.

to/too/two
to = "toward."

They did not go *to* the movie.

too = "also," or "in excess."

My nephew wanted to go *too*.
There were *too* many people who wanted to go.

two = the number 2.

Two of us decided to go somewhere else.

wear/where
wear = 1. "to have on the body, such as clothing."

She wanted to *wear* her new pantsuit.

2. "to use up."

This assignment is going to *wear* me out.

3. "to last."

The new tires will *wear* well.

where = "at what place?"

He could not remember *where* he had been.

were/we're (see Chapter 12)
were = past tense plural form of the verb "be."

We *were* going to go to Florida, but we changed our minds.

we're = contraction of "we are."

The instructor wants to know when *we're* going to complete the assignment.

your/you're (see Chapter 12)
your = possessive form of the pronoun "you."

He wants to borrow *your* lawn mower.

you're = contraction of "you are."

I came over as soon as I heard that *you're* buying a swimming pool.

PRACTICE EXERCISES

*EXERCISE 1 *Fill in the blanks with the appropriate word.*

1–5: *a/an/and*

1. The team made a trade for ________________ pitcher, ________________ outfielder, ________________ a catcher.
2. I found ________________ bottle of soda, but I could not find ________________ opener.
3. She was ________________ diplomat's wife, so she had to be careful not to cause ________________ international incident.
4. He was ________________ suspect because he had once made ________________ attempt to kill ________________ neighbor.
5. The only relatives he has left are ________________ aunt, ________________ cousin, ________________ his sister.

6–10: *its/it's*

6. ________________ an unusual trick; the dog is able to catch ________________ own tail.
7. ________________ right rear fender was badly damaged.
8. ________________ time to file income tax returns.
9. The bird lined ________________ nest with mud and weeds.
10. The dog is alive, but ________________ right hind leg is broken.

11–15: *knew/new*

11. They ______________ that he needed a ______________ chair, so they bought him one for Father's Day.

12. Fred's ______________ jacket cost him a lot of money.

13. The one thing he ______________ for sure was that he could not afford a ______________ house.

14. The ______________ employee is someone we ______________ a long time ago.

15. She ______________ that she needed a ______________ battery for her car.

16–20: *know/no*

16. ______________ one I ______________ will be at the party.

17. We all ______________ the baseball season is over.

18. There is ______________ opportunity for promotion in this job.

19. I ______________ of ______________ better way to fix a flat tire.

20. There is ______________ reason why he has to ______________ about the accident.

21–25: *than/then*

21. The meal he prepared was better ______________ anything I had ever eaten.

22. If you want to be smarter ______________ Jack, you will have to spend more time studying.

23. First she must spend more time practicing, and ________ she can think about being better ________ anyone else in the band.

24. Back ________ , no one had even thought of traveling faster ________ the speed of sound.

25. Since ________ , he has been away on business trips more ________ he has been home.

26–30: *there/their/they're*

26. ________ are several reasons why ________ not going on ________ vacation this year.

27. When he gets ________ , he will try to find out if ________ still living in the same town.

28. ________ friends and neighbors all came to help them rebuild ________ barn.

29. ________ drilling for oil offshore now, hoping that ________ will be oil deposits beneath the ocean floor.

30. ________ is a new car in ________ garage, so everyone assumes that ________ wealthy.

31–35: *to/too/two*

31. ________ of the politicians took up ________ much time in the debate.

32. When they said they were going ________ Europe, their friends said they wanted to go ________ .

33. The price of food is ________ much these days, even with ________ people in a family working.

34. They left the movie ________ go see their ________ friends, Marge and Pete.

35. The ________ players decided ________ sign their contracts before it was ________ late.

36–40: *wear/where*

36. ________ were you going to ________ your new suit?

37. This weather is going to ________ me out. I am moving to a place ________ it never snows.

38. ________ I come from, the people do not ________ their hats indoors.

39. I expect this carpet to ________ well since I know the reputation of the place ________ I bought it.

40. This always happens when I want to ________ something special: I forget ________ I put it away.

41–45: *were/we're*

41. They ________ planning on coming over for dinner, but ________ going out instead.

42. The park rangers said there ________ bears in the area, but ________ going camping there anyway.

43. ________ in the process of planning where ________ going to stay.

44. We ________ not able to finish all of the painting, but ________ hoping some friends will come over to help us tomorrow.

45. The people who ________________ at the restaurant said the food was only average, but ________________ going to go there anyway.

46–50: *your/you're*

46. ________________ neighbors all agree that ________________ the friendliest person on the street.

47. ________________ a lucky person to have ________________ house so close to ________________ job.

48. Everyone says that ________________ working too hard on ________________ project.

49. When ________________ basement is finished, I hope ________________ going to buy a pool table.

50. Although ________________ habits are different, ________________ still one of my best friends.

EXERCISE 2

Write!

Write sentences using each of the words presented in this chapter. You may write a sentence for each word or use several of the words in the same sentence.

1. *a/an/and* ____

____

2. *its/it's* ____

____

3. *knew/new* ____

____

4. *know/no* ____

____

5. *than/then* ____

____

6. *there/their/they're* ____

____

7. *to/too/two* ____

____

8. *wear/where* ____

____

9. *were/we're* ____

____

10. *your/you're* ____

____

EXERCISE 3 *Proofread the following paragraph and correct any errors in the use of the words discussed in this chapter.*

The legal drinking age in New Jersey should be changed from eighteen back to twenty-one. First of all, their has been a significant increase in the number of teenagers involved in serious automobile accidents since New Jersey lowered it's drinking age. Also, New Jersey's legal drinking age is lower then that of Pennsylvania or Delaware. This encourages teenagers from Philadelphia or Wilmington to drive to New Jersey, buy a alcoholic beverage, take it to there home state, and drink illegally. In addition, to many sixteen and seventeen year olds are now attempting to buy alcoholic beverages. Just because a person is eligible to vote when he is eighteen is know reason to allow him to drink at that age.

EXERCISE 4 *Proofread the following paragraph and correct any errors in the use of the words discussed in this chapter.*

I think America and Russia should agree to stop producing nuclear weapons. Its crazy for both countries to just keep making more and more deadly weapons. The latest device is the neutron bomb. This is a bomb which, when it is exploded, kills all living things but does not damage property. Right now the President is trying to decide whether or not we should produce the neutron bomb. Their is every reason to believe that the Russians have this bomb to, but this is not a good enough reason to start making it here. If we do not stop producing more nuclear weapons, the Russians will not stop either. Some people claim the Russians have more bombs then we do, but both countries have enough bombs to destroy everyone on Earth. Its not possible to win a nuclear war, only to lose.

PART FOUR REVIEW

In Part Four you learned to identify and correct errors in the use of mechanics. By "mechanics," we mean punctuation, capitalization, and spelling. While your most important task is still the writing of correct sentences and well-organized paragraphs, it is also important to check your writing for these "minor" errors.

Punctuation The major punctuation errors are in the use of the apostrophe and in the use of the comma. Remember that the apostrophe is used with nouns to indicate possession and to form contractions. The easiest way to avoid errors in the use of the apostrophe is to avoid writing contractions, since contractions are not considered appropriate in formal writing anyway.

There are several rules governing the use of the comma. The major uses of the comma are to separate clauses in compound and complex sentences, to separate items in a list, to set off introductory words and phrases from the rest of the sentence, to set interruptions off from the rest of the sentence, and to separate the different elements in addresses and dates. The key to using the comma correctly is knowing why you are using it.

Capitalization The specific rules of capitalization are presented in Chapter 14, and you should use these rules for reference. The best general rule of capitalization to follow is to capitalize only when someone or something is specifically named.

Spelling In Chapter 15, you studied some of the words that are most often confused and misspelled. The more you use these words in your writing, the more familiar you will become with their spelling. While you are learning them, do not hesitate to refer to the list of definitions and examples in Chapter 15, or to a dictionary. Remember that a paper or a letter with no major errors can be seriously marred by the incorrect spelling of one of these words. Try to check your spelling as part of your regular proofreading procedure.

Answer key

The following key lists the answers to exercises in the text that are indicated by an asterisk (*). Use the key to check your answers only *after* you have completed the exercise.

CHAPTER 2: LEARN THE SENTENCE

Exercise 3 (p. 13)

1. broke
2. prepared
3. loaded
4. mounted
5. struck
6. went
7. spread
8. blew
9. stranded
10. covered

Exercise 6 (p. 16)

1. are
2. are
3. is
4. seem
5. are
6. is
7. is
8. are
9. is
10. are

Exercise 9 (p. 20)

1. are
2. break (down)
3. seem
4. runs
5. is
6. is working
7. seems
8. welcome
9. am
10. are

Exercise 10 (p. 20)

1. are
2. are
3. is
4. is
5. are
6. represent
7. protects
8. stops
9 require
10. is

Exercise 16 (p. 25)

1. have lived
2. has changed
3. was
4. could afford
5. had
6. have taken
7. have moved
8. moved
9. come
10. rush

Exercise 17 (p. 25)

is
oppose
consider
support
conserve
save
is
is
is
race

Exercise 22 (p. 32)

1. divorce
2. money
3. Henry, job
4. desire
5. he
6. wife, he
7. father
8. he
9. fondness
10. problems and disagreements

Exercise 29 (p. 38)

Subjects:

Enrolling	I
I	I
I	I, courses
problems	clerk
instructor	I

Exercise 32 (p. 41)

1.	complete	6.	incomplete
2.	incomplete	7.	incomplete
3.	incomplete	8.	complete
4.	complete	9.	incomplete
5.	incomplete	10.	incomplete

Exercise 33 (p. 43)

1.	goes	6.	enjoys
2.	likes	7.	show
3.	sell	8.	amuse
4.	offer	9.	sees
5.	buys	10.	come

Exercise 34 (p. 44)

1.	was	6.	was
2.	seemed	7.	looked
3.	was	8.	were
4.	were	9.	are
5.	were	10.	seemed

Exercise 38 (p. 46)

1.	People (pl)	6.	students (pl)
2.	college (sg)	7.	students, (pl)
3.	programs (pl)	8.	Going to college (sg)
4.	students (pl)	9.	students, they (pl), (pl)
5.	They (pl)	10.	college (sg)

Exercise 39 (p. 46)

Subject-verb:

students have	Most can complete
class is	students must remember; writing is
they will be asked	Writing requires
fears are	student is willing; he can become
course presents	Writing does come

CHAPTER 3: IDENTIFY AND CORRECT SENTENCE FRAGMENTS

Exercise 4 (p. 52)

1. "Geronimo!," my
2. stop, slipping
3. windows to
4. him, we
5. way to
6. surprised, thanking
7. right, Ralph
8. bathtub, leaving
9. playpen, singing
10. up, pretending

Exercise 5 (p. 53)

Preferred corrections:

Line 1: shower, singing
Line 4: mind to
Line 5: shirt and pulling
Line 7: time, I
Line 8: stop, biting

Exercise 11 (p. 64)

Preferred corrections:

1. Line 2: rowboat even though
2. Line 1: lake, I
3. Line 1: afternoon until
4. Line 1: lake, Cheryl
5. Line 1: time before

Exercise 14 (p. 68)

Preferred responses:

1. before
2. When
3. After
4. If

5.	because	8.	Just as
6.	Although	9.	unless
7.	before	10.	If

Exercise 19 (p. 77)

Preferred responses:

Line 3: sport, I
Line 5: shape for
Line 8: school, has
Line 9: job and
Line 10: job, I

Exercise 24 (p. 80)

Preferred responses:

Line 1: Enforcement, there
Line 5: enforcement in
Line 7: me when
Line 9: curriculum, improving
Line 11: courses because

CHAPTER 4: COMBINE SENTENCES

Exercise 5 (p. 87)

Subject-verb

1. Curt believes
2. He has read
3. He watches
4. He drives
5. Curt considers
6. dream is
7. UFO's bring
8. They fly
9. visitors want
10. it is

Exercise 6 (p. 88)

Subject-verb

1. brothers, I have wanted
2. all would like
3. We decided
4. Jack, Chet wanted
5. Vince, I disagreed
6. mysteries are, do sell
7. idea was
8. Vince, Jack, Chet liked
9. I disagreed, argued
10. All are trying

Exercise 11 (p. 94)

Sentence 1:	house, but
Sentence 3:	wife (no comma)
Sentence 4:	cement (no comma)
Sentence 5:	friends (no comma)
Sentence 6:	carpentry (no comma) plumbing,
Sentence 7:	up,
Sentence 7:	along (no comma)
Sentence 8:	wife (no comma)
Sentence 9:	it (no comma)
Sentence 10:	built, but (no comma)

Exercise 12 (p. 96)

Preferred responses:

1. therefore
2. then
3. in addition
4. however
5. then
6. therefore
7. otherwise
8. thus
9. in addition
10. consequently

Exercise 14 (p. 99)

Independent clause underlined; dependent clause circled.

1. Although I don't look like the outdoor type, camping is my favorite leisure activity.
2. I love camping because I enjoy nature.
3. When I go camping, I get a chance to hike in the woods and observe nature.
4. It brings me special pleasure when I see a wild animal or bird in the woods.
5. While I am in the woods, I feel a closer relationship with nature.
6. Being in the woods gives me the feeling that I am getting away from all the troubles of the world.
7. I also like camping because it requires me to be self-sufficient.
8. Though I take along some modern equipment, I try to keep the whole experience as basic as possible.
9. I don't take a tent along since that would only block out the stars at night.
10. If I didn't go camping once in a while, I would probably go crazy in a very short time.

Exercise 15 (p. 100)

Type of sentence: independent clause underlined; dependent clause circled.

1. Simple
2. Simple

3. Complex: Even if I don't read the newspaper every day, I can still be aware by reading Time.
4. Complex: Time is also good because it has so many sections.
5. Simple
6. Simple
7. Simple
8. Complex: The section consists of four or five paragraphs that report on some minor event.
9. Complex: I like this section because the reports often describe something particularly ridiculous.
10. Complex: When all parts of the magazine are considered, Time is clearly superior to the other weekly news magazines.

Exercise 16 (p. 101)

1.	no comma	6.	no comma
2.	convenient, people	7.	invented, people
3.	relax, people	8.	friends, they
4.	no comma	9.	no comma
5.	television, the	10.	us, far

Exercise 19 (p. 108)

1.	s	6.	cp
2.	s	7.	s
3.	cx	8.	cx
4.	s	9.	cp
5.	cx	10.	cx

Exercise 21 (p. 109)

Line 2:	attractions, I
Line 3:	home, I
Line 5:	play, and
Line 6:	crowd, but
Line 8:	television, I

CHAPTER 5: IDENTIFY AND CORRECT ERRORS IN COMBINATION

Exercise 2 (p. 113)

1.	(no error)	4.	friends, with
2.	different they	5.	worse they
3.	boardwalk last	6.	easy, I

7. jobs that
8. friendly, I
9. minimum not
10. week, I

Exercise 4 (p. 116)

Preferred Responses:

1. Line 4: this. One
2. Line 2: land, but the
3. Line 2: streets, and I
4. Line 4: routine. This
5. Line 3: reins; to

Exercise 6 (p. 119)

Preferred responses:

Line 3: time, for missing
Line 4: hand; this
Line 8: sister; you
Line 10: tray. Your
Line 12: bliss. Now

Exercise 7 (p. 120)

1. Line 2: experience they
2. Line 3: Southerners, many
3. Line 3: threatened it
4. Line 3: language, on
5. Line 1: overlooked small town

Exercise 8 (p. 121)

Preferred responses:

Line 2: Horatio, and he
Line 4: anything, and Horatio
Line 8: champion. He
Line 10: die, for
Line 14: day, but right

Exercise 10 (p. 122)

Preferred responses:

Line 1: life, and I
Line 2: Dooby, and they
Line 7: matter. Scooby

Line 15: them, but she
Line 17: deliberately. There

PART ONE REVIEW

Exercise 4 (p. 126)

Preferred responses:

1. Line 2: job when
2. Line 1: Susan; however,
3. Line 2: parties, both
4. Line 1: country. People
5. Line 2: Players are always
6. Line 3: morning, so students
7. Line 3: tankers to
8. Line 3: work. With
9. Line 1: pizza, all
10. Line 2: edition. I

Exercise 5 (p. 127)

Preferred responses:

Line 2: industry, for more
Line 4: protection because
Line 6: alone, an
Line 6: eat, and, as
Line 9: human, so they

CHAPTER 6: VERBS: LEARN THE PRINCIPAL PARTS

Exercise 3 (p. 141)

	Simple Past	*Past Participle*
1.	did	done
2.	tore	torn
3.	crawled	crawled
4.	set	set
5.	wore	worn
6.	steered	steered
7.	crept	crept
8.	laid	laid
9.	hoped	hoped
10.	hopped	hopped

Exercise 5 (p. 142)

1. According to the company spokesman, the treasurer concealed the truth.
2. The batter hit the ball.
3. According to the child, someone broke the vase.
4. Gerald Finley won the national award.
5. The American president and the Soviet premier signed the treaty.
6. The committee met on Tuesday, January 4.

7. A squirrel bit the boy.
8. The youngest member of the Yugoslavian team broke the world's record in the Olympic event.
9. His dreams of grandeur tormented him.
10. The professional football team in Miami made the first offer.

Exercise 6 (p. 146)

Line 6: used
Line 7: scared
Line 7: used
Line 8: used, played

Exercise 8 (p. 149)

Line 7:	said, knew	Line 16:	tried
Line 8:	bought	Line 18:	kept
Line 9:	loaded	Line 19:	spent
Line 10:	left	Line 21:	drove
		Line 22:	found

Exercise 9 (p. 150)

1. Line 4—past and present
2. Line 2—present and past
3. No shift.
4. Line 2—present and past
5. Line 5—past and present

Exercise 10 (p. 151)

Line 5: live, is get
Line 6: are
Line 12: is

CHAPTER 7: VERBS: LEARN THE PRESENT TENSE

Exercise 1 (p. 154)

1.	deposits	6.	paints
2.	seems	7.	intend
3.	prefer	8.	causes
4.	visit	9.	jog
5.	agrees	10.	find

Exercise 2 (p. 157)

1.	works	6.	is
2.	goes	7.	like
3.	pumps	8.	are
4.	checks	9.	attends
5.	is	10.	has

Exercise 3 (p. 158)

1.	am	6.	are
2.	am	7.	are
3.	is	8.	am
4.	is	9.	are
5.	is	10.	are

Exercise 6 (p. 162)

1. bloom, arrives
2. is, think
3. wants, claims
4. walk, calls
5. states, are

Exercise 8 (p. 164)

1. leaps, grabs, passes
2. takes
3. buys, hopes
4. sings
5. get, forget

Exercise 11 (p. 167)

1. pleads
2. are
3. wait
4. has
5. makes

Exercise 12 (p. 167)

1.	are	6.	(correct)
2.	belong	7.	do
3.	begins	8.	is
4.	is	9.	costs
5.	presents	10.	(correct)

Exercise 16 (p. 172)

1.	are	6.	do
2.	is	7.	are
3.	are	8.	does
4.	are	9.	are
5.	are	10.	am

Exercise 18 (p. 175)

1. meets, discuss
2. has, is
3. hangs, are
4. treats, tries
5. is, are

Exercise 22 (p. 180)

1.	does	6.	charge
2.	is	7.	is
3.	give	8.	increase
4.	cost	9.	have
5.	(correct)	10.	(correct)

Exercise 23 (p. 180)

1. want, hopes
2. turn
3. are, look
4. goes, relaxes
5. is, wants

Exercise 24 (p. 181)

Line 2: gives
Line 4: spend
Line 5: get
Line 7: has
Line 9: joke

Exercise 25 (p. 181)

Line 1: grows
Line 2: happens
Line 3: becomes,

Line 4:	bring	Line 8:	has, cause
Line 5:	increases, end	Line 9:	cause
Line 7:	are		

CHAPTER 8: VERBS: LEARN THE PAST TENSE

Exercise 3 (p. 189)

Line 2:	closed	Line 9:	happened
Line 3:	warned	Line 11:	wanted
Line 6:	started	Line 15:	turned, hoped
Line 7:	kept	Line 16:	hoped
Line 8:	pushed	Line 17:	needed

Exercise 5 (p. 191)

1. was, was
2. was, was
3. were
4. was, was
5. was, was

Exercise 7 (p. 193)

Line 1:	were
Line 3:	were
Line 5:	was
Line 6:	was
Line 9:	was

Exercise 10 (p. 198)

Line 3:	had seen	Line 10:	was
Line 4:	decided	Line 14:	was
Line 6:	was slurped	Line 17:	went
Line 8:	tried	Line 18:	started
Line 9:	kept		

CHAPTER 9: USE PRONOUNS CORRECTLY

Exercise 1 (p. 202)

1. objective—him
2. subjective—he
3. possessive—his
4. subjective—she
5. objective—her
6. possessive—hers
7. subjective—It
8. possessive—its
9. subjective—They
10. objective—them

Exercise 2 (p. 203)

1. us, us
2. our
3. ours
4. their, them
5. theirs
6. me, my
7. me, mine
8. hers
9. your
10. yours

Exercise 3 (p. 205)

1. her and me
2. you and me (us)
3. We
4. ours
5. you and me (us)

Exercise 5 (p. 207)

1. whom
2. who
3. who
4. whose
5. whom

6. Who
7. whose
8. who
9. whom
10. Who

Exercise 8 (p. 213)

1. their
2. his
3. its
4. her
5. an (his or her)

Exercise 10 (p. 214)

1. Competitive *people*
2. *You* must (or, *one has*)
3. *I* just, what *I'm* doing
4. how good *they have* it, *they* feel
5. *you have* (or *one's* friends, *one's* family, even *one's* old dog.)

Exercise 11 (p. 215)

Line 1: High school *athletes*
Line 3: Young *men* and *women . . . practice*
Line 6: if *students are*
Line 8: Student *athletes* often *don't*
Line 8: as *they need*
Line 10: *they* could gain
Line 11: *their* studies

PART TWO REVIEW

Exercise 1 (p. 218)

Line 8: wandered
Line 10: was, was
Line 12: got
Line 13: started

Exercise 4 (p. 220)

Line (1)	there are
Line (4)	he is going to teach writing, but he
Line (5)	his time
Line (6)	He
Line (9)	believes that students
Line (11)	memorize
Line (13)	are correctly
Line (14)	teacher. This
Line (15)	teaches
Line (16)	students need
Line (19)	has his own special talent, I

CHAPTER 10: LEARN PARAGRAPH ORGANIZATION

Exercise 4 (p. 231)

Main Idea: Foreign cars are a better investment than American cars.

Exercise 9 (p. 240)

Irrelevant detail: "It is an old row house that was built sometime after the Second World War." (Does not explain or describe why it is hard to study.)

Exercise 10 (p. 241)

Irrelevant detail: "Most of all I love to play football as much as I love to watch it, but I can never find a group of guys who can organize a good game." (Does not explain or describe why writer likes to watch *Monday Night Football.*)

Exercise 25 (p. 263)

1. opinion
2. effect-cause
3. process (how-to)
4. cause-effect
5. effect-cause
6. contrast
7. comparison
8. opinion

Exercise 26 (p. 264)

Error: irrelevant detail
Correction: delete sentences 4, 5, and 6

Exercise 27 (p. 265)

Error: faulty topic sentence; paragraph consists of *consequences*, not reasons
Correction: new topic sentence: "A lot of unusual things have happened to me as a result of my sleepwalking habit."

Exercise 31 (p. 267)

Topic sentence: There are several reasons why the death penalty should be abolished.

Support:	Reason 1:	inhumane
	Detail:	cruel and unusual punishment
	Reason 2:	death penalty may be given according to a sexual or racial bias
	Detail:	poor are more likely to be sentenced
	Reason 3:	no evidence that death penalty would reduce crime
	Detail:	criminals do not think about the crime before they commit it.

Exercise 32 (p. 267)

Topic sentence: Making an attractive flower bed is a lot of fun, and it does not take very long if these simple steps are followed.

Support: Steps:
1. find a well-lighted location where the soil is loose
2. gather tools
3. clear the area and turn over soil
4. remove weeds and mix in fertilizer—rake smooth
5. plant the seeds; cover and water them
6. water the flower bed every day until the plants are showing

CHAPTER 12: LEARN THE APOSTROPHE

Exercise 1 (p. 283)

1. can't
2. we'd
3. I've
4. wouldn't
5. she'd
6. she's
7. doesn't
8. weren't
9. aren't
10. didn't

Exercise 2 (p. 284)

1.	hasn't	6.	they're
2.	you'll	7.	shouldn't
3.	he'll	8.	you're
4.	he's	9.	I'll
5.	it's	10.	wasn't

Exercise 3 (p. 286)

1.	boy's skateboard	11.	Susan's hair
2.	tree's leaves	12.	Clark's favorite
3.	Bess's car	13.	Mrs. Andrews's job
4.	team's star	14.	Cheryl's ingenuity
5.	school's policy	15.	actor's voice
6.	car's hubcaps	16.	radio's tone
7.	salesman's commission	17.	mistress's complaint
8.	waitress's apron	18.	husband's appearance
9.	singer's performance	19.	museum's reputation
10.	movie's rating	20.	Carol's concern

Exercise 7 (p. 291)

1. They're, their
2. you're, your
3. They're, their
4. It's, its
5. you're, your

Exercise 10 (p. 293)

Line 1:	It's (It is)	Line 8:	I'd (I had), its
Line 4:	we'd (we would)	Line 11:	Florence's
Line 5:	John's, days	Line 12:	couldn't (could not)
Line 6:	He'd (He had), their		

CHAPTER 13: LEARN TO USE THE COMMA

Exercise 1 (p. 296)

1.	stories, he	4.	safer, more
2.	summer, and	5.	job, but
3.	quickly, they	6.	correct

7. dangerous, I
8. carefully, or
9. smoking, I
10. mind, and

Exercise 2 (p. 297)

1. mileage, repair,
2. house, windows, lights,
3. (correct)
4. championship, runs,
5. dishes, laundry,
6. scoutmaster, church,
7. litter, transportation,
8. education, government, people,
9. (correct)
10. bright, sky, blowing,

Exercise 3 (p. 299)

1. all,
2. way,
3. February,
4. (correct)
5. thing,
6. thing,
7. ways,
8. Consequently,
9. Therefore,
10. last,

Exercise 4 (p. 300)

1. problem, however, is
2. living, for example, increases
3. victims, by some kind of miracle, were
4. greener, for some reason, on
5. (correct)
6. ability, in my opinion, is
7. alternative, it seems to me, is
8. appetite, by the way, has
9. (correct)
10. out, in conclusion, that

Exercise 6 (p. 303)

1. Drive, Monterey, California
2. Cortina, Italy
3. February 18, 1972 . . . Buffalo, New York
4. Apartment 112, 1348 West Montoe Boulevard, Cleveland, Ohio on March 22, 1968
5. Murphy, Congressional Office Building, Washington, D.C.
6. (correct)
7. Fairbanks, Alaska, on May 1, 1969
8. Memphis, Seattle, Detroit, and Miami
9. November 12, 1951,
10. Okaloosa County, Florida

CHAPTER 14: LEARN CAPITALIZATION

Exercise 1 (p. 309)

1. Grand Canyon
2. Memorial Day, Uncle Jimmy
3. I, *The Fury of Angels*
4. Sunshine
5. English, Spanish
6. south, Chester River, Cheswick Street
7. Father, summer
8. Dean Ray
9. South, Easter
10. uncle, English
11. *Saturday Evening Post,* "The Saga of American Streets"
12. counselor, Introduction to Sociology
13. family picnic, Fourth of July
14. Congressman
15. Mother, Mother's Day
16. autumn, college classes
17. grandfather's, Lake Pleasant, Senator Kane
18. Officer Geralds, east, Forty-second Street
19. Puritane Chemical Company, Weedgone
20. Italian, father, French, mother, Irish

CHAPTER 15: RECOGNIZE WORDS THAT LOOK OR SOUND ALIKE

Exercise 1 (p. 316)

1. a, an, and
2. a, an
3. a, an
4. a, an, a
5. an, a, and
6. it's, its
7. its
8. it's
9. its
10. its
11. knew, new
12. new
13. knew, new
14. new, knew
15. knew, new
16. No, know
17. know
18. no
19. know, no
20. no, know
21. than
22. than
23. then, than
24. then, than
25. then, than
26. There, they're, their
27. there, they're
28. Their, their
29. They're, there
30. There, their, they're
31. Two, too
32. to, too
33. too, two
34. to, two
35. two, to, too
36. Where, wear
37. wear, where
38. Where, wear
39. wear, where
40. wear, where

41. were, we're
42. were, we're
43. We're, we're
44. were, we're
45. were, we're
46. Your, you're
47. You're, your, your
48. You're, your
49. your, you're
50. your, you're

Index